Emerging Judaism

EMERGING JUDAISM

Studies on the Fourth & Third Centuries B.C.E.

Edited by

Michael E. Stone
& David Satran

FORTRESS PRESS   MINNEAPOLIS

Library of Congress Cataloging-in-Publication Data

Emerging Judaism.

  Bibliography: p.
  1. Judaism—History—Post-exilic period, 586 B.C.–
210 A.D. 2. Jews—Civilization—Greek influences.
I. Stone, Michael E., 1938–   . II. Satran, David.
BM176.E45   1989   296'.09'014   87–45905

3229H88   Printed in the United States of America   1–2090

Contents

Acknowledgments

The following material is used by permission:

1. Elias J. Bickerman, "The Historical Foundations of Postbiblical Judaism," in *The Jews, Their History, Culture, and Religion*, ed. L. Finkelstein (New York: Harper & Row, 1949), 1:70–99, 110–12.

2. Frank Moore Cross, Jr., "Aspects of Samaritan and Jewish History in Late Persian and Hellenistic Times," *HTR* 59 (1966): 201–11.

3. Michael E. Stone, "The Book of Enoch and Judaism in the Third Century B.C.E.," *CBQ* 40 (1978): 479–92.

4. Victor Tcherikover, *Hellenistic Civilization and the Jews*, trans. S. Applebaum (Philadelphia: Jewish Publication Society, 1959), 59–65, 126–28, 131–40, 427–31, 457–58, 459–61.

5. Morton Smith, *Palestinian Parties and Politics That Shaped the Old Testament* (New York: Columbia Univ. Press, 1971), 57– 81, 227–37.

6. Arnaldo Momigliano, *Alien Wisdom: The Limits of Hellenization* (Cambridge: Cambridge Univ. Press, 1975), 74–96.

7. Martin Hengel, *Jews, Greeks, and Barbarians*, trans. J. Bowden (Philadelphia: Fortress Press; London: SCM Press, 1980), 110–26, 170–74.

Preface

The stimulus for this book came from a joint seminar offered at the Hebrew University of Jerusalem. The attempt to address the period under discussion through an assessment of recent discoveries—assisted by a number of outstanding studies devoted to those discoveries—convinced us that students of the history of ancient Judaism might profit from such an anthology. We are grateful to Dr. Harold W. Rast for his encouragement of this project.

The principles underlying selection of the readings are explained in detail in the general introduction to the volume and in the prefatory notes to the individual chapters. We have tried in this manner to stress the interrelatedness of these studies and their cumulative contribution to our new understanding of this historical period. Each of the readings has been presented as closely as possible in the form in which it first appeared.

David Satran was a Visiting Fellow in the Department of Religion at Princeton University while much of the work for this volume was undertaken: he would like to thank the members of that department for their hospitality and to express his gratitude to the Rothschild Foundation (Yad HaNadiv) for its generous support.

Abbreviations

4QEn	Manuscript of the *Book of Enoch* from Qumran Cave 4
4QEnastr	Manuscript of the *Astronomical Book of Enoch* from Qumran Cave 4
11QPsa	Psalm Scroll from Qumran Cave 11
11QPsaDavComp	Compositions of David in Psalm Scroll from Qumran Cave 11
AB	Anchor Bible
ABAW	*Abhandlungen der Bayerischen Akademie der Wissenschaften*
AIPHOS	*Annuaire de l'institut de philosophie et d'histoire orientales et slaves*
AJA	*American Journal of Archaeology*
AJP	*American Journal of Philology*
ANET	J. Pritchard, *Ancient Near Eastern Texts*
Anth.Gr.	*Anthologia Graeca*
Antiquities/Ant.	Josephus *Antiquities of the Jews*
Appian *Syr.*	Appian *Syriake*
Arch. f. Pap.	*Archiv für Papyrusforschung*
ARW	*Archiv für Religionswissenschaft*
b.	*Babylonian Talmud*
BA	*Biblical Archaeologist*
Bar.	Baraitha
BASOR	*Bulletin of the American Schools of Oriental Research*
Ber.	Tractate *Berakot*
BJRL	*Bulletin of the John Rylands Library*
Brooklyn Pap.	E. G. Kraeling, *Brooklyn Museum Aramaic Papyri*
Butler, *Princeton Expedition*	H. C. Butler, *The Princeton University Archaeological Expedition to Syria in 1904–1905*

xi

BZAW	Beiheft zur *ZAW*
CAH	*Cambridge Ancient History*
CBQ	*Catholic Biblical Quarterly*
Charles, *Apocrypha and Pseudepigrapha*	R. H. Charles, *The Apocrypha and Pseudepigrapha of the Old Testament*
CIJ	*Corpus Inscriptionum Judaicarum*
CNI	*Christian News from Israel*
CPJ	*Corpus Papyrorum Judaicarum*
CRAIBL	*Comptes-rendus de l'Académie des inscriptions et belles-lettres*
Deut. R.	*Deuteronomy Rabbah*
Diehl	E. Diehl, *Supplementum Lyricum*
Diod.	Diodorus Siculus
DJDJ	*Discoveries in the Judean Desert of Jordan*
DTC	*Dictionnaire de théologie catholique*
Elephantine P.	*Elephantine Papyri*, ed. A. Cowley
Eusebius *Praep. Ev.*	Eusebius *Praeparatio evangelica*
F.Gr.H.	F. Jacoby, *Fragmente der griechischen Historiker*
Gen. Apoc.	*Genesis Apocryphon*
Gen. R.	*Genesis Rabbah*
HAT	Handbuch zum Alten Testament
Herod.	Herodotus
Homer *Odys.*	Homer *Odyssey*
HR	*History of Religions*
HSM	Harvard Semitic Monographs
HSS	Harvard Semitic Studies
HTR	*Harvard Theological Review*
HTS	*Harvard Theological Studies*
IDB	*Interpreter's Dictionary of the Bible*
IEJ	*Israel Exploration Journal*
j.	*Jerusalem Talmud*
JAOS	*Journal of the American Oriental Society*
JBL	*Journal of Biblical Literature*
JJS	*Journal of Jewish Studies*
Josephus *Ant.*	Josephus *Antiquities of the Jews*
Josephus *C. Ap.*	Josephus *Contra Apionem*
Josephus *War*	Josephus *The Jewish War*
JPOS	*Journal of the Palestine Oriental Society*
JR	*Journal of Religion*

JRS	*Journal of Roman Studies*
JSJ	*Journal for the Study of Judaism in the Persian, Hellenistic, and Roman Period*
JSS	*Journal of Semitic Studies*
Jub.	*Book of Jubilees*
Kidd.	Tractate *Kiddushin*
Kuhn, *Konkordanz*	K. G. Kuhn, *Konkordanz zum Qumran-Texten*
Lev. Rab.	*Leviticus Rabbah*
Lobel and Page	E. Lobel and D. Page, eds., *Poetarum Lesbiarum Fragmenta*
LXX	Septuagint
Marböck *Weisheit*	J. Marböck, *Weisheit im Wandel: Untersuchungen zur Weisheitstheologie bei Ben Sira*
Middendorp, *Stellung*	Th. Middendorp, *Die Stellung Jesu ben Siras zwischen Judentum und Hellenismus*
ms	manuscript
NTS	*New Testament Studies*
'Olam Rab.	*'Olam Rabbah*
OTL	Old Testament Library
P. Col. Zen.	*Zenon Papyri*, ed. Westermann et al.
P. Lon. inv.	*London Papyri*
P. Tebt.	*Tebtunis Papyri*
P. Zen. Mich.	*Zenon Papyri in the University of Michigan*, ed. C. C. Edgar
Pap. Cairo, Zen.	*Zenon Papyri, Cairo*
Pap. Oxy.	*Oxyrhynchus Papyri*
PCZ	*Zenon Papyri*, ed. C. C. Edgar
PEQ	*Palestine Exploration Quarterly*
Persius *Sat.*	Persius *Saturae*
Philo *De Spec. Leg.*	Philo *De specialibus legibus*
PJB	*Palästinajahrbuch*
Pliny *N.H.*	Pliny *Natural History*
Ps.-Callisth.	Pseudo-Callisthenes *Historia*
PSI	*Pubblicazioni della Società italiana*
PW	*Paulys Realencyklopädie für der classischen Altertumswissenschaft*
RA	*Revue d'assyriologie et d'archéologie orientale*
RAC	*Reallexikon für Antike und Christentum*
RB	*Revue biblique*
REJ	*Revue des études juives*

RGG	*Die Religion in Geschichte und Gegenwart*
RheinMus	*Rheinisches Museum für Philologie*
RHR	*Revue de l'histoire des religions*
RSR	*Recherches des sciences religieuses*
Sanh.	Tractate *Sanhedrin*
SB	*Sammelbuch griechischer Urkunden aus Ägypten*
SBAW	*Sitzungsberichte der Deutschen Akademie der Wissenschaften zu Berlin*
Schürer	E. Schürer, *Geschichte des jüdischen Volkes im Zeitalter Jesu Christi*, 3 vols.
SHAW	*Sitzungsberichte der Heidelberger Akademie der Wissenschaften*
SJLA	Studies in Judaism in Late Antiquity
Sulp. Sev.	Sulpicius Severus
SVF	H. von Arnim, ed., *Stoicorum Veterum Fragmenta*
t.	*Tosepta*
Targ. Jer.	Targum Jerushalmi
TDNT	*Theological Dictionary of the New Testament*
TLZ	*Theologische Literaturzeitung*
VT	*Vetus Testamentum*
VTSup	Vetus Testamentum, Supplements
W. Chrest.	L. Mitteis and U. Wilcken, *Grundzüge und Chresomathie der Papyruskunde*
WMANT	Wissenschaftliche Monographien zum Alten und Neuen Testament
ZAW	*Zeitschrift für die alttestamentliche Wissenschaft*
ZDMG	*Zeitschrift der deutschen morgenländischen Gesellschaft*
ZDPV	*Zeitschrift des deutschen Palästina-Vereins*
ZNW	*Zeitschrift für die neutestamentliche Wissenschaft*
ZRG	*Zeitschrift für Religions- und Geistesgeschichte*
ZThK	*Zeitschrift für Theologie und Kirche*

Introduction

This anthology is dedicated to a period in Jewish history clouded in darkness yet crucial for an understanding of the religious and social development of ancient Judaism. The readings in this volume address the span of just over two centuries between the age of Ezra and Nehemiah (the end of the fifth century B.C.E.) and the events surrounding the Maccabean revolt (175–164 B.C.E.). On the political front, this period commenced with Judah a province of the great Persian Achaemenid empire. Before the end of the fourth century the eastern Mediterranean, like most of the then-known world, had been conquered by Alexander the Great (332–323) and divided among his followers, the Diadochoi. At the end of the period under discussion the rule of Palestine passed from the Greek-Egyptian dynasty, the Ptolemies, to Alexander's successors in Syria, the House of Seleucus. This was an age of vast political transformations, yet we know very little about the internal Jewish responses to these momentous events or the enormously influential social and religious movements they brought in their train.

This anthology focuses on the character and diversity of Judaism within Palestine and its outlying regions. The scope is not limited, however, to the administrative province of Judah (*Yahud*) with its center and Temple in Jerusalem, whose inhabitants came to be called Judeans or Jews. In the Persian period, worshipers of the God of Israel were to be found not just in Judah, but also to the north in Samaria and to the east in Ammon. Those to the north, centered about Shechem and the site of Mt. Gerizim, were the Samaritans; across the Jordan to the east there existed a Jewish "barony" presided over by a family known as the Tobiads. The papers presented here relate not only to the people of Judah but to the Samaritans and Tobiads as well. Indeed, one of the aims of this volume is to demonstrate the range and variety of both population and forms of religious life in the land of Israel and its contiguous environs.

The fourth and third centuries B.C.E., it should be stressed, do not form a "period" in conventional Jewish historiography. They fall in the middle of the "Period of the Second Temple," which properly extends from 536 B.C.E. until the destruction in 70 C.E. All too often, however, the period between the return from Exile (536) and that of Ezra (ca. 400) is treated as the "Age of the Restoration," while serious discussion of the Second Temple period commences only with the background to the Maccabean uprising (175).[1] This severe imbalance issues directly from the fact that the two centuries between Ezra and the beginning of the Maccabean revolt have been regarded by scholars and historians as very much of a dark age. The term "dark" is no reflection on the level of cultural or religious development during the period, but an indication of our own lack of knowledge. Too often, though, this lack of knowledge has joined forces with prevailing scholarly assumptions, and the result has been a markedly impoverished portrayal of the period under discussion.

Thus a reading of most histories of Judaism or ancient Israel will reveal a very limited chapter or section on this period, which generally is described as an age of restricted development and of a solidifying of religious institutions. This process is often described in terms of the growth of the legal and cultic aspects of the Jewish religion. A highly influential textbook, for example, presents the treatment of Judaism in this age under the heading "The Religion of the Law" with the following subheadings: The Growth of a Canon of Scripture; Temple, Cult, and Law; Synagogue, Scribe, and Wisdom Teacher; Piety, Righteousness, and the Law; The Absolutizing of the Law.[2] As these subheadings make evident, the picture presented is one of formalization of religion, of a measure of externalization of religious piety, and of the establishment of standardized institutions. The conclusion follows inevitably: "Through the obscurity of the fourth and third centuries, development continued along the lines laid down [by Ezra and Nehemiah] until, by the time of the Maccabean revolt, Judaism, though still in process of

1. Thus, for example, the classic works on the Second Temple period by Wilhelm Bousset and Emil Schürer. This tendency is reflected in recent studies as well: e.g., A. R. C. Leaney, *The Jewish and Christian World 200 B.C. to A.D. 200* (Cambridge: Cambridge Univ. Press, 1984).

2. J. Bright, *A History of Israel*, 3d ed. (Philadelphia: Westminster Press, 1981), 433–42. The quotation which follows is from p. 428.

evolvement, had assumed in all essentials the shape characteristic of it in the centuries to come."

There are two basic issues lurking in this obscurity. The first is the very real absence of evidence; the second is the evaluation of what limited information we do have. Indeed, the generous historical accounts preserved in the Bible peter out after 400 B.C.E., and the next period about which we have detailed knowledge starts about 200 B.C.E. This lack of evidence is already reflected in our ancient sources. Josephus Flavius, the Jewish historian of the close of the first century C.E., treats the period in a highly selective and idiosyncratic manner: he has relatively little information aside from the biblical narrative and certain apocryphal writings. The Rabbis knew even less than Josephus and in their chronology the whole period is shortened to thirty-six years![3] This paucity of evidence from ancient historical sources has been ameliorated by a number of exciting archeological and epigraphical discoveries made during this century. Several of the essays in this book deal with these discoveries and their impact on the amount of information previously at our disposal. Beyond this simple increase of available information lie the broader questions which touch on the second aspect of obscurity—how this new information changes the conventional way in which the development of Judaism in this period has been perceived. It is this issue which lies at the heart of our present concern.

To speak simply in terms of a solidification of belief is to fail to perceive much that transpired between the age of Persian hegemony and the opening decades of the second century. By that time almost all biblical writing was concluded and new, radically different forms of religious literature emerged, of which the apocalypse and the *pesher* commentary are examples. These new forms of writing reflect both new types of religious experience and new modes of social organization. Thus, for example, we encounter for the first time in this period explicit reports of the ascent of a visionary to the heavenly realm—an innovation which surely reflects profound changes in the understanding of human being's position in the cosmos. Changes in the social and religious structure were far-reaching; groups like the Pharisees, Sad-

---

3. For Josephus's sources concerning the period, see M. Smith, *Palestinian Parties and Politics That Shaped the Old Testament* (New York: Columbia Univ. Press, 1971), 148–51. The classic rabbinic treatment is *Seder 'Olam* (29), a work of the second century C.E.; see C. Milikowsky, "*Seder 'Olam* and Jewish Chronography in the Hellenistic and Roman Periods," *Proceedings of the American Academy of Jewish Research* 52 (1982): 115–39.

ducees, and Essenes appeared during the second century; innovations which were to set the patterns for the succeeding millennia were to be found. Indeed, a principal reason why the difference between the fifth and second centuries may appear so acute is the hiatus in our sources during the intervening centuries.

This anthology presents a survey of recent trends in research which have contributed to a fresh understanding of the fourth and third centuries and to a renewed appreciation of their importance. A number of studies have presented the material discoveries which form the very basis of this new understanding. Others have embarked upon the major task of reassessment of the presuppositions according to which historians traditionally have examined this field. Accordingly, the first section (New Discoveries) is devoted to a series of important material discoveries which have enhanced our perception of Judaism during this period. In these studies the twin focuses of this book are unified: the presentation of the direct implications of new material finds and the attempt to integrate what we learn from these finds into a new understanding of the history of Judaism. It is in the nature of the development of learning that the results and implications of certain studies which were published many years ago are only now coming to fruition, while other research reflects the developments of recent decades.

It is, however, not always new material discoveries alone that change our perception of a historical period. Sometimes it is the reassessment of data and evidence that are well known, even deeply familiar. This is often the more difficult innovation to accept, for new perceptions of old evidence are less glamourous than major, new archeological finds such as the Dead Sea Scrolls. We noted above that although we do not have much direct evidence from Jewish sources about the great events of the late fourth century B.C.E., the conquests of Alexander and the Hellenization of the East clearly ushered in a profound and enduring change in the whole social, cultural, and political character of the world west of the Hindu Kush. How did the Jews and Judaism respond to this event? How was Judaism affected by it? The second section of this book will address the question of Hellenistic influence on Jewish culture and literature during the fourth and third centuries in the land of Israel. This is, perhaps, the aspect of Judaism during that period about which we have enjoyed the newest and most striking perceptions in recent years.

A brief explanation should be made concerning the order in which the chapters have been arranged. In both sections of the anthology the material is presented according to the historical development of the period under discussion. This seemed most sensible, yet it harbors a contradiction. What the anthology attempts to illustrate is not just the results of new research, but what it is that makes that research new and important. The reader will gain, we hope, not only fresh ideas about what Judaism of that age was like, but also some truer sense of how the scholars who have taught us these new perceptions did their work. An essential part of their work can only be understood against the background and in the tradition of the scholars who preceded them. It is with predecessors as well as with contemporaries that all important scholarly discourse must be carried out. Yet, the logic of the historical development of the period does not always correspond to the inherent development of the scholarly discourse or the actual progression of discovery and research. The editors have tried, therefore, to address these issues in their remarks preceding the various essays and in the general conclusion to the volume.

The editors are conscious of the subjects not covered by this book. Most obvious is the restriction of this anthology to the history of Judaism in Palestine during the centuries under discussion. Already with the exile of the Jews by Nebuchadnezzar in 586 B.C.E., we hear of Jews transported not only to Babylon, where they eventually formed a flourishing settlement, but also to Egypt (see Jer. 43:7, 44). In the course of the fifth century, for example, we know of Jewish settlers in Elephantini in upper Egypt who were serving as mercenaries in the Persian armies. Payrus scrolls containing many of their legal and other documents have survived. In the period after Alexander's conquest of Egypt and the founding of Alexandria, Jews settled there, and our information about Egyptian Jewry continues for centuries thereafter. Jews lived, what is more, not only in the fertile Nile and Mesopotamian valleys, but throughout the eastern Mediterranean, and also in Media and Persia to the north. The history of this Diaspora Jewry, with the partial exception of the Jewish community of Alexandria, is largely shrouded in obscurity. Not for this reason, however, does the present book limit its scope to Jewish inhabitants of the land of Israel. Imperatives of range and space rather than matters of principle force us to exclude Diaspora Jewry from our purview.

Yet even within these clearly circumscribed geographical and historical boundaries, much remains neglected. We have not included essays dealing with the material culture of the period or with the political and administrative history of Palestine during these centuries. Topics properly appertaining to biblical studies have also been left aside. The reader is asked to show forbearance for these omissions, further indications of which may be found in the concluding chapter. The number of articles that could be included was limited. We have decided to devote them to two central subjects: (1) the major new discoveries and their implications; (2) the great cultural, social, and political event of Hellenization. These two topics are not all that could be treated; however, the period cannot be understood without them.

A brief, annotated bibliography closes the volume. Selection has been guided by the desire to accommodate important surveys of the period under discussion as well as more specialized works which treat some of the central issues introduced in the present book.

Note should be made that all dates and chronological references are to the period Before the Common Era (B.C.E. or B.C.) unless otherwise indicated.

Overview

Elias J. Bickerman

1

The Historical Foundations of Postbiblical Judaism (1949)

Elias Bickerman's groundbreaking essay "The Historical Foundations of Postbiblical Judaism" serves as the frontispiece of the anthology. His discussion of the forces at work during the Persian and Hellenistic period was at once a masterful synthesis of prior research and a daring break with many features of the old consensus. Though the scope of his survey extends somewhat beyond the chronological and geographical limits outlined above, the argument is presented in its entirety in order to preserve its original force and broad perspective.

Bickerman's approach is deeply rooted not only in knowledge of and sensitivity to the particular Jewish or Israelite past, but in the perception of Judea as part of the surrounding Persian or Hellenistic Orient. This leads to a plethora of insights regarding the development of Judaism during the period in question, among which the following may be stressed:

1. The parallel between Persian Judea and contemporary Greek states (including their respective "tyrants")

2. The establishment of the Torah as the Law of the Jews due to Persian influence

3. An absence of religious exclusiveness and binding legalism

4. Substantial Greek influence in Palestine already during the Persian period

5. The development of a Jewish intelligentsia ("scribes") as the result of the impact of Greek civilization on Jewish Palestine in the third century

Bickerman's emphasis on the dynamic and variegated character of Judaism during the fourth and third centuries serves as a particularly appropriate introduction to this anthology. His essay stands, forty years after its initial publication, as the clearest and most convincing short exposition of the history of Judaism during the early Second Temple period. Indeed, a number of the succeeding chapters in this volume were decisively influenced by Bickerman's own research. While his survey invites reassessment in the light of recent discoveries and discussions, it can be argued that the proper appreciation and understanding of those discoveries were made possible by Bickerman's pioneering synthesis.

1

THE SACRED HISTORY of the Chosen People ends chronologically with Nehemiah's prayer: "Remember us, O God, for good." With Nehemiah's name, "glorious in his memory," concludes the praise of the worthies in the Wisdom of Ben Sira, composed in Jerusalem about 190 B.C.E. Thus, even before the Maccabean revolt, the Jews recognized that after Nehemiah and his contemporary prophets, that is, toward the end of the fifth century, in the age of Socrates, the postbiblical period of Jewish history begins. That period is marked by a unique and rewarding polarity: on the one hand, the Jerusalem center and, on the other, the plurality of centers in the Diaspora. The Dispersion saved Judaism from physical extirpation and spiritual inbreeding. Palestine united the dispersed members of the nation and gave them a sense of oneness. This counterpoise of historical forces is without analogy in antiquity. There were, of course, numberless migrations and transportations of peoples and fragments of peoples; but in due time these offshoots lost connection with the main stock. The colonists brought to cities of Syria by Assyrian kings, the men of Cutha or of Erech, were very soon detached psychologically from their respective cities. Likewise, Phoenician or Greek settlements soon separated from the metropolis. At the most, the Phoenicians had refused to follow a Persian king in his campaign against Carthage, their colony.[1] But the Jewish Dispersion continued to consider Jerusalem as the "metropolis" (Philo), turned to the Holy Land for guidance, and in turn, determined the destinies of its inhabitants. Men who established the normative Judaism in Palestine—Zerubbabel, Ezra, Nehemiah—came from the Diaspora, from Babylon and Susa.

The forces which unwittingly enabled Israel to develop into a people

1. Herod. III.19

alike at home in the ancestral land as well as in the lands of the Dispersion were largely external. When Jerusalem was conquered (597 B.C.E.) and, later (586), destroyed by the Babylonians, the court, the warriors, the craftsmen were transferred to Mesopotamia. This device of deportation, invented perhaps by the Hittites, and applied subsequently by all their successors (Babylonians, Persians, Greeks, Romans, Turks, and even Anglo-Americans—as readers of Longfellow's *Evangeline* know) was by no means an attempt at extermination. The distortion of the ancient expedient is an invention of a modern, European nation in the twentieth century. Being Semites and idolators, the Babylonians simply transported a rebellious group elsewhere in order to break its natural cohesion. In new surroundings, mixed with other ethnic elements, the former enemy learned obedience and, once subdued, furnished labor, taxes, and military services. Accordingly, the exiles received land to till, abandoned sites to rebuild and to settle.[2] They remained free and mostly under leadership of native chiefs. Such a *segan* (as he is called in Aramaic documents) of Phrygians, of Carians, etc., is often mentioned in cuneiform records from Babylonia. On the other hand, since the structure of Oriental monarchies was essentially feudal, there was neither the wish nor the need to assimilate. Thus, in 331 B.C.E., there was still near Nippur (in Mesopotamia) a Carian settlement of colonists transported there from Asia Minor at least two hundred years before. Likewise, the Captivity had created numerous Jewish settlements in Mesopotamia. As a later Babylonian historian tells us (according to some lost original records), King Nebuchadnezzar assigned to the captives dwelling places "in the most convenient districts of Babylonia."[3] Later, in 539, when the Persian king Cyrus conquered Babylon, he reversed, quite naturally, the policy of his adversary and allowed gods and men in Babylonian captivity to return home.

At this moment, the restoration of the Holy City, burned fifty years previously, depended on an accidental conjunction. When the Assyrians conquered Samaria in 722 they established a military colony there. As a result, the Ten Tribes, deported to Assyria, could never again come back. Since, however, there were already military colonies of the Assyrians in Palestine (Samaria, Gezer, etc.), Nebuchadnezzar did not need to send new settlers to Jerusalem. Further, although the Babylonians were savage in battle, they took no delight in useless destruc-

2. See my paper "An Edict of Cyrus," *JBL* 65 (1944).
3. Berosus ap. Josephus *Contra Apionem* I.150.

tion and wholesale slaughter. The remnant of Judah was not exterminated or scientifically tortured to death. Nobody desecrated the graves in Jerusalem; noboby prevented the believers from bringing meal offerings and frankincense to the burned-down House of the Lord and from weeping on its ruins. The walls of Jerusalem being broken down by the Babylonians, the ancient capital was now an open Jewish village. So, unlike the case of Samaria, there was a political vacuum which the Restoration could fill. In the same manner, for example, the Thebans, dispersed by Alexander the Great (in 334), returned eighteen years later and rebuilt their commonwealth.[4] The exceptional feature of Jewish history is the reluctance of so many of the exiled to go back. They remained in Mesopotamia but, paradoxically, continued to care for the Holy City generation after generation, for centuries and millennia. Cupbearer before Artaxerxes I, born and reared in the fifth generation in the Diaspora, Nehemiah weeps when he hears of the affliction of the children of Israel in Jerusalem. He risks disgrace to obtain royal favor for the Holy City. How are we to explain this unity between the Dispersion and Jerusalem?

Every transferred group continued, as a matter of course, to worship the ancestral gods on foreign soil. The men of Cutha, transplanted to Samaria, worshiped Nergal, and the men of Sepharvaim in Samaria continued to sacrifice their children to Adrammelech and Anamelech (2 Kings 17:30).[5] "The Jewish force" in Elephantine, mercenaries established there by the Pharaohs about 600 B.C.E.[6] continued to worship the national God on the southern frontier of Egypt. On the other hand, as a matter of course, the colonists feared and worshiped gods of the land in which they dwelt. A priest of Beth-el was sent back from the Captivity to teach the Assyrian colonists in the land of Samaria how to serve the God of Israel. But the latter was a "jealous God." Some Jews at Elephantine, the seat of the Egyptian god Khnum, seem to have accepted this sheep-headed divinity, or other pagan deities. But even to them the God of Zion, "Yahu" or "Yahu Sabaot," as they styled Him, remained the supreme divinity.[7]

The Diaspora clung to its unique God and to Jerusalem, the unique center of lawful worship. But at the same time, the God of Zion, the

4. Maurice Holleaux, *Etudes d'épigraphie et d'histoire grecques* (Paris, 1938), I:1.

5. On Sephararvain, cf. William Foxwell Albright, *Archaeology and the Religion of Israel* (Baltimore, 1942), 163.

6. On chronology, cf. ibid., 168.

7. See A. Dupont-Sommer, *RHR* 130 (1945): 17–28, and *CRAIBL* (1947): 175–91.

"great and terrible God," was not only the God of the Jews; He was the sole God in heaven and earth, the so-called deities of the pagans were nothing but vain idols. Hence, the polarity of Jerusalem and the Dispersion had its ideological counterpart in the paradoxical combination of universal monotheism and particularism, in the conception that the sole Lord of the Universe dwells on the hillock of Zion. This theological paradox held the Jews in the Dispersion together, and from all points of the compass they directed their eyes to the Lord's Temple in Jerusalem.

But here, in turn, we have to consider the political aspect of the situation. The spiritual unity of the Jews could hardly be established around Jerusalem if the whole Orient, from the Indus to Ethiopia, had not been one world obeying the orders issued by the Persian king. By its influence at the royal court, the Diaspora in Babylonia and Persia could act in behalf of Jewry everywhere and impose a uniform standard of faith and behavior. In a papyrus unearthed in Elephantine we can still read a communication, sent in 419, to the Jewish settlement at this other end of the world, giving rules as to the observance of the Feast of Unleavened Bread. These instructions were forwarded to the satrap of Egypt by King Darius of Persia. On the other hand, in their troubles with the Egyptians, the Jews in Elephantine wrote to the Jewish authorities in Jerusalem.

Or again, the reestablishment of normative Judaism after the Exile is connected by both Jewish tradition and modern scholarship with the name of Ezra, who restored the Law of Moses. But unlike Moses, Ezra's authority to promulgate and administer the Torah in Jerusalem was not derived from a Divine Revelation. Ezra arrived at Jerusalem as a Persian commissioner with a royal letter placing "the Law of thy God" on the same compulsory level as the law of the king, and threatening the offender of Mosaic precepts with death, banishment, confiscation of goods, and imprisonment. In this way the perpetual character of the Torah was established and the Divine Law made known and imposed on all Jewry under the Persian scepter. When, after the dissolution of the empire of Alexander the Great, about 300 B.C.E., the unity of the political world of which the Jews were part had been broken, their religious and spiritual cohesion remained firmly established on the foundations laid down during the Persian age by Ezra and Nehemiah, King Darius and King Artaxerxes.

The imperial protection shielded the Palestinian Jewry from the Arabs and the Philistines, Edom and Moab. In the background of Jewish history in Palestine, from the time of the Judges, there was a constant drive of Aramaic and Arab nomads against the settled country whose comforts they envied. Persian, and later, Macedonian, frontier guards secured from now on the peace of the Jewish peasant. If Jerusalem had not been a part of a Gentile empire, the nomads would have driven the Jews into the sea or swallowed up Palestine, and the rock of Zion would have been the foundation of an Arabian sanctuary a thousand years before Omar's mosque.

2

Let us now take a look at Judaism in the last century of Persian rule, after Nehemiah (432) and before Alexander's conquest of Asia (332). During this period, Jerusalem and a strip of land around it formed a small district of Judea (*Yehûd*) lost in the enormous satrapy "Across the River," that is, west of the Euphrates. The district of Judea was approximately a quadrilateral, about thirty miles long, from Beth-el to Beth-zur, and from twenty-five to thirty-five miles broad, the plateau between the Dead Sea and the lowland in the west. Its area was about a thousand square miles, of which a good part was desert. Of the political history of Judea during our period there is virtually no record. An accidental notice informs us that Artaxerxes III of Persia had deported many Jews to the Caspian Sea during his campaign against Egypt. In all probability, Jerusalem, like Sidon, sided with Egypt in this conflict. A cuneiform tablet records the transport of prisoners from Sidon to Babylonia in the autumn of 345.[8] Thirteen years later Jerusalem as well as Sidon opened the gates to Alexander the Macedonian.

There was a Persian governor in Jerusalem; there was a provincial fiscus; jar handles bearing stamps of "Judea" and "Jerusalem" in Hebrew (and later Aramaic) characters show that tribute was paid in kind.[9] The governors received "bread and wine" from the people (Neh. 5:15) and since the governor had to provide a free table for his officers and the nobles of the land, each day he had to slay one ox and six choice sheep, exclusive of fowl. No wonder, then, that the governor expected a sheep as a present in behalf of suppliants (Mal. 1:8). Monetary economy, nevertheless, began to grow in Palestine. In the time of

---

8. Sidney Smith, *Babylonian Historical Texts* (London, 1924), 145.
9. William Foxwell Albright "Light on the Jewish State in Persian Times," *BASOR*, 53, p. 20.

Nehemiah there are people borrowing money to pay the royal taxes. It is worth noting that Persian royal coins have not been found until now in the numerous and rich coin hoards of the fourth century in this region.[10] Likewise, the Book Ezra-Nehemiah does not mention any coin; when it mentions precious metals and objects made of the metals, it reports their weight. There is no certain record of troops from Judea in Persian service. The contingent from "the Solymian hills" in Xerxes' expedition against Greece, mentioned in the epic poem of Choerilus, a friend of Herodotus, refers probably to the "eastern Ethiopians." But the Jews had arms and had to appear with their swords, their spears, and their bows by order of the governor. The latter had his personal guard, and the castle in which he lived commanded the Temple Hill.

Like every city and nation in the Persian Empire the Jews enjoyed a more or less large autonomy, amplified by bribes and diminished from time to time by arbitrary interference of the Persian authorities. For instance, when once a murder had been committed in the Temple, the governor inflicted on the Jewish nation the fine of fifty shekels for every lamb used in the daily offering; this payment was enforced for seven years, that is, probably, until a new governor came to Jerusalem. The Jews were represented by "the nobles of the Jews," the heads of the clans. On the other hand, there was the High Priest, "and his colleagues the priests who are in Jerusalem," as a document of 409 says. All the sacred personnel, the priests, Levites, singers, doorkeepers, slaves, and servants of the Temple were free of tolls, tributes, and customs. Here as elsewhere the Persian government favored the priesthood among its subjects as against the military aristocracy. The introduction of the Torah as "the law of the Jews" by a royal decree in 445 served the same purpose. Nevertheless, it would be erroneous to regard the district of Yehûd in the fourth century as an ecclesiastical state. While in Egypt, at the same date, a very large part of the soil belonged to the temples, and even a tithe of custom duties was assigned to them,[11] the sanctuary of Jerusalem does not appear to have possessed any real estate outside its own site, and the emoluments of the priests were offerings of the believers. Even the voluntary contribution of a

10. M. Rostovtzeff, *Social and Economic History of the Hellenistic World* (Oxford, 1941), 3:1324.

11. On the so-called Naucratis inscription, see the literature quoted by G. Posener in *Annales du Servicer des Antiquités de l'Egypte* (Paris, 1934): 141.

third of a shekel by every male Israelite, established under Nehemiah to defray the expenses of public worship, fell into disuse.[12] But the influence of the priests continues to rise. In Nehemiah's time lay rulers of Judah led in public affairs, for example, in the dedication of the walls of Jerusalem, while the priests and the Levites purified the people; likewise plots against Nehemiah were devised among "the nobles of Judah." A century after him, a Greek traveler learned from his Jewish informant that public affairs of the Jews were administered by priests.[13]

It is a widely spread error that Judaism after Ezra was under the yoke of the Law, that the Jews were a community governed by an extreme strictness, that they were immune to foreign contagion and, until the Macedonian conquest, separated from the Greek world. As a matter of fact, excavations have shown that in the fifth and fourth centuries B.C.E., Palestine belonged to the belt of an eclectic, Greco-Egyptian-Asiatic culture, which extended from the Nile Delta to Cilicia.[14] The kitchen pots, as well as heavy bronze anklets worn by girls, or weapons of men, were now the same in the whole Levant, united under Persian sway. Greek painted pottery, Phoenician amulets and Egyptian idols are equally typical of Palestine in the fourth century. A Jerusalemite who went down to the coastal cities, let us say to Ascalon, could not help seeing a Greek cup showing Oedipus in conversation with the Sphinx or small bronzes of Egyptian deities. And when he returned with earthenware for his household, it might happen that he introduced into the Holy City reminiscence of a Greek mythos. An Attic black-figured cup with a sphinx has been found at Tel-En-Nashbeh, some six miles north of Jerusalem. The story, related by a pupil of Aristotle, that the master had met in Asia Minor (ca. 345 B.C.E.) a Hellenized Greek-speaking Jew is probably a fiction, but not one which is improbable.[15] The commercial influence of Greece in Palestine was so great that the Athenian coins became the principal currency for trade transactions in the fifth century. This currency was gradually replaced in the fourth century by local imitations of the Athenian "owls." The authorities in Palestine also struck such imitations.[16] As their small denominations show, these

12. See E. Bickerman, "Héliodore au Temple de Jérusalem," in *Annuaire de l'Institut de Philologie et d'Histoire Orientale* 7 (Université de Bruxelles, 1939–42): 14.

13. Hecataeus ap. Josephus *Contra Apionem* I.188.

14. For archaeological evidence, cf. Rostovtzeff, *Social and Economic History* 3:1325; see also C. C. McCown, *Tell En-Nashbeh* (Berkeley, 1947), vol. 1.

15. Clearchus ap. Josephus *Contra Apionem* I.176; cf. Hans Lewy, "Aristotle and the Jewish Sage According to Clearchus of Soli," *HTR* 31/3, p.205.

16. A. Reifenberg, *Ancient Jewish Coins* (Jerusalem, 1947).

coins were destined for local use and for business transactions on market days. Nevertheless, used by pious Jews and even bearing the stamp of a Jewish agent of the Persian government (Hezekiah), these first Jewish coins show not only the owl of the Athenian model but also human figures,[17] and even the image of a divinity seated on a winged wheel.[18] Whether the die cutter simply imitated here the Baal of the Tarsian coins or intended to represent in this way the "Lord of Hosts," these coins are hardly in accord with the biblical interdiction of "graven images." In fact, being real men and not puppets like the characters portrayed in conventional textbooks, the Jews of the Restoration, like those of every generation, were entangled in contradictions and in conflicting patterns of real life.

They were convinced that God set them apart from the nations (Lev. 20:24), but they called Him the God of Heaven, which was the title of Ahuramazda, the deity of their Persian rulers. They regarded as Israel's heritage the whole land from Dan to Beer-sheba, even from Egypt to the Orontes (1 Chron. 13:5), but did not establish friendly relations with the remnants of Ephraim who worshiped the same God and consecrated His priests according to the prescriptions of the Torah (2 Chron. 13:9). In Jerusalem in the fourth century the priesthood was considered firmly organized by David himself, but among these ancient priestly families were some like the clan Hakoz, which had been regarded as of doubtful lineage only a hundred years before. The Jews imagined that they were living according to the Law of Moses, while the synagogue, unknown to the Torah, became a fundamental part of their devotional life. So "the congregation of the Lord" became the basic element of the nation[19] and a Jerusalemite could not imagine the national kings of the past acting otherwise than in agreement with the Holy Community (1 Chron. 13:1; 16:1; 28:8; 29:1; 2 Chron. 30:4). Of still greater significance was another innovation: how the Torah came to be taught "throughout all the cities of Judah" (2 Chron. 17:9). Before this the priests had kept to themselves the decision on matters of ritual and of morals. The knowledge comes from the priest's lips, says an author of the age of Ezra and Nehemiah, and law from the priest's mouth, because he is the messenger of the Lord (Mal. 2:7). But the democratization of the instruction in the Law in the fourth century opened the

17. Ibid., #1a. A Hebrew shekel (3.88 gr.) in silver, obv.: male head bearded; rv.: female head; inscr. (in Hebrew): "one half."

18. Ibid., Pl. I, #3.

19. Louis Finkelstein, *The Pharisees* (Philadelphia, 1938), 2:566.

way to the coming of the scribe, and imperceptibly compromised the supremacy of the priest. From now on, the superiority of learned argument over authoritative decree prevailed. The First Psalm presents as the model of happiness not the officiating priest in the Temple, but rather the Sage who meditates on the Torah day and night. Scribes and Sages, clergy and laymen, the Jews were expected to be "saints," holy unto the Lord (Lev. 20:26). But the Law of God which gave the standard of holiness was imposed upon the saints by the decree of their pagan sovereign.

Another widespread and mistaken conception is that of postexilic exclusiveness.[20] As a matter of fact, in the Persian period, the Jews were first of all peoples we know to open wide the gates to proselytes. Every ancient cult was exclusive; none but the members of a family participated in the worship of its tutelary gods; no foreigner was able to sacrifice to the deities of a city.[21] When Orestes, masked as a stranger, returns to his ancestral home, he asks permission to take part in religious ceremonies, "if strangers may sacrifice with citizens."[22] In the fifth century B.C.E., the Athenians equally assume that it is a "calamity" to have an alien father.[23] They were proud of being autochthonous, and not immigrants of mixed blood. In 333 B.C.E., when Alexander the Great was already making war in Asia, a special law was necessary in Athens to authorize the shrine of a foreign deity on the sacred soil of Pallas.[24] But the Jewish law allowed a stranger sojourning among the Jews to keep the Passover with the congregation of Israel (Ezra 6:21). "One law shall be to him that is homeborn, and unto the stranger who sojourns among you" (Exod. 12:49). And again: "The stranger who sojourns with you shall be to you as the homeborn among you, and thou shalt love him as thyself" (Lev. 19:34). An Athenian contemporary of Ezra would be astonished to hear that he has to love the *Metoeci*. Equally startling for the ancient world was the idea of proselytism, the appeal to the nations to join themselves to the Lord, which began with Second Isaiah and was repeated by later prophets again and again. "Thus says the Lord of hosts: In those days it shall come to pass, that ten men shall

20. C. C. Torrey, *The Second Isaiah* (New York, 1928), 126, has already vigorously protested against this misconception. Cf. Finkelstein, *Pharisees*, 461.

21. It is a pity that N. D. Fustel de Coulanges's *La Cité Antique*, first published in 1864, is almost unknown outside of France.

22. Euripides *Electra* 795.

23. Euripides *Ion* 588.

24. Cf. A. D. Nock, *Conversion* (London, 1933), 20.

take hold, out of all the languages of the nations, shall even take hold of the skirt of him that is a Jew, saying: We will go with you, for we have heard that God is with you" (Zech. 8:23). So, the postexilic community establishes the new and really revolutionary principle: "Thus says the Lord: My house shall be called a house of prayer for all peoples" (Isa. 56:7).

Again we meet with the fact that every historical situation is many-sided and full of contradictions. The heathens were tolerant and their gods lived amicably side by side because each nation had its own gods who did not care for other people. An Argive refugee in Athens is told not to be afraid of the Argive gods: "We have gods who fight on our side and who are not weaker than these on the side of the Argives."[25] Thus, the pagans made no efforts to convert a stranger but, for the same reason, excluded him from their own religion. Everybody was a true believer, in the opinion of the heathen, if he worshiped his ancestral gods. Thus, each city was exclusive and intolerant within its walls, but recognized the other gods outside. On the other hand, knowing that the Lord is the One True God, the Jews naturally proselytized among the heathen and admitted the converted to the universal religion. And for that same reason they were intolerant of those outside the congregation and rejected the folly of idolatry. Only a Jew was a true believer, but everybody could enter the congregation of the Chosen People.

The thought of this period is illustrated in an anonymous historical composition which now appears in the Bible as Ezra-Nehemiah and Chronicles.[26] The arrangement reveals that the latter part of the original work (Ezra-Nehemiah) found its way into the scriptural canon before the portion (Chronicles) which related the preexilic history already covered by the Books of Samuel and Kings. But the work originally formed a single, continuous narrative from Adam to Nehemiah; it was still read in this edition by the compiler of a Greek version (the so-called First Esdras) in the second century B.C.E.

For the preexilic period the Chronicler draws for the most part on the Books of Samuel and Kings, but adds a great deal of information from other sources. Historians usually discount this additional material and blame the Chronicler for his little regard for facts. He can, for instance, state coolly that David had 1,570,000 warriors, exclusive of the troops of Levi and Benjamin (1 Chron. 21:5). But the same exuber-

25. Euripides Heracleidae, 348.
26. William Foxwell Albright, "The Biblical Period," in Archaeology, 50ff.

ance in numbers is displayed by Assyrian records, and the source of the Chronicler (2 Sam. 24) gives a number no less fantastic for David's army: 1,300,000. Fact-hunting critics overlook a very important feature of the work: its emancipation from the authority of tradition.

Oriental historiography is strictly traditional. An Assyrian reviser of royal annals may transform a booty of 1,235 sheep into one of 100,225,[27] or attribute to the king a successful campaign of his predecessor; but in the main he simply summarizes his source. The compiler of Kings closely follows his authorities, although he adds personal comments to the events. The Chronicler, like Hecataeus of Miletus or Herodotus, gives such information concerning the past as appears to him most probable, and corrects the sources in conformity with his own historical standards. For instance, when he asserts that the Levites carried the Ark in accordance with David's order (1 Chron. 15:1), he interpolates something into his source (2 Sam. 6:12) because he assumes as self-evident that the pious king could not but act according to the Law of Moses (Exod. 25:13). For the same reason he says "Levites" (2 Chron. 5:4) when his source (1 Kings 8:3) speaks of "priests" taking up the Ark under Solomon. Following his rule of historical probability, he cannot believe that Solomon turned over some cities to Hiram of Tyre (1 Kings 9:12); so he changes the text: the cities were given by Hiram to Solomon (2 Chron. 8:2). In the same manner, he attributes to ancient kings, David and Josiah, the organization of the priesthood and of the sacred services as they existed in his own time. Since Israel had ceased to be an independent state, the author treats with predilection all matters concerning the Temple, which now became the center of national life, and devotes a long description to religious measures of King Hezekiah which are hardly mentioned in Kings. Owing to the shift of historical interest, he passes over in silence the Northern Kingdom, which had rebelled against the house of David. He does not hesitate to use the term "Israel" when he speaks of Judah, which alone remained faithful to the covenant of the fathers.

The critics have often stressed the Chronicler's practice of viewing the past as the realization in Israel of the rules and principles of the Torah, his tendency to find the origins of the Judaism of his own day in remote antiquity. In fact, his purpose is not to give a mere chronicle but to provide a clue to the meaning and direction of Israel's history. The same attempt, with regard to Greek (and even world) history, was made

27. A. T. Olmstead, *History of Assyria* (New York, 1923), 580.

by Herodotus, who wrote about a hundred years before the Chronicler. Herodotus seems to feel that the gods, envious of human greatness and happiness, use man's wrongdoings to punish him or his posterity. It is the doctrine of Nemesis, exemplified, for instance, in Polycrates's fate. The moral of history is, therefore, to remain an average man; its lesson is that of moderation and submission to destiny, the "nothing in excess" of the Seven Sages.

The Jewish author finds in divine pragmatism the principle for understanding the past; his clue is the idea of retribution. That is, of course, nothing new. Herodotus explains Croesus's fall by the sin of his ancestor in the fifth generation. In a cuneiform text Nabonidus's evildoing explains his fall and the catastrophe of Babylon.[28] But the Chronicler describes the whole of human history from this standpoint. According to his conception, the pious kings always enjoyed prosperity, while punishment necessarily befell the wicked and unfaithful ones. The idea is applied to the reinterpretation of the past with the same constancy and disregard of facts as when some modern books describe history in terms of class struggle or racial changes. From Saul to the last king, Zedekiah, the evildoers die for their transgressions. But, since the Chronicler conceives of Divine Necessity in human history as the work of the personal God and not of a machinelike Fate of the Greeks, he seeks to justify the visitations sent upon Israel. In the first place, he stresses the idea of personal responsibility. He follows and repeats (2 Chron. 25:4) the principle established in Deuteronomy (24:16) that "the fathers shall not be put to death for the children, neither shall the children be put to death for the fathers; every man shall be put to death for his own sin," a conception which appears about the same time in Greece too. But the principle of collective responsibility remained active in Greece, except for Athens, with regard to political crimes.[29] In Judaism, the Book of Kings still presents the hand of God visiting the sins of the fathers upon their children and striking peoples for the transgressions of their kings. Jehoiachin is carried away and Judah is destroyed in 597 "for the sins of Manasseh" who had reigned almost fifty years before (2 Kings 24:3; Jer. 15:4). The Chronicler assumes that Manasseh had received a due punishment from the Assyrians, who led him about in fetters and held on to him by a hook thrust into his nostrils

28. Cf. William Foxwell Albright, *From the Stone Age to Christianity* (Baltimore, 1940), 242, 245.

29. G. Glotz, *The Greek City and Its Institutions* (New York, 1929), 258.

(2 Chron. 33:11). On the other hand, the destruction of Jerusalem in 587 is explained in Kings (2 Kings 24:20) as an expression of God's anger against the last king, Zedekiah. The Chronicler adds that "all the chiefs of the priests, and the people, transgressed very greatly after all the abominations of the nations; and they polluted the house of the Lord which He had hallowed in Jerusalem" (2 Chron. 36:14). The Syrian invasion in the reign of Joash is a judgment on the people, "because they had forsaken the Lord, the God of their fathers" (2 Chron. 24:24). The invasion of Shishak happened because all Israel had transgressed along with King Rehoboam (2 Chron. 12:1). Consequently, the deliverance from Sennacherib is caused by the reconciliation of the people with God, and the author is fond of associating the people with the king in religious reformations (1 Chron. 13:4; 2 Chron. 30:4–5).

This conception of personal responsibility for transgression explains the role of the prophets in Chronicles. Herodotus uses the Oriental theme of the wise counselor to show how man in his blindness neglects prudent advice and runs to his doom. The Chronicler knows that God sent His prophets "because He had compassion on His people" (2 Chron. 36:15); but they mocked His messengers and despised His words. So the culprit was fully conscious of the culpability of his deed and duly warned, a proviso which later talmudic jurisprudence requires for legal conviction and punishment of a capital offender. Thus, warned by God, the wicked kings sinned with malice and God's wrath was fully justified. Accordingly, the Chronicler's standard in judging the ancient kings is their obedience to the Divine Message sent through the prophets. Jerusalem was destroyed because Israel scoffed at the warnings of the prophets. The Temple was rebuilt by Cyrus, in order that the Word of the Lord by the mouth of Jeremiah might be accomplished (2 Chron. 36:22). This, "the Chronicle of the whole of sacred history," as Jerome calls it, leads to the Restoration under Persian rule. When the adversaries of Jerusalem frustrate the building of the Temple, King Darius intervenes, and the Jews dedicate the sanctuary and prosper "through the prophesying of Haggai . . . and Zechariah" (Ezra 6:14).

In keeping with ancient historiography, the recital becomes fuller when the compiler approaches his own time. But some features of the latter part of his work are peculiar. In the first place, we note that while the author considers Nehemiah's days as being in the past (Neh. 12:47), he does not continue the narrative until his own time but ends with the account of Nehemiah's measures which concluded the Restoration in 432 B.C.E. In the same way, Heodotus (and other Greek historians in the fifth century) did not deal with the events after the Persian wars.[30] Again, while for the preexilic period the Chronicler refers to many sources, for the Persian epoch he gives hardly anything other than a reproduction of official records: lists, letters and memoranda of royal administration, memorials of Ezra and of Nehemiah. He scarcely provides notes of his own for a chronological and logical framework. And, while he freely passes judgment on ancient persons and times, he refrains from expressing his personal views in the account of the Persian period. One is reminded of Greek *logographi* of the fifth century who, as an ancient critic says, repeated "the written records that they found preserved in temples or secular buildings in the form in which they found them, neither adding nor taking away anything."[31]

This dependence on source material leads, quite naturally, to some confusion. As the Chronicler confuses, for instance, Darius I with Darius II, he places a dossier referring to Xerxes and Artaxerxes I before their predecessor Darius I. The Chronicler quotes Ezra's and Nehemiah's accounts in their own words, a feature which involved the change from the third person to the first person and vice versa. This device served to authenticate the narrative and came into historical writing from the diplomatic style, where exactness of quotation was absolutely necessary. In Egypt the story of the war of King Kamose in the sixteenth century B.C.E., or the epic of the victory of Rameses II at Kadesh, ca. 1300 B.C.E., presents the same change from a subjective account to objective praise by the hero of his own deeds.[32] The so-called "Letters to God Assur" in Assyrian historiography likewise show the use of the third person when the king is spoken of in the introduction composed by a scribe, while in the body of the text the king speaks in the first person.[33] In a Persian tract composed after the conquest of Babylon in 538 B.C.E., the so-called Cyrus cylinder, the author relates the evildoings of Nabonidus, the last king of Babylon, and the conquest of the city by Cyrus. Then, without any transition, exactly as in Ezra-Nehemiah, the author introduces Cyrus's proclamation, beginning "I am Cyrus," which gives Cyrus's own account of the

30. C. N. Cochrane, *Christianity and Classical Culture* (Oxford, 1944), 462.
31. Dionysius of Halicarnassus *De Thucydide* 5. I quote the translation of the passage in Lionel Pearson, *Early Ionian Historians* (Oxford, 1939), 3.
32. Adolf Erman, *The Literature of the Ancient Egyptians* (London, 1927), 58, 95.
33. Cf., too, an inscription of Shalmaneser III in D. D. Luckenbill, *Ancient Records of Assyria and Babylonia* (Chicago, 1926–27), II. The narrative begins in the first person (#623) and continues in the third person (#624).

events.[34] When the Chronicler quotes documents verbatim, he again follows the style of chancelleries. He introduces even in his narratives of preexilic history such compositions couched in official form, for example, a circular communication of King Hezekiah (2 Chron. 30) and even a letter of the prophet Elijah (2 Chron. 21:12).[35]

Ezra's and Nehemiah's prayers, the national confession of sins, the covenants made with God under the leadership of Ezra and Nehemiah are presented as proof that there is a difference between the wicked Jerusalem of the kings and the new Israel which decided to follow the way of righteousness. That accounts for the blessing of the present state under the protection of the Persian kings. The Temple is restored "according to the commandment of the God of Israel, and according to the decree of Cyrus, and Darius, and Artaxerxes king of Persia" (Ezra 6:14).

The whole conception of the Chronicler shows that he wrote when Persian rule seemed destined for eternity and the union between the altar in Jerusalem and the throne of Susa seemed to be natural and indestructible. The Chronicler wrote before Alexander the Great, that is, in the first half of the fourth century. Accordingly, the tendency of his work is to recommend a kind of political quietism which should please the court of Susa as well as the High Priest's mansion in Jerusalem. The idea of the Messianic age which was destined to come after the overthrow of the Persian world power, finds no place in the work of the Chronicler. Armies are superfluous for Israel, the Jews need not fight when the Lord is with them; the Chronicler does not tire of stressing this conception. But "the Lord is with you while you are with Him" (2 Chron. 15:2). Zedekiah was punished and Jerusalem destroyed not only because the king did evil and did not give heed to Jeremiah's words, but also because "he rebelled against King Nebuchadnezzar, who had made him swear by God." That is taken from Ezekiel (17:13) but the lesson could hardly escape the attention of the Chronicler's readers, subjects of the Persian king.

The Chronicler's historical work, Attic pottery unearthed in Palestine, Jewish coins bearing a Divine Image, universalism and exclusiveness, all these together create a picture of Jewish life after the Restora-

---

34. R. W. Rogers, *Cuneiform Parallels to the Old Testament* (New York, 1912), 380.

35. Such fictitious documents are already included in the Egyptian cycle of stories of Petubastis, a kind of historical novel which is presented as a work of historiography. See G. Maspero, *Popular Stories of Ancient Egypt* (New York, 1915), 242, 256.

tion rather different from what is conveyed by the conventional clichés. They indicate that life was more vivid, more diversified than the rules of conduct as formulated in Scripture might suggest.

3

A postexilic oracle, included in the Book of Isaiah (11:11) promises the return of the Diaspora from Elam, Assyria, Babylonia, Lower and Upper Egypt, from North Syria and "from the islands of the sea." This Jewish Diaspora encountered everywhere the Hellenic Diaspora. Greek trading stations existed in the fifth and fourth centuries, for example, at Ugarit (near modern Lattakie) and at the mouth of the Orontes in Syria.[36] When in 586 Jewish refugees from Palestine, Jeremiah among them, went to "Tahpanhes" in the Egyptian Delta, they entered a settlement of Greek mercenaries, established here (Daphne) by Psammetichus.[37] Payments of rations listed in a Babylonian account between 595 and 570 B.C.E. were provided not only to King Joiachin [Jehoiachin] and numerous other men of Judah in exile, but also to Ionian carpenters and shipbuilders.[38] As cuneiform business documents of the Persian period show, the Jews in the Babylonian Diaspora rubbed shoulders with men from India and Armenia and Turkestan and, of course, Lydians and Ionians.[39] When later Greek authors supposed that Pythagoras, that ancient sage of Samos, was indebted not only to Egypt and Chaldea, but to Jewish wisdom, too, when a later Jewish author thought that the Greek sages had learned loftier conceptions of God from Moses, they were probably wrong, but the surmise does not any longer appear absurd in the light of recent discoveries. One may fancy Ezekiel talking with Pythagoras in Babylon; they speak of Homer and of Moses. What a topic for an *Imaginary Conversation* in Landor's fashion!

But our information concerning the Diaspora in the Persian period is scanty and accidental. To be sure, we still have numerous records from Babylonia, written between 464 and 404 B.C.E., with many Jewish names.[40] But, since these tablets are business documents of one pagan firm in Nippur, in southern Babylonia, we do not really learn anything substantial of the life of the Jews from these contracts and receipts.

---

36. See Rostovtzeff, *Social and Economic History* 3:1326.
37. Herod. II.30, 154.
38. William Foxwell Albright, "King Joachim in Exile," *BA* 5/4 (1942): 51.
39. W. Eilers, in *ZDMG* (1940), 225.
40. See S. Daiches, *The Jews of Babylonia* (London, 1910).

Nevertheless, these archives show that the *golah* of 597 and 587 still remained on the same place where the exiled had been settled by Nebuchadnezzar, namely, "by the river Chebar" (Ezek. 1:1), which is the "large canal" of the cuneiform tablets, a watercourse on which Nippur was situated. The Jews in the documents often bear Babylonian and Persian names, some of them combined with the names of pagan deities. For instance, the father of a Hanana is called Ardi-Gula, that is, "servant of [the Goddess] Gula." But about seventy per cent of the Jews had genuine Hebrew names. The Jews in the district of Nippur were for the most part farmers; but they were also tax collectors and royal officials; they held military tenures and transacted business with the Babylonians and the Persians. A Jewish claimant opposes a Babylonian merchant house "in the judicial assembly of Nippur."

There were many Jewish settlements in Egypt, too; for instance, in the Delta, near Pelusium, at Memphis, and in upper Egypt. The Egyptian Diaspora was preexilic. Even before the Exile an oracle signifies five cities in the land of Egypt that speak the language of Canaan and swear to the Lord of Hosts (Isa. 19:18), and the Second Isaiah (49:12) mentions the Jews in the land of Sinim, that is, Syene, at the first cataract of the Nile, at the southern border of Egypt. To this place Jewish mercenaries were sent by one of their kings in the beginning of the sixth century to help the Pharaoh. Guardian of the Ethiopian boundary, "the Jewish force" came into Persian service after Cambyses's conquest of Egypt (525 B.C.E.), and obeyed the Pharaohs again after the defection of Egypt in 404. Numerous documents in Aramaic of the fifth century, belonging to this military settlement, have been unearthed at Elephantine.[41]

The Jewish force (as the regiment is officially styled) was divided into companies, the captains of which bear Babylonian or Persian names; a Persian was "the chief of the force." The settlers received pay and rations (barley, lentils, etc.) from the royal treasury. But the colony was civilian in its way of life. The Jews at Elephantine bought and sold their tenures, transacted business, defended their claims in civil courts, although everyone, even women, was styled as belonging to the regiment. The Jews dealt with military colonists of other nations settled in the neighborhood, as well as with Egyptians. There were mixed mar-

---

41. A. E. Cowley, *Aramaic Papyri of the Fifth Century* (Oxford, 1923). Some 125 ostraca will be published by A. Dupont-Sommer. See his paper quoted above in n.7.

riages. Independently of the military organization the Jews formed a religious community of the kind later, in the Hellenistic period, called *politeuma*. A president "with his colleagues" represented the community which was gathered in "assembly" whenever wanted. The president was also the treasurer of the local Temple of the national God, whom these Jews called "Yahu" and regarded as "the God of Heaven." Likewise, their system of sacrifices and the terms referring to them were the same as in the Bible: holocaust, meal offering, incense; they offered libations and immolated sheep, oxen and goats. They observed the Passover. Their faith was rather homely and plain. They suggested in a letter that their enemy was killed, "and the dogs tore off the anklets from his legs," because they had prayed for it to the God of Heaven and fasted "with our wives and our children" in sackcloth. They did not doubt that merit before God may be obtained with expensive sacrifices, and would hardly appreciate the prophetic word that God desires mercy and not sacrifices (Hos. 6:6). But equally, they did not suspect that their place of worship was a violation of Divine Law proclaimed in Deuteronomy, which forbids altars and immolations outside of the one chosen place at Jerusalem. With the same "provincial" naiveté, they uttered blessings in the name of "Yahu and Khnum."

While the religion of the Jews of Elephantine was primitive their business activity was highly modern. The wrote, and probably talked, not Hebrew but Aramaic, which had become the common and official language of the Persian Empire. Accordingly, while contemporary demotic documents reflect Egyptian law, and while Mesopotamian settlers near Aleppo (Syria) and at Gezer (Palestine) continued to draw cuneiform deeds in harmony with the Babylonian system,[42] the Aramaic records from Elephantine manifest the formation and development of a new common law of the Levant. The form of these instruments is that of a declaration made before witnesses and reproduced in direct speech; this is modeled on Egyptian formularies. The same form is used in an Aramaic lease agreement of 515 B.C.E. entered into in Egypt by two parties not of Jewish origin. Some stipulations in business documents from Elephantine reproduce Egyptian formulae also, for example, the abandonment of the claims to a ceded property. But the term "hate" for separation of spouses is Babylonian and biblical (Deut. 21:15), although it was also borrowed by the Egyptians. Babylonian too

---

42. E. Dhorme in *RA* (1928).

are the contracts of renunciation arising from a previous decision of the court, the legal term for "instituting a suit" and the standard of weight. This syncretistic common law was built up partly by precedents set by the Persian king's judges, partly by way of customary agreements. The Persian court adopted, for instance, the Egyptian practice of imposing an oath (formulated by the judge) upon the party in support of the claim when there was no other evidence, even when the litigants were of different nationalities, for example, a Jew and a Persian. Everybody was required, of course, to swear by his own deity; when a Jewess became the wife of an Egyptian, she was supposed to follow the status of her husband and she took oath by an Egyptian goddess. On the other hand, polygamy, allowed in Jewish law, was prohibited in marriage contracts of Elephantine by a stipulation agreed upon by the parties and guaranteed by a fine. While Egyptian marriage was based on mere consensus, the Jews at Elephantine still regarded a union as valid only when the bride's father received from the groom a "marriage price" (*mohar*). But this conveyance of rights to the husband became here an antiquated formality. The new common law established an almost complete equality between spouses. Both had the right to divorce at his or her pleasure, provided the declaration of "hating" was made "in the congregation." The power to divorce was given to the bride in Egyptian marriage contracts, but it was limited to the husband alone in Jewish (and Babylonian) law. Egyptian too was the status of women with regard to her legal capacity; married or not, she was able at Elephantine to conduct business, hold property in her own right and resort to law about it. No less surprising was the stipulation that either spouse would inherit from the other when there were no children. Thus, the Aramaic papyri from Elephantine of the fifth century B.C.E. are the earliest evidence we have for the transformation of the Jewish behavior in the Dispersion. Living on equal terms with the natives, transacting business with peoples of various races, intermarrying, the Diaspora began to diverge from the course followed at Jerusalem.

But living together with other people rarely continues untroubled. Although the priest of the Egyptian god Khnum was a neighbor of the Jewish sanctuary at Elephantine for many decades, in 411 the Egyptian clergy bribed the Persian governor to order the Jewish temple destroyed. One may doubt whether that was really "the first anti-Semitic outbreak," as the action is now considered by historians. When we read the endless complaints of a certain Peteesi, an Egyptian (513 B.C.E.), about vexations he was forced to suffer from Egyptian priests on account of some litigation,[43] we are rather prepared to believe that the conflict of 411 at Elephantine was a local incident, and not a symptom of general anti-Semitism. When the Persian governor refused to allow the reconstruction of the temple, the Jews of Elephantine sent an appeal to Jerusalem. But the existence of a temple outside Zion could hardly please the authorities at Jerusalem. Consequently, in 408, the Jews of Elephantine wrote to Bagoas, the Persian governor of Judea, and to the sons of Sanballat, governor of Samaria, hinting also at a forthcoming bribe. The addressees prepared a memorandum recommending to the satrap of Egypt the reestablishment of the temple, without animal offerings, however: a compromise which would please both the Egyptians, who at this time worshiped almost every animal, and the Jerusalemites, who in this manner reduced the altar of Elephantine to a lower rank.

But there were again intrigues and counterintrigues, bribes and favors at the court of the Persian satrap of Egypt; and since, toward the end of the fifth century, Egypt rebelled against Persia, the temple at Elephantine was never rebuilt, although the Jewish military settlement continued and was ultimately taken over by Alexander the Great.

4

The Persian Empire fell in 333. When Alexander the Great proceeded down the coast of Syria toward Egypt, most peoples and cities on his route, Jerusalem among them, readily submitted to the Macedonian. The meeting of Jewish deputies, sent to offer the surrender of the Holy City, with the world conqueror later became a choice topic of Jewish legend. In fact, the Macedonian, who considered himself the legitimate heir of the Persian kings, here as elsewhere simply accepted and confirmed the statutes and privileges granted by his Iranian predecessors. But an accidental order of Alexander's deeply influenced the history of Palestine.

The city of Samaria revolted in 332, and the king, having taken it, settled Macedonians there. This punishment, inflicted on Samaria, brought about the break between Judah and Ephraim. Captured by the Assyrians in 722, the city of Samaria had become a military colony. The men from Babylonia and northern Syria transplanted here, brought

---

43. F. L. Griffith, *Catalogue of the Demotic Papyri in the John Rylands Library* (Manchester, 1909), 60.

along their own gods, such as the god of pestilence, Nergal of Cutha, who at the same time appeared in Sidon, a city also resettled by the Assyrians after the rebellion of 677. Being polytheists, the settlers in due course adopted the deity of the land in which they dwelt and learned to worship the God of Israel with great zeal. Since Sargon in 722 deported only the higher classes of the district of Samaria, the countryside was not denuded of the original population. Sargon himself refers to the tribute imposed on this remnant of Israel.

The newcomers intermingled and intermarried with the former inhabitants of the land of Samaria and accepted their religion. In 586, men of Shiloh and Samaria came and worshiped at the ruined site of the Temple of Jerusalem. In 520 the Samaritans claimed a share in the rebuilding of this Temple. As already noted, in 408 the Jews at Elephantine wrote to the leaders in both Jerusalem and Samaria as to coreligionists. Still later there were people of Ephraim who celebrated the Passover at Jerusalem (2 Chron. 34:6). It seems that the conversion of the heathen immigrants to the service of the God of Israel was complete and that both Samaria and Jerusalem worshiped the same God with the same rites in the fourth century B.C.E. There is no mention of any pagan cult among the Samaritans. Accordingly, prophets in Jerusalem expected the redemption of both "prisoners of hope" (Zech. 9:13), Judah and Ephraim. The conflict between the two cities under Persian rule was primarily a political one. Samaria opposed the rebuilding of the walls of Jerusalem because the resurrected capital in the south would be a natural rival of the northern fortress. In the same way, the Assyrian settlers in Sidon, who became completely assimilated with the natives, inherited their quarrel with Tyre, another Phoenician capital.

But when Alexander planted Macedonian colonists in the city of Samaria, he destroyed the fusion between "the force at Samaria" and the countryside. The new masters of the stronghold did not know anything about the God of Israel. They did not care for Nergal either. They were at home rather in Athens, where in the third century B.C.E. a pagan association crowned a certain "Samaritan" as its benefactor. If the new inhabitants were inclined to adopt some elements of the religion of the former settlers, they could hardly succeed because the God of Israel did not tolerate any rival.

It often happened that when a Greek colony was established, native villages under its control formed a union around an ancestral sanctuary. Following the same pattern, the countryside of (now Macedonian)

Samaria constituted an organization, in Greek style, "Sidonians of Shechem," for the purpose of serving the God of Israel.[44] Shechem, the most ancient capital and the most sacred site of Israel, became the natural center of the confederation. The name "Sidonians," that is, "Canaanites," was probably chosen in opposition to the newcomers; it emphasized the fact that the members of the League were aboriginal inhabitants of Canaan. The geographical term "Samaritans" was appropriated by the Macedonian intruders, and the religious term "Israel" now belonged to Jerusalem. The descendants of the Assyrian settlers, men like Sanballat, Nehemiah's adversary, who had been the leaders in Palestine for four centuries and who were now dispossessed, could neither accept the predominance of the Macedonian colony nor become a dependency of Jerusalem. They repeated to the Jews, "we seek your God as you do" (Ezra 4:2), but were not prepared to recognize the demands of Jerusalem that the common Deity may not be rightfully worshiped away from the summit of Zion. As the Chronicler emphasized (2 Chron. 30:10), such claims were received with derision in the north.

The new union around Shechem, therefore, founded its own sanctuary. It was consecrated to the God of both Jerusalem and Shechem, and stood on the summit of Gerizim, overlooking Shechem, on the site where the Chosen People were commanded to "set the blessing," according to the precept of Deuteronomy (11:29). Deuteronomy was originally a Jerusalemite book, published in 621 B.C.E., but since 722 B.C.E. there had been no center of religion of the fathers outside Jerusalem, and the worshipers of God, in Samaria or elsewhere, had to seek guidance at Jerusalem. The choice of Gerizim shows the dependence of the Shechemites on Jerusalem in spiritual matters and, at the same time, it proves that only the pride of the former Assyrian aristocrats, loath to acknowledge the supremacy of the southern rival, was responsible for the foundation of the Samaritan temple, and, consequently, for the break between Judah and Ephraim. The whole controversy between Jews and Samaritans was now subordinated to the question: Which place was chosen by God for His inhabitation, Zion or Gerizim? Later propagandist inventions obscured the origin of the schism and confused its dating which, for this reason, remains controversial. The Samaritans glorified their temple by attributing its founding to Alex-

44. See E. Bickerman, "Un Document relatif à la persécution d'Antiochus IV Epiphane," *RHR* 115, p. 188.

ander the Great. The Jews associated the separation with Nehemiah's expulsion of a scion of the high-priestly family for his marriage to a Samaritan girl (Neh. 13:28). This combination provided a "rational" account for the schism, and conveniently branded the priesthood at Gerizim as illegitimate. But the Jewish tradition itself, repeated by Josephus, states that the Samaritan temple was founded at the time of Alexander the Great. The fact that it did not receive any subvention from the Macedonian rulers, as well as the fact that it belonged not to Samaria but to "that foolish nation which dwells in Shechem" (as Ben Sira says), offers the definitive proof of its foundation after the Macedonian conquest.

Jerusalem was situated far away from the main trade routes which crossed Palestine and ran along the coast. Thus, while the Greeks knew the Palestinian shore very well, no Greek writer before the time of Alexander the Great mentions the Jews, with the exception of Herodotus, who alludes to the circumcision practiced by "the Phoenicians and the Syrians of Palestine." But even after Alexander the Great, the first Greek authors who took cognizance of the Jews got their information from the Diaspora, from Jewish immigrants or Jewish soldiers in the service of Alexander and his successors. That is by no means surprising. Why should a Greek author, at a time when the whole fabulous Orient was open to his inquiry, concentrate on a Lilliputian place in the arid mountains? Let us note, by the way, that the first Greek book (by Aristotle's pupil Theophrastus) giving some exact information about Rome, appeared in 314–313 B.C.E. Some years later another student of philosophy, Hecataeus of Abdera, who had accompanied Ptolemy I of Egypt in his Syrian campaign of 312 B.C.E., published in a report of his journey the first Greek account of the Jews, based particularly on data given to the author by a Jewish priest who, in 312, accompanied the Ptolemaic army to Egypt.[45] Hecataeus's narrative was used by Theophrastus,[46] while another pupil of Aristotle, Clearchus, described what is probably a fictitious meeting between his master and a Jewish magician in Asia Minor.[47]

Let us consider the picture of the Jews as seen with Greek eyes at the end of the fourth century. For the reason just stated, a Greek writer

45. H. Lewy, "Hekataios von Abdera," *ZNW* 31, p. 117.

46. W. Jaeger, "Greeks and Jews: The First Greek Records of Jewish Religion and Civilization," *JR* 18, p. 38.

47. Lewy, "Hekataios," n. 15.

must have had a particular motive to take an interest in the Jews. Now, the philosophers, and the school of Aristotle in particular, looked for empirical confirmation of their social theories in the newly opened Orient. Similarly, the discovery of America was utilized by European scholars of the sixteenth century to identify the Red Indians with the lost Ten Tribes. Greek scholars of Alexander's time thought that the peoples untouched by the dissolving influence of modern (that is, Greek) civilization must have conserved the purity of religion and the perfection of social organization which the philosophers attributed to man in a state of nature. On the other hand, the Greeks knew that in the Orient knowledge was the monopoly of the priestly caste. Having discovered a people led by priests and obeying the Law coming directly from the Divinity, the Greeks ranged the Jews beside the Indian Brahmans and Persian Magi. The Jews are a "philosophical race," says Theophrastus; they descend from the Indian philosophers, says Clearchus, Just as a Greek author (Megasthenes) claimed that the doctrines of the ancient Greek philosophers concerning nature had been formulated by the Indians, other writers ascribed the origins of philosophy to the Jews. Clearchus presents a Jewish sage who furnished Aristotle with the experimental proof of the Platonic doctrine of immortality. Some decades later, Hermippus, another follower of Aristotle, mentions the (supposed) Jewish belief in the soul's immortality as a well-known fact, and adds that Pythagoras borrowed from the Jews and the Thracians his opinions about it. Since the Jews named their Deity "God of Heaven," they provided the philosophers with the desired proof that natural theology of mankind had identified God with the heavens. Likewise, monotheism, as well as the absence of divine images, agreed with the philosophical conceptions. Other data were interpreted accordingly. For instance, Theophrastus states that the Jews celebrate their festivals at night in contemplation of the stars (the order of heavenly bodies was for the philosophers the most important proof against atheism) and discourse about the Divine. In the same way, Hecataeus ascribes to the Egyptian priests philosophical conversations during the banquets where wine was not served.

The political organization of the Jews was viewed from the same standpoint, as the realization of an ideal state governed by the Sages, the philosophers according to Plato and the priests according to the Palestinians. The Torah is presented as a narrative of the settlement of the Jews in Palestine and as their constitution. Moses, as law giver, could establish his system only after the conquest; so, according to

Hecataeus, he had conquered the Promised Land and founded Jerusalem. As in Sparta, his system is based on military virtues of bravery, endurance and discipline. As is fit for the perfect state, the legislator forbade the sale of the land distributed among the Jews of Palestine in order to prevent the concentration of wealth and its sinister consequence, the decrease of population. This Greek interpretation of Lev. 25:23 clearly shows that Hecataeus's inquiry was oriented by his philosophic aims; he elicited from his Jewish informants answers which could serve his theory. For this reason it is a very delicate task to appreciate the earliest Greek records as testimony regarding the state of Judaism in Alexander's time. When Hecataeus affirms that the priests receive a tithe of the income of the people, he idealizes the realities. When he adds that the priests administer public affairs, he surely gives a one-sided view of the subject. But when he emphatically states that the High Priest was regarded as the mouthpiece of God and messenger of divine oracles, we suspect that the Greek writer attributes to the Jews the behavior they should have in his opinion, in order to represent the ideal scheme of the philosophical commonwealth. Hecataeus's High Priest, by the way, is chosen as the most able leader among the priests.

Some features stressed in the Greek records are worth noting. The importance of the priesthood and the role of the High Priest in Jerusalem, the obstinacy of the Jews in defense of the Law and the slander of their neighbors and foreign visitors with regard to antialien sentiments of the Jews, already point in Hecataeus's narrative to characteristic features of Hellenistic Jewry. We learn that already before 300 B.C.E. the Jews in Palestine did not tolerate pagan shrines and altars on the holy soil and that, at the same time, the Jews in the Diaspora freely scoffed at the superstitions of the Gentiles. This attitude was inevitable because the Jews were in possession of the Truth. They might have said to the pagans: We claim liberty for ourselves in accordance with your principles and refuse it to you in accordance with our principles. In the polytheist world of Hellenism, where all beliefs were admitted as different refractions of the same eternal light, the Jewish claim to the oneness of the Divine Revelation must have appeared as a provocation.

Nevertheless, Alexander and his successors accepted the Jews among the citizens of the new settlements founded in the East. When the experiment of founding commonwealths of Greek type in the Orient succeeded, later descendants of the settlers became "Aristocrats" but the first settlers were no more respected by their contemporaries than the passengers of the *Mayflower* were by the English of 1620. The conquest of Alexander, welding East and West into a single economic whole, brought wealth to Greece and to many Oriental towns. Why should a craftsman from Athens or a moneylender from Babylon enroll in the list of settlers of a new city far away, let us say Europos on the Euphrates? As the kings needed cities to safeguard the military communications and as strongholds against the indigenous population, settlers were at a premium. For instance, Alexander transferred some contingents from (still Assyrian) Samaria to Egypt, where they received allotments of land. There is no reason to suspect Josephus's statement that the early Hellenistic rulers gave the Jews equal status with the Macedonians and Greeks who settled in the new colonies. He fails to make it clear that these privileges were individual and did not bear on the position of Jewry as a community in the new colony. This was a point on which hinged the later struggle between the Greeks and the Jews in Hellenistic cities. We do not know how Alexander and his successors reconciled Jewish exclusiveness with the obligations of the Greek citizen. Probably, the antinomy was solved in each case empirically. There were Jews, like the magician spoken of by Clearchus, who "not only spoke Greek, but had the soul of a Greek," and thus were inclined to mutual tolerance. Sometimes the king exempted the Jews; thus Alexander pardoned the Jewish soldiers who had refused to build a heathen temple in Babylon, and Seleucus I ordered money to be given for oil to those Jews, citizens of Antiochia, who were unwilling to use pagan oil. As oil was given by the "gymnasiarchs" for anointing during athletic games, the notice seems to imply that in Greek cities of the Diaspora, Jewish youth about 300 B.C.E. already took part in exercises of the "gymnasia," naked like their Hellenic comrades.[48] Physical training was the foundation of Greek life and mentality in all Greek cities, and the gymnasia became the centers of Greek intellectual activity and the principal instrument of Hellenization. Through the palaestra, by way of sports, the Jewish settlers became recognized members of the community. They learned to take pride in the city long before Paul proclaimed at Jerusalem his double title of honor, "I am a Jew, a Tarsian of Cilicia, citizen of no mean city." And conversely, the Jews of Alexandria could not but imagine that Alexander had become a worshiper of the true God at the time of his founding of their city and had brought the bones of the prophet Jeremiah to Alexandria as its palladium.[49]

48. We do not know whether oil was also distributed to the people who did not frequent the "gymnasia." Cf. Jeanne and Louis Robert, *Inscriptions grecques de Lydie* (Paris, 1948), 129.

49. F. Pfister, "Eine jüdische Gründungsgeschichte Alexandrias," *SHAW* 11, (July 1914).

5

After Alexander's death (324 B.C.E.) wars between his generals ended in the dismemberment of his empire. After 301 there were three great powers governed by Macedonian dynasties: Asia (that is substantially Syria, Mesopotamia, Persia, and a large portion of Asia Minor) under the sway of the Seleucids, Egypt of the Ptolemies, and the realm of Macedonia in Europe. Thus, the political unity of the world where the Jews lived was broken. Even the Roman Empire did not reestablish the lost oneness, since an important Jewry remained in the Parthian kingdom, outside the laws of the Caesars.

Palestine became a dominion of Egypt but was reconquered by Antiochus III of Asia in 200 B.C.E. Since the government of both the Ptolemies and the Seleucids rested on the same political principles, we may view as an entity the period of Ptolemaic and Seleucid domination over Jerusalem until the Maccabean struggle, that is, some 125 years between 301 and 175 B.C.E. The district of Judea, called "the nation of Jews," under the Seleucids, was still a very small part of the province of Syria.[50] When a traveler passed the Jordan or the town of Modein in the north, or went south beyond Beth-zur, or toward the west descended into the coastal plain, he left the Jewish territory. Frontier guards, for instance, at Antipatris, customhouses, custom duties for export and import reminded the Jerusalemite of this fact. Thus, even in Palestine, the political term "Jew" did not include all the religious adherents of the Temple of Zion. With respect to religion there were many Jews and Jewries elsewhere, in Galilee or in Trans-Jordan or, for instance, where the powerful clan of the Tobiads was located. But politically these were not considered "Jews." The term "Jew" applied only to those "who lived around the Temple of Jerusalem," and so a Greek historian calls them.[51] Jerusalem was the only "city" of the Jews; other settlements in Judea were politically "villages." Judea continued to be a self-governing unit; there was no royal governor in Jerusalem, although the citadel of the Holy City was garrisoned by royal troops. The Jews, too, had to furnish contingents to the royal forces; Jewish soldiers are mentioned in Alexander's army, a Jewish regiment of cavalry under Ptolemy. It may be that fortresses on the frontier, such as that at Beth-zur, excavated recently, were occupied by native forces; about 200 B.C.E. the walls of Jerusalem were rebuilt by the Jewish authorities.

50. See E. Bickerman, *Institutions des Séleucides* (Paris, 1938), 165.
51. Polybius, XVI. 39.5.

In 200 the Jewish militia helped Antiochus III to dislodge the Egyptian garrison from the citadel of Jerusalem. But more important for the central government was the collection of taxes, such as the poll tax, or taxes on houses or gate tolls, etc., to which was added the tribute, that is, the annual payment of a lump sum by the Jewish commonwealth as such. In the third century Judea, as a province of the Egyptian Empire, was part of the highly complicated system of planned economy that was built up by the Ptolemies. Like all natives of the province, "Syria and Phoenicia," the Jews had to declare their movable property and cattle for the purpose of taxation. Likewise, the Ptolemies introduced their subtle system of collecting the revenue by tax farmers. The Ptolemies favored the local notables as farmers of revenue, since in this way the native aristocracy had a stake in the Ptolemaic domination.

As regards self-government, Jerusalem was an "aristocratic" commonwealth. The "council of Elders" was the ruling body, composed of laymen and priests. But the aristocracy as a social class was priestly, just as in Hellenistic Egypt. When Antiochus III granted exemption from personal taxes to the upper class in Jerusalem, he named the council of Elders, the officers of the Temple with respect to their functions, and the sacerdotal caste as such. The intermediary between the royal government and the Jews was the High Priest, appointed by the king. Practically, the office was hereditary and was held for life. The High Priests, responsible primarily for the tribute, also became accustomed under Egyptian domination to farm the other taxes. In this way, the High Priest became the political head of the nation as well. About 190, Ben Sira spoke of the High Priest Simeon in terms appropriate to a prince: he was the glory of his people, in his time the Temple was fortified, he protected his people. As to the common people, they were sometimes summoned to the Temple court to hear official reports on the situation and to acclaim the official speaker. Nevertheless, as Ben Sira shows, the "assembly of Elders" and even the popular "assembly in the gate" continued to regulate social life and still had judicial and administrative functions.

While politically the situation of the "nation of the Jews" was essentially the same in 175 B.C.E. as had been that of the district *Yehûd* two centuries earlier, there was a decisive change as to the state of civilization.[52] There was a mixture of population and language and a diffusion of the foreign (Hellenic) culture unparalleled in the Persian period. To begin with, there were now many Hellenic cities in Palestine. The

52. Rostovtzeff, *Social and Economic History*, index s.v. Palestine.

Jewish territory was practically in the midst of Hellenic cities: Ascalon, Akko (Ptolemais), Joppa (Jaffa), Apollonia, and others on the coast; Samaria, Scythoplis, and Gadara in the north; Pella, Gerasa, Philadelphia (Rabbath-Amana) beyond the river Jordan; and Marisa in the south. Here the Jews came into contact with Greek men, institutions, arts, soldiers from Aetolia or Macedonia, Greek poetasters, and sculptors like the creator of the fine statue of the nude Aphrodite found at Carmel recently. They could see in Marisa, for instance, the Greek system of paved streets forming quadrangular blocks with a large open place at the main street, enlarged by colonnades, a view quite different from the maze that constituted an Oriental town. In Trans-Jordan there was a mixed settlement of Jewish and Greek soldiers under the command of a Jewish sheikh. There, in 259 B.C.E., a Greek from Cnidus in the service of this sheikh sold a Babylonian girl to a Greek traveler from Egypt. Among the guarantors and witnesses were a son of one Ananias and a Macedonian "of the cavalrymen of Tobias."

The Jewish territory itself was crowded with Greek officers, civil agents and traders, as the papyri show. Greek residents loaned money, bought and sold slaves, oil, wine, honey, figs, dates, while wheat was exported from Galilee. Greek caravans came up to Jerusalem too. On the other hand, the kings had inherited from the Persian monarchs crown lands, and there were in Judea estates belonging to royal courtiers. It happened, of course, as a papyrus tells, that a Greek usurer was driven out of a Jewish village when he tried to collect money for a debt; but, as this instance shows, even the village could not avoid the Greek commercial penetration. Another important factor was that now a foreign language, Greek, became that of business and administration. Even in the villages there must have been persons able to draft a contract in Greek, or to write a request in the style required by a Greek petition.

The influence of a new, foreign, and technologically superior civilization acted, as usual, as a powerful dissolvent which destroyed the traditional discipline of life. The author of the Book of Jubilees[53] gives us insight into the moral situation of Palestinian Jewry after one and a half centuries of intensive contact with the Greeks. He fulminates against the evil generation who forgot the commandments and sabbaths. He repeatedly warns against associating with the pagans or eating with them. He lets Abraham implore his sons "not to take to themselves

53. On the Book of Jubilees: Louis Finkelstein, "Pre-Maccabean Documents in the Passover Haggadah," *HTR* 36, p. 19.

wives from the daughters of Canaan," nor to make idols and worship them. He even speaks of children of Israel "who will not circumcise their sons," and stresses the prohibition against appearing naked, that is, participating in Greek athletic games. It is particularly notable that he claims that the commandments were already observed by the Patriarchs and stresses again and again that ritual prescriptions are eternal ordinances. In fact, "every mouth speaking iniquity" already began to deny the perpetual force of the biblical regulations. As Esau says in the Book of Jubilees, "neither the children of men nor the beasts of the earth" have any oath valid forever: an echo of Greek philosophical criticism. Another contemporary writer, Ben Sira, speaks of the Jews who are ashamed of the Torah and its regulations, of ungodly men who have forsaken the Law of the Most High God. At the same time, probably unknown to Ben Sira, in Rome another adversary of Hellenism, Cato the Censor, applied himself to the reformation of the lax morals of Hellenized Rome where the newly coined word *pergraecari*, "act as a Greek," was used to signify the licentious way of life. But Cato surpassed the Jewish moralists in his antialien feelings. Ben Sira knows that wisdom has gained possession of every people and every antion, and he considers the physician ordained by God. Cato insists that Greek physicians came to Rome with the purpose of killing Romans by treatment, and under his influence Greek philosophers were expelled from Rome.

Nevertheless, it is rather difficult to gauge the impact of Greek civilization on Jewish thought in the third century B.C.E. Even if the Book of Kohelet (Ecclesiastes) was composed in this period, as the critics generally agree, it hardly shows any trace of Greek speculation. The outlook of the author is rather anti-intellectual: "he that increaseth knowledge, increaseth sorrow" (Eccles. 1:18). The whole philosophy of expediency which the author preaches, and even his lesson—make the best of the present day—belongs to the traditional teaching of wise men in the Orient. Significant only is his omission of traditional values. He does not attack these, but he emphatically denies their value: it is the same whether one sacrifices or not, "all things come alike to all" (Eccles. 9:2), "moment and chance" rule life (Eccles. 3:19). Ecclesiastes is prepared to accept anything because he doubts the value of everything. He mentions God thirty-eight times, but he also repeats thirty times that "all is vanity." It is in opposition to such a philosophy of relativity, dear to the "sons of Beliar," that the author of Jubilees stresses the heavenly origin of the traditional precepts of belief and ritual.

As it often happens, in order to uphold traditional values, their apologists themselves propose the most radical innovations. The author of the Book of Jubilees outdoes the later talmudic teaching in his severity as to the observance of ritual prescriptions. But to assert the everlasting validity of the Torah, this traditionalist places his own composition beside and even above Scripture, claims for his book a divine origin, and gives precepts which differ widely from those set forth in the Torah. The Bible says that the sun and the moon shall regulate seasons and days. In his paraphrase the author of Jubilees attacks the lunisolar calendar and strongly urges the adoption of his own system of a year of 364 days in which each holiday always falls on the same day of the week as ordained by God. Since the Jewish ecclesiastic calendar was built on the observation of the physical reappearance of the new moon, the apologist of orthodoxy simply proposes to turn upside down the whole structure of the ritual. The reason for his revolutionary idea is significant: the irregularity of the moon confuses the times. Thus, without realizing it, this traditionalist succumbs to the seduction of the Greek penchant for rationalization.

In the face of innovators, Hellenistic or pseudo-orthodox, the conservative forces, grouped around the Temple, stood fast and tried to uphold the established way of life.[54]

The literary representative of this conservative class was Jesus Ben Sira, a warm admirer of the High Priest Simeon. He realized that with him a venerable line of pious maxim writers came to an end: "I, indeed, came last of all," he says, "as one that gleaneth after the grape-gatherers." His social and religious ideas are conventional and the advice he addresses to his "son" (that is, pupil) aims at making him accept the present order. "The works of God are all good and He provides for every need in its time." Although he sharply denounces the oppressors who, by the multitude of their sacrifices, try to pacify God for sins—he that deprives the hireling of his hire sheds blood—he is convinced that poverty and wealth alike come from God. In these views, Ben Sira reproduces the traditional wisdom of the Orient. This traditional Oriental wisdom is further reflected in such general dicta as "he that runs after gold will not be guiltless." He also keeps the traditional tenets of religion, and implicitly rejects the new doctrine of the future life. He maintains that man can dominate his evil nature by strictly following the Law, he clings to the principle that the moral

54. On the phantom of the so-called Great Synagogue, which is often evoked by modern writers on this period, see my note in *RB* 31 (1948).

govern the world, that the wicked are punished, and that virtue leads to well-being while laziness and dissolution bring disaster. He strongly stresses man's own responsibility for his sins and his advice to his pupils is biblical: "with all thy strength love Him that made thee."

Historians classify, but life's strands are inextricably interwoven. The traditionalist Ben Sira is at the same time the first Jewish author to put his own name to his work and to emphasize his literary personality and individuality. He claims no prophetic inspiration, nor any apocalyptic revelation. He is bringing doctrine "for all those who seek instruction" and, like a Greek wandering philosopher of his time, proclaims: "Hear me, you great ones of the people and give ear to me, you, rulers of the congregation." He not only accepts the figure of personified wisdom (an originally Canaanite goddess), which appears in Proverbs, but puts this profane knowledge on a level with "the book of the Covenant of the Most High, the law which Moses commanded"—a rather bold effort to reconcile the synagogue with the Greek Academy, Jerusalem with Athens. Even the literary form of his book reflects the modernism which he combats. Ben Sira is fond of utilizing passages of Scripture as texts to comment upon in putting forth his own views on the subject. This practice was probably influenced by synagogue preaching.

The process of action and reaction produced in the third century B.C.E. by the suddenly intensified contact between Judaism and Hellenism led to curious changes in the usage of the Divine Name. The proper name of the national God (YHWH) ceased to be pronounced by the Jews in the course of the fifth century except in the Temple service and in taking an oath. The latter usage is attested to by a source used by Philo,[55] and it was preserved by the Samaritans as late as the fifth century of the Common Era. As the exceptions show, the motive for the disuse of the proper name was the idea that its utterance had magical power. The general belief in the magical efficacy of the proper name is well known, but in Canaan it became dominant about the beginning of the first millennium B.C.E. Thus, the Phoenician gods are anonymous[56] while the deities of the "Proto-Phoenicians" in the fourteenth century B.C.E. had proper names, as the texts of Ugarit show. The Jews accepted the idea of the unpronounceable Divine Name, only after the Exile. Their national God was now "the God in Jerusalem" or the "God of Heaven," a name which identified Him with the supreme

---

55. W. L. Knox, *Some Hellenistic Elements in Primitive Christianity* (London, 1944), 48.
56. See E. Bickerman, "Anonymous Gods," *Journal of the Warburg Institute* 1, p. 58.

deity of the Persians and the Syrian peoples. Accordingly, the pronunciation *Elohim* (God), and afterward *Adonai* (my Lord), was substituted for
the tetragrammaton YHWH. When the Greeks came, the abstract term
"God" perfectly corresponded to their philosophical conception of the
Supreme Being, *ho Theos,* the God, or *to Theion*, the Divine. So they
accepted this indefinite designation for the God of the Jews. By a kind
of reversed attraction, the Greek speculative term then influenced
Hebrew writers. The Book of Kohelet speaks of God only as *Elohim*. One
would expect, therefore, that when speaking Greek the Jews would
designate their God as *ho Theos* or *to Theion*. As a matter of fact, they said
Kyrios, a legal term meaning the legitimate master of someone or
something, a word which as a substantive was not used in Greek
religious language. It is simply a literal translation of the Hebrew
appellative *Adonai* (the Lord), which became in the meantime the standard pronunciation of the awe-inspiring tetragrammaton. Since *Kyrios*
was not intelligible to the Greeks and the term *Theos* had a rather
general meaning, the Jews speaking or writing Greek in Palestine began
in the third century B.C.E. to speak of their God as *Hypsistos,* the "Most
High." In the same way, in the fifth century B.C.E., the Hellenized
Thracians identified their supreme deity, *Sabazios*, with Zeus. And again,
the Greek term reacted upon the Hebrew style. Already in Ben Sira the
designation, "Most High God," is found forty-eight times, although the
corresponding Hebrew term *Elyon* is very rare in the Bible. The same
circumlocution is frequently used by the very anti-Greek author of the
Book of Jubilees, and the same title was chosen by the Maccabean
priest-kings to designate the God of Zion in their official Hebrew
utterances. The Talmud quotes the formula: "In such a year of Johanan,
priest of the Most High God."

But the most important result of the Greek impact on Palestinian
Judaism was the formation of a Jewish intelligentsia, different from the
clergy and not dependent on the sanctuary. The new class was known as
"scribes." "Scribe," if not simply penman, was the technical term for a
public official who entered the civil service as a profession. Accordingly, there were in the ancient Orient preparatory schools for future
officeholders. From these institutions came the works of the mundane
"wisdom" literature (like the biblical Proverbs), advising, as a Babylonian text says, "to fear God and the Law." But in the Hellenistic age
Greek became the universal language of administration and business,
and native writing and learning were rapidly becoming confined to the
temples. The cuneiform documents of the Hellenistic age use the

ideogram "priest" to denote the native notaries, and the latter act in Ptolemaic Egypt "in behalf" of a priest. Likewise, the native law in Ptolemaic Egypt was administered by a court of three priests. In both Egypt and Babylonia, so far as the native writing was still used, the priest was now the scribe, the judge and the sole teacher of the people, and the temples were only centers of native learning. The "Chaldeans," astrologers and astronomers who preserved the ancient science in Babylonia, were part of the clergy. At the same time as in Egypt and Mesopotamia the polytheistic Orient shrinks into a priestly dependence, there begins a cleavage between the sacerdotal and the secular interpreters of the Divine Law in Judaism. About 190 B.C.E. Ben Sira urges his hearers to honor the priest and to give him his portion according to the Law. He acknowledges the authority of the High Priest "over statutes and judgment," but it is the scribe who advises the rulers, and the assembly in the gate sits in the seat of the judge and expounds righteousness and judgment. The scribe is not a lawyer acting in behalf of a client; but like the Roman *juris periti* of the same period, a person who has such knowledge of the laws and customs as to act as authority for the judge to follow in his decisions. In both Jerusalem and Rome, the administration of justice was no longer in the hands of the priests in the third century B.C.E. Ecclesiastes mentions the "ten rulers" of the city who are not worth one Sage (Eccles. 7:19). Ben Sira mentions the jurisdiction of the popular assembly in the punishment of adultery. But for the most part he speaks of the "rulers." He advises his reader: Gain instruction so that you may "serve the potentate." Ben Sira has in mind the agents of the Macedonian kings, such as Zenon, well known on account of recently discovered papyri. As servant of his Greek master, the Jewish scribe becomes a legitimate interpreter of the Divine Law. In fact, still at the time of Malachi, that is, toward the end of the fifth century B.C.E., knowledge comes from the priest's lips and the people "seek the law at his mouth; for he is the messenger of the Lord of hosts" (Mal. 2:7). It is the priest who answers the questions concerning ritual cleanliness (Hag. 2:12). The Chronicler still regards instruction in the Law as the privilege and duty of the Levites and considers the "scribes" as a class of Levites (2 Chron. 34:13). But in the royal charter given to Jerusalem in 200 B.C.E. the "scribes of the sanctuary" form a special and privileged body. The foreign rulers of the Orient needed, of course, expert advice as to the laws and customs of their subjects. Antiochus III's proclamation concerning the ritual arrangements at Jerusalem could not be drafted without the collaboration of Jewish jurists. At the same time, the lay scribe, powerful in the council of the Greek potentates, became, owing to his influence with the foreign master, an authority in the Jewish assembly. "The utterance of a prudent man," says Ben Sira, "is sought for in the congregation," and he mentions in opposition to the scribe, the craftsman, whose opinion is not asked in the council of the people. Since all Jewish law and legal customs were derived from the Torah, the scribe became the authority as to the Law of Moses. He meditated on the Law of the Most High. But still, in the time of Ben Sira the knowledge of the Torah was considered only part of the intellectual qualifications required of the scribe. He had also to find out the hidden sense of parables and to search out the wisdom of all the ancients. Daniel, who explains the secret and meaning of royal dreams at the Babylonian court, is the ideal scribe as visualized by Ben Sira. On the other hand, the scribe is not only counselor of kings and assemblies, but also wise man and teacher. "Turn to me, you ignorant," says Ben Sira, "and tarry in my school." He promises as the fruit of his teaching the acquisition by the pupil of "much silver and gold." But he gives to his pupils "wisdom," "and all wisdom is from the Lord, and is with Him forever." So his scribe and his school of wisdom prepare for the coming of the Pharisaic scholar in the next generation. This Pharisaic scholar regards learning as the highest of human values and teaches that the fear of the Lord is the beginning of wisdom, but is prepared to serve his Master not for the sake of reward. However, between Ben Sira and the first Pharisees, there is the persecution of Antiochus and the revolution of the Maccabees.

Bibliography

Albright, William Foxwell. *Archaeology and the Religion of Israel*. Baltimore, 1942.

_____. *From the Stone Age to Christianity*. Baltimore, 1940.

_____. "King Joachin in Exile." *BA* 5/4 (1942).

Bickerman, Elias. *Institutions des Séleucides*. Paris, 1938.

_____. *The Maccabees*. New York, 1947.

Cochrane, Charles Norris. *Christianity and Classical Culture*. Oxford, 1944.

Coulanges, Fustel N. D. de. *La Cité Antique*. 28th ed. Paris, 1924.

Cowley, A. E. *Aramaic Papyri of the Fifth Century*. Oxford, 1923.

Cumont, Franz. *Les religions orientales dans le paganisme romain*. 4th ed. Paris, 1929.

Daiches, Samuel. *The Jews of Babylonia*. London, 1910.

Erman, Adolf. *The Literature of the Ancient Egyptians*. London, 1927.

Finkelstein, Louis. *The Pharisees.* 2 vols. Philadelphia, 1938.

Glotz, G. *The Greek City and Its Institutions.* New York, 1929.

Griffith, F. L. *Catalogue of the Demotic Papyri in the John Rylands Library,* Manchester, 1909.

Holleaux, Maurice. *Etudes d'épigraphie et d'histoire grecques.* Paris, 1938.

Knox, Wilfred L. *Some Hellenistic Elements in Primitive Christianity.* London, 1944.

Lieberman, S. *Greeks in Jewish Palestine.* Philadelphia, 1942.

Luckenbill, D. D. *Ancient Records of Assyria and Babylonia.* 2 vols. Chicago, 1926–27.

Maspero, G. *Popular Stories of Ancient Egypt.* New York, 1915.

McCown, C. C. *Tel-En-Nasbeh.* Vol 1. Berkeley, 1947.

Nock, A. D. *Conversion.* London, 1933.

Olmstead, A. T. *History of Assyria.* New York, 1923.

Pearson, Lionel. *Early Ionian Historians.* Oxford, 1939.

Reifenberg, A. *Ancient Jewish Coins.* 2d ed. Jerusalem, 1947.

Reitzenstein, R. *Die hellenistischen Mysterienreligionen.* 3d ed. Leipzig, 1927.

Robert, Jeanne and Louis. *Inscriptions grecques de Lydie.* Hellencia 6. Paris, 1948.

Rogers, R. W. *Cuneiform Parallels to the Old Testament.* New York, 1912.

Rostovtzeff. M. *Social and Economic History of the Hellenistic World.* Oxford, 1941.

Smith, Sidney, trans. *Babylonian Historical Texts.* London, 1924.

Torrey, Charles C. *The Second Isaiah.* New York, 1928.

New Discoveries

Frank Moore Cross, Jr.

2

Aspects of Samaritan and Jewish History in Late Persian and Hellenistic Times* (1966)

The discovery of a cache of papyri in Wadi Daliyeh, north of Jericho in the Jordan valley, in 1962, has enriched our appreciation of various aspects of Judaism in Palestine in the Persian period. The papyri stem from the period immediately preceding Alexander's conquest: their very date makes them a major new contribution to the material evidence. The dry, legal character of the documents may serve initially to disguise their full impact, yet the seminal article by Frank Moore Cross lays bare the importance of the papyri for our understanding of the development of Jewish history and religion.

The point of departure is a knotty chronological problem which has long confronted students of the history of the Samaritan community. By showing the prevalence of papponymy, the naming of children after their grandfathers, Cross uncovers one of the keys to the foreshortening of the Persian and early Hellenistic periods in the ancient historical accounts, Josephus and the Rabbis alike (see above). Grandfathers became confused with their grandsons and the record of whole generations was lost. From the resolution of this specific historical crux, the key to which was provided by the Daliyeh papyri, Cross draws basic implications for the evaluation of relationships between the Samaritans and the Jews. The final break, he is able to propose, took place much later than expected—indeed, the aristocracies of the two communities intermarried for centuries.

*A paper read at the Symposium on Biblical Archaeology held in Berkeley and San Anselmo, March 16, 1966. My thanks are due to Professor David Noel Freedman for permission to publish it.

Finally, Cross brings into play not just the new epigraphic material from Wadi Daliyeh, but the implications of the excavations at
Schechem by G. E. Wright. The new archaeological evidence is
used to show how much more complicated Jewish society and
religion were than we had been accustomed to think. Seemingly
dry dating formulae and archeological finds have combined here to
supplement the meager historical record and to lift a small and
tantalizing corner of the veil of darkness.

In 1962, papyri of the fourth century B.C. were discovered by Beduin in a
desolate canyon north of Jericho on the rim of the Jordan rift. These
documents, known by their place of discovery as the Wâdi Dâliyeh
Papyri, were inscribed in Samaria during the half century before the
conquest of Alexander the Great.[1] The papyri are without exception
legal documents, not a few executed before the governor and prefect
of Samaria. Among the surprises to be found in the new documents is
the appearance twice of the name Sanballat, or more properly Sin'ubal-
liṭ. In each instance Sanballat is listed as father of the governor of
Samaria, once on an official sealing inscribed in Paleo-Hebrew script,
once in Aramaic in the context of a document of about the mid-fourth
century.

The appearance of a Sanballat who flourished in Samaria in the first
half of the fourth century gives an unexpected answer to a question
debated for generations by students of the history of the Jews and
Samaritans in the postexilic era. Sanballat of Beth Horon is well known
as the devious and malicious enemy of Nehemiah, mentioned frequently in the memoirs of Nehemiah, and once in a papyrus from
Elephantine in Upper Egypt.[2] He was governor of the province of
Samaria in 445 B.C., when Nehemiah arrived in Zion, and by 410 B.C. was
an aged man, whose son Delaiah acted in his name. Sanballat gained
notoriety in the Bible for his opposition to the restoration of the walls
of Jerusalem, and for conspiring against the life of Nehemiah, in league
with Tobiah, the Jewish governor of Ammon, and Gashmu, king of the
Qedarite league, whose territory extended from northern Arabia into
southern Palestine.

1. See F. M. Cross, "The Discovery of the Samaria Papyri," *BA* 26 (1963): 110–21.
2. Cf. Neh. 2:10, 19; 3:33; 4:1; 6:1, 2, 5, 12, 14; 13:28 (*snblṭ*); Elephantine *P.*
30:29 (*sn'blṭ*). The gentilic "Horonite" is best explained as derived from Bêt Ḥôrôn.

Nehemiah prevailed, of course, proving as wily as he was pious. He fortified the city, increased its population, and completed his first tour of duty as governor in 433 B.C. After a sojourn of indeterminate length, he returned to the Holy City. At the close of his memoirs, recounting the details of his reforms in Judah, he relates a last episode in which Sanballat plays a role. Nehemiah discovered that the son of Joiada the Zadokite high priest and the daughter of Sanballat the Horonite had been joined in a diplomatic marriage uniting the two great families of Judah and Samaria.[3] Nehemiah in righteous indignation chased the young man out of Jerusalem. Unhappily, we do not know his name. According to Josephus, however, after Johanan, son of Joiada, became high priest, he killed his brother Jesus in the Temple. So dreadful was the event that Bagoas, the Persian governor of Judah, a successor to Nehemiah, entered the Temple by force, defiling it, and imposed a heavy tribute on the Jews for seven years.[4] Jesus evidently had been laying claim to the high priesthood with the aid of Bagoas. It would not be surprising if Jesus were the elder brother, son-in-law of Sanballat, who had proper claims to the diadem.[5]

In the Antiquities, Josephus tells a similar story with similar names, but the plot is played out in the era of Darius III and Alexander the Great. Sanballat, appointed governor of Samaria by Darius III, arranged a marriage between his daughter Nikaso and a certain Manasseh identified as the brother of Jonanan the high priest. Manasseh was expelled from the altar, and retired to Samaria. This was the occasion, according to Josephus, for the building of the Samaritan temple on Mount Gerizim. Sanballat set up his son-in-law in business, so to speak, providing him with his own Temple. According to the tradition received by Josephus, Alexander the Great himself commissioned its building on his arrival in Palestine in 332.[6]

In the past, scholars viewing these two similar accounts were incredulous. Cowley's sentiment was typical: "The view that there were two Sanballats, each governor of Samaria, and each with a daughter who married a brother of a High Priest at Jerusalem is a solution too

---

3. Neh. 13:28.

4. *Antiquities* XI.297–301. This event probably must be dated before 404, since according to Neh. 12:22 Jaddua I (see below) came to the throne during the reign of Darius (II). Josephus identifies him as the *stratēgos* of Artaxerxes, presumably confusing him with the notorious eunuch of Artaxerxes III.

5. Cf. N. H. Smith, *Studies in the Psalter* (London, 1934), 13–14; H. H. Rowley, "Sanballat and the Samaritan Temple," *BJRL* 38 (1955): 184–85.

6. *Antiquities* XI.302–12, 321–25.

desperate to be entertained."[7] Many historical constructions were attempted to provide a solution. Most saw the account of Josephus as a secondary reflex of biblical Sanballat and the intermarriage of the fifth century. A few gave credence to an Alexandrine date for the founding of the Samaritan temple. In a bizarre attempt to salvage Josephus's reputation as a historian, C. C. Torrey moved Nehemiah down into the fourth century, claiming that the Sanballat of Samaria mentioned in the Elephantine Papyri was grandfather of Sanballat the Horonite, enemy of Nehemiah and father of two (!) marriageable daughters.[8] Some scholars even moved the building of the temple on Gerizim back into the fifth century, despite the silence of the Chronicler on the question of a separate Samaritan cultus.[9]

If I mistake not, no scholar has proposed the existence of a Sanballat who flourished in the first half of the fourth century, after Sanballat the Horonite was dead, before the day of the Sanballat of Josephus's account, laid in the reign of Darius the Third (335–330 b.c.). However, once the existence of a second Sanballat, father of governors of Samaria, is firmly established, paradoxically it becomes far easier to accept a third Sanballat in the age of Alexander. That is to say, with the appearance of Sanballat II in the Dâliyeh Papyri, most if not all objections to a Sanballat III melt away. The point is this. We know well that it was a regular practice in the Achaemenid empire for high offices, that of satrap or governor, to become hereditary. It is evident that the Sanballatids held the governorship of Samaria for several generations, as did the Tobiads of Ammon. Moreover, we know that the practice of papponymy (naming a child for its grandfather) was much in vogue among the Jews and surrounding nations precisely in this era.[10] One may refer to the Tobiads where papponymy is documented for about nine generations.[11] The high priests of Judah in the Hellenistic era present almost as striking a picture. The Oniads alternate the names Onias and Simon over five generations.

We can reconstruct with some plausibility, therefore, the sequence

7. A. E. Cowley, *Aramaic Papyri of the Fifth Century b.c.* (Oxford, 1923), 110 (quoted by Rowley, "Sanballat," 173 n.1).

8. See, e.g., Rowley's discussion in *The Second Isaiah* (New York, 1928), 456–60, and references.

9. For detailed bibliographical references, see Rowley, "Sanballat," passim.

10. Cf. W. F. Albright, "Dedan," in *Geschichte und altes Testament,* ed. G. Ebeling (Tübingen, 1953), 6 n. 3.

11. On papponymy in the Tobiad family, see B. Mazar, "The Tobiads," *IEJ* 7 (1957): 137–45, 229–38, and esp. 235 and n.73.

of governors of Samaria in the fifth and fourth century. Sanballat the Horonite is evidently the founder of the line, to judge by the fact that he bears a gentilic, not a patronymic. He was a Yahwist, giving good Yahwistic names to his sons Delaiah and Shelemiah. Sanballat I must have been a mature man to gain the governorship, and in 445, when Nehemiah arrived, no doubt was already in his middle years. His son Delaiah acted for his aged father as early as 410. The grandson of Sanballat, Sanballat II, evidently inherited the governorship early in the fourth century, to be succeeded by an elder son (Yeshūa'?), and later by his son Hananiah. Hananiah was governor by 354 B.C., and his son, or his brother's son, Sanballat III, succeeded to the governorship in the time of Darius III and Alexander the Great.[12]

Josephus is not wholly vindicated. It is clear that he identified biblical Sanballat and Sanballat III, jumping from the fifth to the late fourth century. Moreover, it is highly likely that a similar haplography occurred in Josephus's sources for the sequence of Zadokite high priests. From the Elephantine letters we know that Bagoas had become governor and that Johanan, son of Joiada, had taken the high priestly office no later than 410. Nehemiah furnished us with the name of his son Jaddua, a caritative form of his grandfather's name, Joiada. Unless the name of Darius in Neh. 12:10, 22, is added by a late editor, we must suppose that Jaddua took priestly office before 404 B.C.[13] It is hardly conceivable therefore that he exercised the priestly office until 332, much less had a brother of marriageable age in 332, as we should have

12. This is not counter to probabilities. Sanballat I no doubt died ripe in years, his eldest already advanced in age. This construction is, of course, hypothetical. Our evidence is tantalizingly limited to the following set of readings in the Dâliyeh Papyri.

(1) [yš]w' (or [yd]w') br sn'blt whnn sgn' . . .
(2) qdm [Ḥ]nnyh pht šmryn . . .
(3) [yš'?]yhw bn [sn']
    blt pht šmrn
(4) ly[š/dw]'

The last two readings are in Paleo-Hebrew on sealings. They are the only inscribed seals in the lot of more than 125 impressions and seal rings. Evidently, in Persian fashion, only officials had inscribed seals.

The Sanballat seal (which we earlier reconstructed to read [ḥnn]yhw) more likely read yd'yhw or yš'yhw, the formal name as against the caritative yaddū' or yešū'. There are no traces of the long tails of the nuns on the seal. Hannan the prefect probably must be equated with the governor Hananiah, suggesting that he succeeded an elder brother Yešūa' (?) in the governorship.

13. See above, n.4; see also W. F. Albright, *The Biblical Period* (Pittsburgh, 1950), 54.

to affirm if biblical Jaddua is identified with Jaddua the high priest whose brother married Nikaso, daughter of Sanballat III. It seems highly probably that we must insert a Johanan (?) and a Jaddua III in the series of high priests.[14]

What, then, are we to say about the marriage of the son of Joiada to a daughter of Sanballat I, and the marriage of the brother of Jaddua to the daughter of Sanballat III? Certainly we can no longer look at the episode with the same historical skepticism. After all, the names and relationships are by no means identical. It appears that the noble houses of Samaria and Jerusalem were willing to intermarry despite the ire of certain strict Jews, presumably the progeny of the reforms of Nehemiah and Ezra.

In the past it has been difficult to reckon with the possibility of repeated intermarriage between the aristocracy of Samaria and the theocratic family of Jerusalem. We are inclined to read back into the era of Nehemiah and Ezra the extreme alienation, indeed the hatred, which marked the relationship of Jews and Samaritans in Roman times, and to attribute to Ezra the developed legal tradition related to the Kutîm in Rabbinic sources. There has been mounting evidence, however, that the schism which separated the Samaritans finally, and irreversibly, from their Jewish coreligionists came much later, long after the end of Persian rule. For one thing, it is evident that the religion of Samaria derived from Judaism. Its feasts and law, conservatism toward Torah and theological development, show few survivals from the old Israelite religion as distinct from Judean religion, and no real evidence of religious syncretism. Even the late Jewish apocalyptic has left a firm imprint on Samaritanism.[15] For this and other reasons, scholars have increasingly been inclined to lower the Samaritan schism into the last half of the fourth century, and some would discover the occasion of the radical break of Jews and Samaritans as falling precisely in the era of Alexander the Great. After the Samaritan revolt of 331 when nobles of Samaria burned to death Andromachus, the prefect of Alexander in Syria, Alexander marched north from Egypt against Samaria. Curtius tells us that the rebels were "delivered up to him" when he reached the city. This appears to have been the occasion of the

---

14. Counting Joiada as I. Cf. P. W. Lapp, "Ptolemaic Stamped Handles from Judah," *BASOR* 172 (1963): 33, no. 54.

15. See E. Bickerman, *From Ezra to the Last of the Maccabees* (New York, 1962), 42–43. He observes that the conflicts of the Persian period between Samaria and Jerusalem were largely political, rather than religious.

patricians' flight into the wastelands of the Wâdi Dâliyeh, where they were massacred by Macedonian troops, leaving to us a cache of papyri strewn among Samaritan bones.[16] Thereupon Alexander or his deputy Perdiccas (our sources are in conflict) resettled the city as a Macedonian colony. Elias Bickerman writes, "It often happened that when a Greek colony was established, native villages under its control formed a union around an ancestral sanctuary. Folowing the same pattern, the country-side of (now Macedonian) Samaria constituted an organization, in Greek Style, the Sidonians of Shechem, for the purpose of serving the god of Israel. Shechem, the most ancient capital and the most sacred site of Israel, became the natural center of the confederation."[17]

The recent excavations at Shechem directed by my colleague, G. Ernest Wright, have given substance to the view that the Samaritans rallied together at Shechem. After a long abandonment of the city, the city was rebuilt and fortified in the last third of the fourth century.[18] There can be little doubt that the city was rebuilt by the remnant of the Samaritans driven out of their newer capital at Samaria. More recently, the expedition to Shechem has uncovered the remains of Hadrian's temple on a peak of Mt. Gerizim, and under it the remains of an earlier structure. Probably it is the Samaritan temple of the era of Alexander. There cannot be certainty until much larger excavations are undertaken (now scheduled for the summer of 1966.)[19] Whether the Temple was finished shortly before the destruction of Samaria by Alexander, or shortly after, we may never know. At all events, the early Hellenistic date of its founding recorded by Josephus appears to be confirmed.

There can be little doubt that the erection of the temple of Gerizim as a rival to Zerubbabel's temple in Jerusalem further aggravated the traditional bad relations between Samaritan and Jew. It need not, however, be regarded as the final event leading to total estrangement.

---

16. Cf. Cross, "Discovery of the Samaria Papyri," 118–19 and n. 22. The reconstruction of the background of the deposit of the Dâliyeh Papyri was worked out by the writer on the basis of a preliminary study of the papyri and associated artifacts, notably coins. The subsequent campaigns of excavation led by Professor Lapp have tended to confirm this hypothesis. Certainly the deposit is homogeneous, a series of artifacts including pottery from ± 331 B.C. The latest papyrus, with a date formula preserved, comes from March 18, 335 B.C.

17. Bickerman, *From Ezra*, 43–44 [see above, p. 30].

18. G. Ernest Wright, "The Samaritans at Shechem," *HTR* 55 (1962): 357–66; cf. idem, *Shechem: The Biography of a Biblical City* (New York: 1965), 170–81.

19. Robert J. Bull and G. Ernest Wright, "Newly Discovered Temples on Mt. Gerizim in Jordan," *HTR* 58 (1965): 234–37.

Curious to say, the Hellenistic era added at least three, perhaps four, rival cults to that of Jerusalem. In the second century B.C. Onias IV, pretender to the Zadokite high priesthood, built a temple in Leontopolis in Egypt.[20] At the beginning of the second century, Hyrcanus of the Tobiad family built a temple in 'Arâq el-'Emîr in Trans-Jordan.[21] If Josephus is correct, the Essenes conducted a sacrificial cultus by the Dead Sea.[22]

It is difficult to speak of the Samaritans as a fully separated sect, so long as direct Jewish influence shaped their doctrine and practice, so long as the biblical text which they used was held in common with the Jews, so long as Jew and Samaritan used a common national style of script. In other terms, when do Samaritan and Jewish theology and discipline begin separate, increasingly diverging lines of development? When does the textual tradition of the Samaritan Pentateuch branch apart from the textual tradition established in Jerusalem? When does the Samaritan script begin to evolve in its distinctive path?

In 1940, W. F. Albright wrote as follows: "If we compare the oldest lapidary examples of Samaritan writing with the coins of the Hasmonaeans . . . , dated between 135 and 37 B.C., a relatively late date for the origin of the Samaritan script as such seems highly probable. Moreover, since Shechem and Samaria were conquered by the Jews between 129 and 110 B.C., and were lost to the Romans in 63 B.C., it would only be natural to date the final schism between the sects somewhere in the early first century B.C."[23]

With the discovery of the Qumran scrolls, especially the hundred or more biblical rolls from Cave 4 Qumran, Albright's position was confirmed in principle. The writer drew on a number of new lines of evidence which appear to establish firmly that the Samaritan Pentateuch, its textual type, orthographic style, Paleo-Hebrew script, and linguistic usage, all developed in the Maccabean and early Hasmonean periods.[24] Recently two of my students have developed in detail these

20. Josephus *War* I.31, 33; VII.422–35.

21. See P. W. Lapp, "The Second and Third Campaigns at 'Arâq el-'Emîr," *BASOR* 171 (1963): 8–38; and idem, "The Qasr el-'Abd: A Proposed Reconstruction," ibid., 39–45.

22. On a possible sacrificial cult at Qumran, see F. M. Cross, *The Ancient Library of Qumran*, 2d ed. (New York, 1961), 100–106.

23. W. F. Albright, *From the Stone Age to Christianity* (Baltimore, 1940; 2d ed., 1946), 336 n.12. Cf. idem, *BASOR* 140 (1955): 33 n.29; and *BASOR* 81 (1941): 5–6.

24. On the textual and paleographical aspects of "Proto-Samaritan" texts from Qumran, see my early comments in *BASOR* 141 (1956): 12 n.5a; *The Ancient Library of*

and other positions relating to the Samaritan Pentateuch in Harvard dissertations: Bruce K. Waltke, Prolegomena to the Samaritan Pentateuch (1965); and James D. Purvis, The Samaritan Pentateuch and the Origin of the Samaritan Sect, to be published soon in the series, Harvard Semitic Monographs.

We can now place the Samaritan Pentateuch in the history of the Hebrew biblical text.[25] It stems from an old Palestinian tradition which had begun to develop distinctive traits as early as the time of the Chronicler, and which can be traced in Jewish works and in the manuscripts of Qumran as late as the first century of the Christian era. This tradition was set aside in the course of the first century in Jerusalem in favor of a tradition of wholly different origin (presumably from Babylon), which provided the base of the Masoretic Recension. The Samaritan Pentateuchal tradition breaks off very late in the development of the Palestinian text. Early exemplars of this tradition lack most of the long additions from synoptic passages, as well as exhibiting stronger affinities with the Egyptian textual tradition, which broke off and began its separate development much earlier than the Samaritan. The Samaritan text-type thus is a late and full exemplar of the common Palestinian tradition, in use both in Jerusalem and in Samaria.

The Palestinian textual tradition of the Pentateuch sometimes comes in special dress. Often at Qumran it is inscribed in the Paleo-Hebrew script. This script is now known from seals of the fourth century from Samaria (via Dâliyeh), an unpublished seal from Makmish,[26] and from late in the century from the so-called Hezekiah coin.[27] It is frequent in the official jar stamps of the third century B.C. from Judah, both in the stamps inscribed with *Yehūd plus symbol*[28] and in the pentagram stamps bearing the legend *Jerusalem*.[29] In the second and first centuries B.C., this

Qumran, 172–73; and "Development of the Jewish Scripts," in *The Bible and the Ancient Near East*, ed. G. Ernest Wright (New York, 1961), 189 n.4.

25. See provisionally my paper, "The History of the Biblical Text . . . ," *HTR* 57 (1964): 281–99; and "The Contribution of the Discoveries at Qumran to the Study of the Biblical Text," *IEJ*.

26. My knowledge of this seal is thanks to Professor Nahman Avigad, who will publish it. Its script shows a number of special traits in common with the Samaritan seals.

27. Published by Ovid R. Sellers, *The Citadel of Beth-zur* (Philadelphia, 1933), 73–74.

28. See most recently Lapp, "Ptolemaic Stamped Handles from Judah," 22–35.

29. J. S. Holladay, in a letter dated December 2, 1965, has called my attention to stamps on wine jars of the Greek islands, notably Thasos, which bear the pentagram, and evidently influenced Jewish potters.

old national script is well known from published and unpublished manuscripts from Qumran as well as from Hasmonean coins. It is now possible to date roughly the periods in the typological sequence of the Paleo-Hebrew scripts.[30]

In this sequence of scripts, it is evident that the ancestral Samaritan character branches off from the Paleo-Hebrew script in the course of the first century B.C. There is no question of pushing the date higher. It may be noted that the Paleo-Hebrew script is used only in copying Palestinian texts. Texts of other traditions never are copied in the script; on the other hand, Palestinian texts of the Pentateuch are also inscribed in the ordinary Jewish character.

A similar typology can be drawn in the development of spelling practices. The earliest Palestinian texts follow a highly defective mode of orthography. In the course of the early second century a special "Maccabean" spelling system emerged, which expands the use of vowel letters, sometimes in a startling fashion. This baroque style of spelling, in a relatively restrained mode well known in late manuscripts from Qumran, characterized the Samaritan Pentateuch.[31]

The language of the Samaritan Pentateuch also includes archaizing forms and pseudo-archaic forms which surely point to the post-Maccabean age for its date.

From whatever side we examine the Samaritan Pentateuch, by whatever typological development we measure it, we are forced to the Hasmonean period at earliest for the origins of the Samaritan recension of the Pentateuch.

This evidence suggests strongly that the definitive breach between the Jews and Samaritans must be sought in the special events of the Hasmonean era, before the Roman period when Jew and Samaritan look upon each other in loathing, or as corrupters of the faith.

Once again we may look to the excavations at Shechem which yield evidence which, when correlated with texts from Josephus, provides a convincing setting. In 128 B.C. John Hyrcanus laid waste to the Temple of Mt. Gerizim and imposed Judean Judaism, so to speak, on the Samaritans; on the same campaign, he went so far as to circumcize by

---

30. See R. H. Hanson, "Paleo-Hebrew Scripts in the Hasmonaean Age," *BASOR* 175 (1964): 26–42. With the publication of the full lot of Cave 4 manuscripts, more precision in dating these Qumran hands will become possible.

31. On the orthography of Palestinian texts, see my paper on "The Contribution of the Discoveries at Qumran" (n.25, above), and D. N. Freedman, "The Massoretic Text and the Qumran Scrolls: A Study in Orthography," *Textus* 2 (1962): 87–103.

force the Idumeans living to the south of Judah. It is clear that his goal was to establish orthodoxy in the realm which once made up Israel. In 107 B.C. Hyrcanus again stormed north, destroying Samaria and probably Shechem as well.[32] Hyrcanus's attempt to extirpate the Samaritan cultus failed as signally as Spanish attempts to baptize Jews in another age. When Pompey in 64 B.C. freed Samaria from vassalage to the Hasmonean priest-kings, we may be sure the Samaritans severed all ties with Judaism, to traverse their own isolated and involuted path.

This reconstruction of the history of the Samaritans solves many problems which have perplexed us in the past. As we have suggested, it dissolves the mystery of the specifically Jewish character of Samaritanism. It explains the close ties of Samaritanism to Zadokite traditions, provides the background of Essene or apocalyptic Zadokite strains in late Samaritan law and doctrine. The historian is no longer required to contend with a parallel, but unrelated, evolution within two sects over a half milennium after their separation.

Similarly, the new reconstruction of the history of the Samaritans clears up confusion concerning the history of the text of the Pentateuch. In the distorted picture of this development still being defended in most circles, we were required to suppose that the Samaritan Pentateuch branched off as early as the fifth century, yet preserved a text exceedingly like the *textus receptus* of the Roman age, indeed a secondary or inferior form of the received text. The Greek version, branching off about the same time or slightly later, on the other hand, preserved a remarkably variant tradition, sometimes superior, sometimes inferior to the Rabbinic text of the first century of the common era. The Greek tradition conforms to all analogies in the transmission of ancient texts. The development of the Samaritan seemed at all points anomalous. These anomalies now disappear, with the happy result that the text critic's task is greatly facilitated.

---

32. See E. F. Campbell in Toombs and G. E. Wright, "The Third Campaign at Balâṭah (Shechem)," *BASOR* 161 (1961): 47; and Wright, "Samaritans at Shechem," 358–59.

Michael E. Stone

3

The Book of Enoch and Judaism in the Third Century B.C.E.* (1978)

This chapter turns to a discussion of a number of scrolls found in the famous series of discoveries at Khirbet Qumran nearly forty years ago. These Dead Sea Scrolls, as they came to be called, were deposited in caves near an Essene communal settlement on the northwestern coast of the Dead Sea. Although the Essene settlement at Qumran started in the second century B.C.E., certain of the manuscripts that they brought with them were considerably older. Among these earliest scrolls, which are numbered among the most ancient Hebrew and Aramaic manuscripts in general, are portions of the *Book of Enoch* in Aramaic. The *Book of Enoch* was previously known only in its later Greek and Ethiopic versions. These Aramaic fragments date from the third and early second centuries B.C.E. Certain sections of the *Book of Enoch* (chaps. 1–36, 72–83), then, stand unquestionably as the oldest, extrabiblical Jewish religious literature.

The contents of these oldest writings are very surprising, not corresponding at all with our preconceptions of what Jewish religious development was like in the fourth and third centuries. Michael E. Stone explores the implications of this early dating of the Enoch manuscripts for the existence of circles devoted to speculative wisdom, scientific and mystical, within third-century Palestinian Judaism. This is another example of how implications drawn from an epigraphic discovery can force a reassessment of conventional views of the development of Judaism in this age.

*R. A. Kraft, J. J. Collins, and H. Attridge kindly read earlier forms of this paper and made a number of most helpful comments.

IT HAS LONG been true that a major difficulty in writing the history of Judaism in the pre-Christian era is the paucity of information relating directly to the fourth and third centuries. Certain of the biblical writings were doubtless redacted in this age and a few others composed in it. Nonetheless, we lack a clear picture of how Judaism developed throughout this period.[1] Rabbinic chronology radically foreshortens this era and Josephus's brevity too reflects the poverty of the historical accounts.[2] It is not surprising then that when the sources become plentiful once more, after the start of the second century B.C.E., the picture of Judaism they present differs considerably from that which can be constructed for the period down to the age of Ezra and Nehemiah.[3] .

The chief cultural and political event that had taken place in the interim was the conquest of the East by Alexander of Macedon and the concommitant advance of Hellenization.[4] When the curtain lifts once more on Palestinian Judaism, it is more than a century after this event; the Judaism it uncovers differs greatly from that which preceded it. Quite new forms of religious writing had emerged and far-reaching changes in the religious structure of society had taken place, as well as innovations in the history of ideas that were to set patterns for the succeeding millennia.[5]

There have been various attempts in recent scholarship to recon-

---

1. On the dates of redaction of the biblical books, see O. Eissfeldt, *The Old Testament: An Introduction* (New York: Harper & Row, 1965). He also cites an extensive bibliography for each book.

2. *'Olam Rab.* 29; *Lev. Rab.* 29:2; Josephus *Ant.*11–12.

3. Papponymy may have been one of the causes of the foreshortening of this period in the historical records; a recent reconstruction taking account of this is by F. M. Cross, Jr. ("A Reconstruction of the Judean Restoration," *JBL* 94 [1975]: 4–18). In this article Cross uses the rather meager evidence gained from the study of the Dâliyeh papyri to recover certain of the names and dates of leaders of Judea and Samaria throughout this age and thus to establish a historical framework for it.

4. M. Hengel (*Judaism and Hellenism* 2 vols. [Philadelphia: Fortress Press, 1974; London: SCM Press, 1974]) has provided a compendious collection of evidence relating to the interaction between Judaism and Hellenism in the pre-Maccabean period. The strictures of L. H. Feldman ("Hengel's *Judaism and Hellenism* in Retrospect, *JBL* 69 [1977]: 371–82) do not affect the value of the rich resources which Hengel lays before his reader.

5. Indeed, a case may be made that this transformation of Judaism was deeper and far more pervasive than that of Judah before the Babylonian exile to the community of the Restoration. In the earlier period the changes were gradual and the older institutions developed or disappeared slowly. After 200 the structure of society and the nature of religious thinking changed very fundamentally.

struct something of the character of Judaism in the third century. The most extensive is that of Martin Hengel. Intending to tell the history of Judaism and Hellenism down to the time of the Maccabean revolt, Hengel draws on existing sources to outline the interplay and conflict between these civilizations in the late fourth and third centuries. He points out that Hellenization was extensive in pre-Maccabean Judea and that it must have had opponents as well as supporters. In these conflicts, he sees the background to the Maccabean revolt.[6]

Thus, Hengel surmises rather plausibly that the various pietistic groups that opposed the Antiochian decrees must have originated in the third century. Perhaps some biblical psalms and more certainly some of the apocryphal psalms were composed in the third century by such groups.[7] A large body of apocalyptic literature too, Hengel claims, stemmed from one of these groups called the Hasideans. This literature arose from the impact on them of the persecution by Antiochus IV Epiphanes.[8] For various reasons one might deny that the Hasideans (about whom we know very little) were responsible for the apocalypses. Still, it would accord with the thrust of Hengel's analysis to regard some of the apocalypses, such as Daniel and *The Dream Visions of Enoch*, as having arisen out of the conflict between Judaism (particularly pietistic Judaism) and Hellenism which peaked in the earlier part of the second century.[9] This conflict must have been the eruption of a long-standing

6. *Judaism and Hellenism* 1:107–217.

7. Scholars most commonly cast biblical Psalm 149 and apocryphal psalm 154 (11QPsa 18:1–16) in this role.

8. *Judaism and Hellenism* 1:175–217. Considerable similarity exists between the apocalypses of the Maccabean period. Nonetheless, to make them all, or even most of them, compositions of the Hasideans is to go far beyond what is warranted by the meager evidence for the views and attitudes of this particular group. Yet it seems extremely likely that many of these writings arose from the circles of the pietistic opponents of Hellenism, of which the Hasideans were part. Most recently J. J. Collins has commented on these problems in his book *The Apocalyptic Vision of the Book of Daniel* (HSM 16; Missoula, Mont.: Scholars Press, 1977), 201–18.

9. P. D. Hanson (*The Dawn of Apocalyptic* [Philadelphia: Fortress Press, 1975]) traces the origins of apocalyptic eschatology back to the fifth century B.C.E. He sees it as arising out of the tensions between "visionary" and "hierocratic" groups in the exilic and postexilic communities and the gradual transfer of the hopes of the "visionary" group to the metahistorical realm. Note particularly his succinct formulation on pp. 6–12, 24–29. There are certain difficulties in this analysis, see nn. 13, 14, below. G. W. E. Nickelsburg (*Resurrection, Immortality and Eternal Life in Intertestamental Judaism* [HTS 26; Cambridge: Harvard Univ. Press, 1972]) has emphasized the role that the experience of martyrdom under the Antiochian persecution had in moving the future hope to the hope of immortalilty. J. J. Collins ("Apocalyptic Eschatology as

tension which can also be discerned at points in the Wisdom of Ben Sira. Yet, Ben Sira's audience was not pietistic zealots but the well-to-do youth, which serves to remind us that faithful adherence to the traditions of Judaism was not the exclusive prerogative of the pietists.[10] Thus, simply to contrast pietistic opponents of Hellenism and rich, priestly or aristocratic assimilationists is surely to oversimplify.

Other evidence hints at differing positions in pre-Maccabean times. J. J. Collins has pointed to the importance of the attitude to the gentile rulers in the court-stories of Daniel, Esther, and the like as an indicator of Jewish attitudes to the gentile world. Without following necessarily his arguments to all of their conclusions,[11] it seems clear that most of the Danielic stories, like the Book of Esther, are open to the possibility of Jews playing a role at the pagan courts. No ritual difficulties are raised;[12] the advance of the Jew to the highest position in the land; the marriage of a Jewess to the king; the fortunes of the wise Jewish

the Transcendence of Death," *CBQ* 36 [1974]: 21–43) identified the transcendence of death as the unique and particular element of apocalyptic eschatology. None of these studies deals with the origins of apocalyptic literature; even Hanson's work is concerned primarily with the development of apocalyptic eschatology and not of the litetary form of the apocalypse. The question of apocalyptic origins has been much debated, see in summary M. E. Stone, "Lists of Revealed Things in Apocalyptic Literature," *Magnalia Dei: The Mighty Acts of God—Essays on the Bible and Archaeology in Memory of G. Ernest Wright*, ed. F. M. Cross, W. Lemke, P. D. Miller (New York: Doubleday & Co., 1976), 436–44. Hengel's historical reconstruction is much indebted to the important work by E. Bickerman, *Der Gott der Makkabäer* (Berlin: Schocken Books, 1937). Compare also the book by V. Tcherikover, *Hellenistic Civilization and the Jews* (Philadelphia: Jewish Publication Society, 1959). Hengel's view has not been accepted by all scholars; see, e.g., the review by M. Stern, *Kirjath Sepher* 47 (1971): 94–99. A new view of the events, debatable at points, is that of J. A. Goldstein, *1 Maccabees* (AB 41; New York: Doubleday & Co., 1976).

10. On Ben Sira and Hellenism see Hengel, *Judaism and Hellenism* 1:131–53. On the character of Jewish piety, see A. Bücher, *Types of Palestinian Jewish Peity* (London: Oxford Univ. Press, 1922); see also S. Safrai, "The Teaching of Pietists in Mishnaic Literature," *JJS* 16 (1965): 15–33.

11. See Collins (*Daniel*, 36–54) where he suggests that the attitudes of the stories in Daniel range from sympathy for the gentile ruler to open hostility. We would query his conclusion (pp.29–33) that Daniel 1 is part of the old story style; see n.12. On the setting of the stories, see W. L. Humphreys, "A Life-style for the Diaspora: A Study of the Tales of Esther and Daniel,"*JBL* 92 (1973): 211–23. Hengel (*Judaism and Hellenism* 1:29–30) also points to the changes in attitude reflected by these stories. See further the bibliography which he cites (2:24–25).

12. Contrast the Book of Judith and see E. Haag *Studien zum Buch Judith* (Trier: Paulinusverlag, 1963). The similar character of Daniel 1, e.g., in its concern for the dietary laws, as well as its Hebrew language, argue for its belonging to a later level of material than the Aramaic court stories.

courtier and the wisdom of the Jewish page—all these themes imply a positive attitude towards a Jew functioning in gentile society. The vindication of the God of Israel against the idolatry of the heathen is presented as the king's acknowledgment of the superiority of God and glorification of His servant, who is the king's own courtier. The events of the first quarter of the second century B.C.E. changed these attitudes and this is indicated by the different types of stories emanating from this later period.

P. D. Hanson suggests that the hierocratic tendency or group, which is one of the two that he discerns in postexilic Judaism, was predominant during the fourth and third centuries. Only the events of the early second century, according to him, renewed the impetus of the "prophetic" or "visionary" trend that developed apocalyptic eschatology. Significantly, he does not suggest any lines of genetic or other direct connection between the bearers of these traditions in the fifth century and those in the second century.[13] In a recent paper he attempted to characterize the different stages of development of *1 Enoch* 6–11, a section of *1 Enoch* that must stem from the third century (see below). Here again he avoids formulating any relationship between the bearers of the different tendencies he discerns in *1 Enoch* 6–11 and those groups he had identified in the earlier, postexilic period. Yet he would attribute each of the three layers he discerns in these chapters of *1 Enoch* to circles cultivating "apocalyptic eschatology" and suggests some connections between such sectarian apocalyptic movements and second-century Hasideans and Essenes.[14] Caution in such matters is

---

13. *Apocalyptic*, 402–9. One difficulty in his presentation is that he underestimates the role played by the Temple in all types of Judaism. Particular attitudes towards the Temple and its cult may have varied, but all of them presume its central role. An analogous difficulty is in the article cited in the next note in which he maintains that the group responsible for one of the sections of *1 Enoch* 6–11 (and so, it seems, to be dated in the third century at the latest) rejected or judged ineffectual the Day of Atonement ritual of the Temple (p. 226). This part of his argument, which is intrinsically unlikely, is also beset by philological difficulties. Some of these were pointed out by G. W. E. Nickelsburg ("Apocalyptic and Myth in 1 Enoch 6–11," *JBL* 96 [1977]: 401–3).

14. P. D. Hanson "Rebellion in Heaven, Azazel and Euhemeristic Heroes in 1 Enoch 6–11," *JBL* 96 (1977): 219–20, 224–25, 231–32. This article contains much of interest to the student of *1 Enoch*. It is marred by an overly uncritical acceptance of the literary analysis by others as a basis for discussion. Furthermore, Hanson's view that ancient Near Eastern mythical patterns predominate in *1 Enoch* 6–11 has not been sufficiently demonstrated. The relationship between ancient Near Eastern, Hellenistic, and other elements in this writing needs further study. One might also differ from Hanson on a number of matters of detail in his arguments.

wise, for the movement from tendencies of thought discerned in the analysis of texts to the positing of the existence of otherwise unattested social groups is fraught with peril. Yet, that danger is one that the scholar must brave if his analysis is conducted in terms that imply a sociological matrix for the development of ideas.[15]

One feature, however, more than any other has made the description of Judaism in this period so difficult and made the picture of Judaism in the following age so surprising. That is the transmission of the sources. As for the period of the First Temple, so for the age of the Restoration we are dependent almost solely on the biblical sources. No other ancient Jewish books have survived and even the epigraphic material is sparse and of little interest to the historian of Judaism. In contrast, the sources for that "surprising" Judaism of the second century are all extrabiblical: the Book of Daniel is a sole exception. Indeed, almost all of them were preserved outside the Jewish tradition, either by the various Christian churches or by archaeological chance.

When this extrabiblical literature exhibits aspects of religious thought that are new if contrasted with the biblical literature of the age of the Restoration, various sorts of explanation may be sought. These features could be new, indigenous developments of Judaism. They could also have come into being under the influence of foreign cultures—Greek, Persian, or even Phoenician. But they might also be the first surfacing in literature of points of view and teachings that survived from earlier days, excluded from the biblical sources by the selectivity of their transmission.

In his recently published book, J. T. Milik has made available for the first time detailed information about and photographs of most of the manuscripts of *1 Enoch* that were discovered at Qumran. The oldest of these is 4QEnastr, a manuscript of *The Astronomical Book* which he dates to "the end of the third or else the beginning of the second century B.C."[16] Next oldest is 4QEn, a manuscript of *The Book of the Watchers*

---

15. A further indication of the complexity of Judaism at this time is the series of temples that existed outside Jerusalem, such as in Elephantine (somewhat earlier), Leontopolis, and Araq el-Amir. These remind us that the Deuteronomic reform and its consequences were not universally accepted. The evidence has been marshaled well by M. Smith (*Palestinian Parties and Politics That Shaped the Old Testament* [New York: Columbia Univ. Press, 1971], 83–98), even if one does not wish to accept all his conclusions. Smith's work is also important as it attempts to reconstruct the cults to which the prophets voiced their opposition.

16. J. T. Milik, *The Books of Enoch* (Oxford: Clarendon Press, 1976), 273. Unfortunately, he did not publish the photographs of this manuscript; so for the present the dating is dependent on his uncorroborated judgment.

which he dates to "the first half of the second century."[17] Neither of these manuscripts appears to be an author's autograph, and it is reasonable, therefore, to date the composition of the writings that they contain to the third century. There seems to be no basis upon which to dispute these dates, since they are founded upon firmly established paleographic criteria.[18] Moreover, *The Book of the Watchers* does not stem from a single pen, but was composed by a writer who utilized diverse source-documents. At least one of these, chaps. 6–11, is itself composite. Consequently, the sources of *The Book of the Watchers* may be inferred to be even older than the writing down of its present form which, as said above, took place some time in the third century B.C.E. These dates are very significant for they mean that *The Book of the Watchers (1 Enoch 1–36)* and *The Astronomical Book (1 Enoch 72–82)* are the oldest, extrabiblical Jewish religious literature.

This dating is corroborated by the antiquity of the evidence for the existence of the developed view of Enoch as the primordial sage. The oldest of the numerous sources attesting to this are *Jub.* 4:16–25 and Sir. 44:16 as well as the material contained in *1 Enoch* itself.[19] When these sources are assessed, one certain conclusion emerges. Their delineation of Enoch is not an exegetical extrusion from Gen. 5:22–24.

17. Ibid., 104; see pls. I–IV. This is also the view of F. M. Cross in a letter dated 13 January 1978.

18. See F. M. Cross, Jr., "The Development of the Jewish Scripts," in *The Bible and the Ancient Near East: Essays in Honor of William Foxwell Albright,* ed. G. E. Wright (Garden City, N. Y.: Doubleday & Co., 1961), 170–264. A quite different sort of argument for the third-century date of *The Book of the Watchers* is advanced by T. F. Glasson ("The Son of Man Imagery: Enoch xiv and Daniel vii," *NTS* 23 [1976]: 81–90). He argues unconvincingly for the literary dependence of Daniel 7 on *1 Enoch* 14, thus requiring a third-century date for the latter. His treatment is deliberately narrow in scope, not even taking the full character of *1 Enoch* 14 into account. It is possible, however, that other literary analyses will be more successful in supporting such hypotheses.

19. P. Grelot. ("La légende d'Hénoch dans les apocryphes et dans la bible: origine et significance," *RSR* 46 [1958]: 19–21) suggested that antiquity of *Jub.* 4:17–23 and discussed its relationship to parts of *1 Enoch*. More recently ("Hénoch et ses écritures," *RB* 82 [1975]: 481–500), he concludes that the author of *Jubilees* knew *The Book of the Watchers, The Astronomical Book,* and *The Dream Visions. Jubilees* is usually dated to the first part of the second century; the Wisdom of Ben Sira to the period between 198 and 175 B.C.E. It may be remarked parenthetically that the meaning of Sir.44:16 now seems clear, in light of the dates of the Enoch books. Milik's attempt (*Enoch,* 8–9) to show that the pseudo-Eupolemus fragment was in fact used by a Eupolemus who lived in the early second century must be judged inconclusive. See J. C. Greenfield and M. E. Stone, "The Books of Enoch and the Traditions of Enoch," *Numen* 26 (1979), 89–103. This Samaritan text is preserved in Eusebius, *Praep. Ev.* 9.17, 2–9, and in it astronomical knowledge seems to be attributed to Enoch.

He is presented in these diverse sources with new, distinct and clearly articulated features that are by no means hinted at in Genesis. Some decades ago, H. L. Jansen strongly urged the view that the figure of Enoch as the sage of heavenly wisdom draws on Mesopotamian sources. According to this view, Enoch the seventh from Adam was modeled after the wise, seventh antediluvian Mesopotamian monarch or after other Mesopotamian wisdom figures.[20] In any case, it is impossible to know whether this tradition about Enoch is a development of that already found referred to by the author of Genesis 5 some centuries before. It might be, or it might have been a new growth in the interim. A careful study of the Mesopotamian evidence may prove decisive in favor of the former hypothesis.

Such a development in the late Persian or Ptolemaic periods is not without parallels. At least one other figure can be shown to have evolved during this age and to have taken on great significance in the creation of literature, and that is Daniel. Although he might be connected in some remote way with the wise Canaanite king Dan'il, known

20. See H. L. Jansen, *Die Henochgestalt* (Papers of the Norwegian Academy in Oslo, Hist.-Phil. Class, 1939, no.1; Oslo: Dybwad, 1939). Jansen discussed a number of different Mesopotamian wisdom figures and culture heroes whose depiction may have influenced that of Enoch. Earlier scholars had already made suggestions of this sort, see the sources cited by Jansen (ibid., 1–4). He particularly emphasized the influence of the Hellenistic Chaldean teachings that were widespread in the last pre-Christian centuries. This point has been taken up again most recently by J. J. Collins, "Cosmos and Salvation: Jewish Wisdom and Apocalyptic in the Hellenistic Age," *HR* 17 (1977): 131–32. A clear presentation and evaluation of the evidence for Mesopotamian influence on the figure of Enoch is that by P. Grelot, who had not seen Jansen's book; see Grelot, "La légend," 5–26, 181–210. He concludes (pp. 23–25) that the Jewish Enoch figure combines a number of Mesopotamian motifs and ventures to suggest that this borrowing is of considerable antiquity; see particularly pp. 193–95. These views doubtlessly need reevaluation in the light of the new evidence that has accumulated since their formulation, but the general thrust of the hypotheses of Jansen and Grelot could well be correct. This may be corroborated by the observations made by some scholars on the Mesopotamian character of the astronomical theories propounded by *The Astronomical Book* (*1 Enoch* 72–82). See Hengel, *Judaism and Hellenism* 1:209 and references there. This subject should now be reexamined by an expert in the history of science, since the Qumran Enoch manuscripts with their extensive astronomical and calendar contents have been published. In an important article P. Grelot pointed out the Mesopotamian character of the map of the world presumed by the various parts of Enoch: see "La géographie mythique d'Hénoch et ses sources orientales," *RB* 65 (1958): 33–69. This point was taken up once more by Milik, *Enoch*, 13–19. See additional bibliography there. Milik (p. 29) also reports that Mesopotamian names and mythological personages figure in *The Book of the Giants* which also belongs to the Qumran Enoch corpus. See the texts he has published on pp. 311–13.

from the Ugaritic epic and from the Book of Ezekiel, or else with Enoch's father-in-law (*Jub.* 4:20), still the hero of the Book of Daniel has no obvious antecedent in biblical literature. The Moses of a Moses pseudepigraphon or the Elijah or Ezra of books attributed to them were personalities already well established in biblical literature. In the Book of Daniel, however, the hero is unknown. Moreover, he is also the putative author of a number of other works. The Qumran Danielic writings as well as certain of the additions to the Greek translations of Daniel are most likely independent of the Book of Daniel.[21] As was true of Enoch, so also the figure of Daniel apparently underwent extensive development during the fourth and third centuries. This parallel between them is heightened by the special wisdom features shared by these two figures.[22]

From these considerations it follows that a careful examination of *1 Enoch* 1–36 and 72–82 together with the fragmentary Qumran manuscripts of these chapters can provide some insights into the character of Judaism in the third century. Chaps. 1–36 seem to be a literary whole embodying various sources and can be divided into the following chief parts. They open with a prophecy by Enoch of God's coming visitation (chap. 1). An exhortation to men to pattern their righteous conduct on the regularity of the natural phenomena, and the blessings and curses of the righteous and wicked follow this (chaps. 2–5). The story of the fallen angels, their corruption of men and their wicked teaching, their punishment and the ideal state that will ensue are next (chaps. 6–11). Enoch's translation to heaven, his consideration of the watchers' petition and his ascent to the heavenly palace where he receives God's answer to the petition come next (chaps. 12–16). Visions of the underworld and the secrets of meteorology and the place of punishment of the fallen angels follow (chaps. 17–19). Then Enoch learns the names of

21. See most recently Collins, *Daniel*, 1–7, and further bibliography there. His views as to the possible Babylonian origin of the stories in the Book of Daniel provide an intriguing parallel to features of *The Book of Enoch* discussed above: see ibid., 54–59.

22. For Daniel see ibid., 55–58 and earlier bibliography there; Collins, "Cosmos and Salvation," 134–35. On Enoch see the material presented by Grelot, "La légende," 14–17. For a similar, contemporary development in the Greco-Oriental sphere, we may look to the growth of the figure of Hermes-Thoth: see A.-J. Festugière, *La révélation d'Hermès Trismégiste* (Paris: Firmin-Didot, 1944), 1:67–88. Apparently similar is also Phoenician Taautos, who is equated with Hermes-Thoth by Philo Byblus (apud Eusebius *Praep. Ev.* 1.9; I am indebted to H. Attridge for this comment).

the archangels and their functions (chap. 20). He journeys for a second time and sees the place where the angels are punished, Sheol and the Underworld and sundry distant regions of the earth and its mythical geography to the northwest, center, east, north and south. In particular, meteorological and astronomical features of these regions are stressed (chaps. 21–36).

The Astronomical Book is much more extensive in the form in which it has survived at Qumran than in the Ethiopic version. In addition to preserving a longer form of the astronomical and meteorological material contained in Ethiopic 1 Enoch 72–82, the Qumran manuscripts also contain fragments of an extensive calendar replete with additional astronomical and meteorological information. Unfortunately none of the Qumran fragments coincides with chaps. 80–81 which deal with the perversion of the order of nature by the deeds of men, Enoch's receipt of a more general revelation about the future of men, and his return to his house. There is, however, no reason to doubt the antiquity of these chapters.

When this material and its range of interests are considered, certain things strike the reader immediately. The first is that chaps. 1–36, clearly a composite of various source-documents and traditions, are in parts eschatological in character, chaps. 1–6 and 10:14–11 being particularly notable in this respect.[23] Nevertheless, chaps. 6–11 are chiefly interested in the origins of evil and of certain types of knowledge, in the fallen angels and their offspring and in the cause of the flood. Eschatological matters are presented only incidentally in the rest of chaps. 12–36. Chap. 14 is an ascent vision, exhibiting a developed view of the heavenly abode of the Godhead. A detailed angelology, much interest in the geography of the Underworld, the earth and its hidden parts, astronomy, meteorology, and uranography characterize the rest of these chapters. This subject is even more prominent in The Astronomical Book which, however, also has some eschatological concerns.

Thus, as a result of the publication by Milik of these particularly

23. Hanson and Nickelsburg are both convinced of the primarily eschatological intent of chaps. 6–11. See details in their articles cited above, nn.13, 14. The present paper does not pretend to resolve the knotty issues raised by these two provocative articles. It should be observed, however, that the "eschatological" prophecy of 10:14ff. is strange. It seems to refer to events that will ensue on the binding of the Watchers which apparently took place before the flood. This implies, it seems, that the eschatological time too was antediluvian, which was patently not so. The general range of interests of chaps. 6–11 is notable, however their final verses are interpreted.

ancient manuscripts, a developed "scientific" lore about astronomy, calendar, cosmology, and angelology is now known to have existed in the third century B.C.E. Prior to this discovery there was no reason to suppose that within Judaism the cosmos and all its parts were the object of detailed learned speculation at that time. For some years now the present writer has maintained, on quite different grounds, that speculative interests of this sort are one of the core elements of the Jewish apocalypses.[24] These interests arose neither out of biblical nor out of apocryphal wisdom literature, at least insofar as the surviving books are at all representative of the concerns of the schools of didactic wisdom.[25]

Of equal importance is the fact that from *1 Enoch* 14 it is clear that a tradition (and apparently the practice) of ascent to the heavenly environs of the deity was also well established by that time. In the early 1940's, G. Scholem showed that a line of continuity could be traced back from the earliest body of Jewish mystical texts, the Hekalot and Merkabah books of the mid-first millennium C.E., through certain passages in Tannaitic literature and into certain of the pseudepigrapha.[26] Prominent among the passages that he located within this terminological tradition was *1 Enoch* 14. Another document that appertains to it became available only later, the Angelic Liturgy from Qumran.[27] All of these texts describe the heavenly realm and the environs of the Godhead, under profound influence of Ezekiel 1, which was the central text for contemplation. Nearly all of these passages are ascent texts. So it is that *1 Enoch* 14 is remarkable in two respects at least. First, it is the oldest Jewish ascent vision. Its very existence shows the changes that had taken place in the view of man and the norms of religious experience in comparison with those found in the Hebrew Bible,[28] Second, and even more surprisingly, it shows that the utilization of Ezekiel 1 as

24. See Stone, "Lists," passim.

25. *Pace* Gerhard von Rad. See Stone, "Lists," 435–38, and see also Collins, *Daniel*, 56–59. He emphasized the elements of mantic wisdom that were brought into the discussion of apocalyptic literature by H.-P. Müller, "Mantische Weisheit und Apokalyptik," VTSup 22 (1972): 268–93. See most recently Collins, "Cosmos and Salvation," 135–40.

26. G. G. Scholem, *Major Trends in Jewish Mysticism* (New York: Schocken Books, 1941), 40–63.

27. The Angelic Liturgy was published by J. Strugnell, "The Angelic Liturgy at Qumran," VTSup 7 (1960): 318–46. Further relevant studies may be found in G. G. Scholem, *Jewish Gnosticism, Merkabah Mysticism and Talmudic Tradition* (2d ed.; New York: Jewish Theological Seminary, 1965), esp. 14–19.

28. See D. S. Russell (*The Method and Message of Jewish Apocalyptic* [London: SCM Press, 1964], 164–69) who has assembled many of the sources.

the basic text for description of the heavenly realm and the ascent through it was already well established by the third century.[29] The ascent, which is one of the main vision types found in the Jewish apocalypses, is already prevalent in the oldest surviving exemplar.

It seems to be quite clear that the "scientific" or speculative interests that play a predominant role in these oldest parts of *1 Enoch* were beyond the pale for the tradents of biblical literature. The Book of Daniel, notable among the apocalypses for its lack of interest in these subjects, is an eloquent witness to this: it is the only apocalypse included in the Hebrew Bible.[30] This seems to mean that to trace the eschatological axis as the chief or indeed the sole axis along which apocalyptic literature developed is to lay upon the evidence those same censorial rules that were laid upon the material by the biblical tradents themselves. The role of the speculative knowledge and of the early Merkabah-type ascent contemplation must be accepted as part of Judaism from its oldest extrabiblical literature on.

The implications of these observations must be worked out in some further detail, particularly as they affect the account of Judaism and of the development of Jewish literature in the third century B.C.E. Those conflicts that have so far served as a basis for positing the existence of different groups within the Jewish community have centered around assimilation, syncretism, or eschatological hope. These lines of analysis have been determined partly by the configuration that the concerns of the biblical authors and tradents laid upon the surviving literary remains and partly by the interests of modern scholarship (themselves also deeply influenced by the former factor). The speculative element is

29. This is not to claim that *1 Enoch* 14 is a mystical text, properly speaking. The purpose of the ascent in it is the revelation of certain information rather than the "perception of (God's) appearance on the Throne, as described by Ezekiel, and cognition of the mysteries of the celestial throne world" (Scholem, *Major Tends*, 44). Should the use of the term *merkabah* by Ben Sira (49:8, ms B), referring to Ezekiel's vision, now be considered technical?

30. On this matter see Stone, "Lists," 440–43. Some other apocalypses of the Maccabean period are also predominantly eschatological in content, such as *The Dream Visions of Enoch* and the oldest form of *The Testament of Moses*. The absence of such material from 4 Ezra, which was written in a later age, is deliberate and probably polemical. See M. E. Stone, "Paradise in IV Ezra iv.8 and vii.36, viii.52," *JJS* 17 (1966): 85–88 and "Lists," 419–21. It is possible that *The Apocalypse of Weeks (1 Enoch* 93:1–10 + 91:12–17) is another example of a predominantly eschatological apocalypse of this era, but the time of its composition and its interpretation remain open issues.

alien to biblical literature (except, to some extent, for Job) and is also excluded from the NT. For reasons that arise from that, scholars have made a few attempts to investigate this material or to understand it.[31]

Among the groups of assimilationists and the pious, the wise and the Hasideans, a place must now be found for those who cultivated sacred speculations on subjects represented in the early part of *1 Enoch*. It is of course impossible to know whether these people formed a group or sect that was distinct from all those already mentioned. At the very least, however, they reflected an intellectual tradition and the likely relationships of that tradition can be studied. Its bearers must have been well-educated men and may possibly have been associated with the traditional intellectual groups, the wise and the priests. Enoch is the archetypical wise man, the founder of wisdom and, moreover, there exist intriguing connections between certain aspects of apocalyptic learning and Mesopotamian mantic wisdom.[32] Certain other features suggest that such circles were connected with the priests. The intense interest in the calendar is a priestly concern. After all, the 364-day solar calendar must now be dated back to the third century at least, although its role and function remain mysterious. At a somewhat later date the Qumran sectaries related their calendary interests to the calculation of the priestly courses of the Temple.[33] In many ways also, the first section of *1 Enoch* (particularly chaps. 21–36) resembles Ezekiel 40–44. This serves to remind us of another possible priestly connection. Interest in heavenly objects is ancient when it is related to the idea of the celestial pattern of the sanctuary and its furnishing.[34]

A central element of the apocalypses is their visionary character. This is also true of the Enoch books and it is this element more than any other that has argued in favor of seeing the origins of apocalyptic literature within the prophetic tradition. Certainly, G. von Rad argued for years that the apocalyptic literature originated in the traditions and

31. Stone, "Lists," 440–43.

32. See n.25.

33. See Milik (*Enoch*, 274–78) on the calendar. His conclusions on the Samaritan origins of this calendar (pp. 7–10) are open to dispute. See Greenfield and Stone, "Books of Enoch."

34. See Exod. 25:9–10, 1 Chron. 28:19, Ezek. 40:2 and perhaps Zech. 2:5–9; see further Stone, "Lists," 445–46. The similarity to Ezekiel is in the "guided tour" type of revelation. Moreover, connections between *1 Enoch* 14 and Ezekiel 1 were mentioned above. J. Maier (*Vom Kultus zur Gnosis* [Salzburg: Müller, 1964]) has emphasized this aspect of the origins of speculative traditions.

schools of didactic wisdom, but this view has been shown to be inadequate as an exclusive explanation of apocalyptic origins.[35]

In light of the new manuscripts and their dates, however, it may be deceptive to seek an exclusively prophetic origin for the apocalypses either as far as their form is concerned or their content. In principle, there is no reason to think that the body of literature that is transmitted as the Hebrew Bible is a representative collection of all types of Jewish literary creativity down to the fourth century. It is a selection of texts and the process of transmission and preservation that created this selection reflects the theological judgment of certain groups in Judah and Jerusalem before and after the Babylonian exile. It is specious, therefore, when faced by a third-century phenomenon, either to seek its roots in the Bible or to relegate it to foreign influence. Circles other than those transmitting the biblical books existed, or else those involved in transmitting the biblical books did not allow a considerable part of the intellectual culture of their day to be expressed in them. From *The Book of the Watchers* and the *The Astronomical Book* we learn that some men were deeply involved in sacred science and speculative ascent experiences and that these had already taken on a complex written form by the third century.

It seems to follow that in third-century Judea there were circles profoundly interested in the range of subjects dealt with by *The Book of the Watchers* and *The Astronomical Book*. These circles nurtured a developed intellectual and literary tradition and this tradition drew upon sources not rooted in biblical exegesis.[36] It is true that parts of *1 Enoch* 6–11 are the oldest pieces of Jewish biblical exegesis we possess outside the Bible. Nonetheless we venture to say that the speculative aspects of the interests of such circles drew on material that is not found in the Bible or its exegesis.

---

35. A good deal has been written on these issues. The views of von Rad are dealt with perceptively by P. von der Osten-Sacken, *Die Apokalyptik in ihrem Verhältnis zu Prophetie und Weisheit* (Munich: Kaiser, 1969). See also Collins (*Daniel*, 57) whose opinion is typical of the present consensus on this issue.

36. On *1 Enoch* 6–11 as exegesis, see Hanson, "Rebellion in Heaven," 197–202. The intellectual tradition that is expressed in these and other parts of *The Book of the Watchers* and *The Astronomical Book* does not derive from the biblical text. It should be noted that if *1 Enoch* 6–11 is treated as an independent writing, then it is not an apocalypse in form. Notably also none of the other apocalypses are as intimately tied to the biblical text as are the earlier parts of those chapters. For a recent attempt to delineate the form of apocalypses, see K. Koch, *The Rediscovery of Apocalyptic* (London: SCM Press, 1972), 23–28.

It has been observed in the past that those sections of the Hebrew Bible that have the closest relations with the apocalypses in form have little contact with them in content, while those texts in which the development of apocalyptic eschatology can be traced tend to lack the formal elements of the apocalypses.[37] Could it be that the part taken by the eschatological elements was magnified, or even became predominant, as a result of the crises of the Maccabean revolt? It is from that time, indeed, that we find the largely eschatological writings such as Daniel 7–12 and *The Dream Visions of Enoch* (see n.30). This shift of emphasis might have been the result of the persecutions and martyrdoms that accompanied the revolt. Here the issue is not the presence of eschatological material in the more ancient documents; it is that they contain so very much that is not eschatological.

However the question raised in the preceding paragraph is answered, it is clear that an additional stage in the development of the apocalyptic literature can be traced. The biblical texts that are precursory either in form or content can be designated proto-apocalyptic. A newly isolated and dated type of apocalyptic speculative writing containing some eschatological elements and much other material is now known from the third century. The writings stemming from the age of the Maccabean revolt embody the "eschatological leap" and the schematizations of history that have so long been considered to be the very essence of apocalyptic. A final group of writings can be tied down chronologically, those books written in the aftermath of the destruction of 70 B.C.E.

The Similitudes of Enoch (*1 Enoch* chaps. 37–71) probably came from the last century B.C.E. and the final form of *The Assumption of Moses* must have been written shortly thereafter. Undatable, but now more comprehensive in light of the speculative roots of apocalyptic literature are *2 Enoch* (Slavonic) and *The Greek Apocalypse of Baruch*. The status of later writings like *The Testament of Abraham* still awaits clarification, partly at least in the context of the development of Jewish traditions in the early church.

37. Formally close to the apocalypses are, e.g., Ezekiel 16–19, Proto-Zechariah, Ezekiel 40–48. Close to them in eschatological content are Ezekiel 38–39, Isaiah 24–27, 40–56, Deutero-Zechariah.

Victor Tcherikover

4

The Tobiads in Light
of the Zenon Papyri (1959)

The Zenon papyri, discovered in 1915 in the Fayum region of Egypt, are an exceptional source for the economic and political history of the Ptolemaic dynasty. Within this archive are records of the visit made by Zenon, a senior official of the Ptolemaic administration, to Palestine and Transjordan in the year 259 B.C.E. Here we find mention of a certain Tobiah, the head of a wealthy and powerful family whose members also are mentioned by Josephus. Indeed, Josephus's account of this period—full of problems though it be—provides rich material about the stormy history of Tobiah's sons and grandsons (*Antiquities XII*).

Victor Tcherikover presents the evidence of the papyri and then proceeds to a detailed analysis of Josephus's narrative. His reconsideration of the basic motives underlying the "Tobiad romance" (as Josephus's text is often called) provides important insights into the social and religious temperament of certain circles in late Ptolemaic Palestine. The Tobiads were feudal lords, and their holdings in Ammon (Transjordan) formed, in essence, a military colony. They intermarried with the Jerusalem priestly aristocracy—not unlike the complex Judahite and Samaritan relations discussed by Cross—and had extensive contacts with the Ptolemaic court in Alexandria. Furthermore, the Tobiads provide an interesting perspective on the meeting of Jewish and Greek culture: the Tobiad aristocracy was far from an intellectual group, and their contacts with the Greeks and their assimilation to Greek ways were commercial and social. Tcherikover's discussion of both epigraphic and literary sources contributes impressively to our knowledge of the social and religious forces in third-century Palestine and its environs.

THE PTOLEMIES ruled Palestine for a hundred years. Politically these were years of peace and quiet. Apart from the destruction of Samaria by Demetrius in 296, we hear of no military or political event (prior to 219) which involved the country directly. The wars between the Ptolemies and the Seleucids, which continued at intervals from 275 to 240, approximately, were waged at various places in the great empire and did not penetrate the interior of the country. It is indeed difficult to express this opinion with complete confidence, since we know scarcely anything whatever of these hundred years; mutilated fragments of information preserved in Josephus and in Alexandrian literature do not provide sufficient material for an account of the period, and what they do provide is very suspect in the eyes of the modern scholar. Thus, for example, Josephus says (C. Ap. II.48) of Ptolemy III Euergetes, that he visited the Temple at Jerusalem to render thanks to God for his victory in the war against the Seleucids, and Josephus explains explicitly why he poured out his heart to the God of Israel and not to the gods of Egypt. Naturally such statements have to be treated with the utmost caution. Nor does what Josephus relates of Joseph son of Tobiah and his son Hyrcanus always bear scientific criticism.

But luckily we now have another source at hand, whose historical trustworthiness is beyond doubt, namely, the Zenon papyri, part of which concerns the affairs of Palestine in the period of Ptolemy II Philadelphus. This Zenon, whose extensive archives were discovered in Egypt in 1915 in the territory of the ancient village of Philadelpheia in the Fayûm, was one of the most diligent and dexterous officials of Philadelphus's time. He stood under the orders of the *dioiketes* (finance minister) Apollonius, himself a man of great energy and one of the best administrators of Ptolemaic Egypt. Zenon's chief task involved the management of Apollonius's large estate near Philadelpheia in the Fayûm; but prior to obtaining it, he had discharged several missions on behalf of Apollonius, and among them in the year 259 had visited Palestine and stayed there a whole year. He brought back with him from this journey various documents and letters which were preserved among his records; and after his return to Egypt maintained touch with Palestine for some time and kept the various letters that arrived from there for Apollonius and his officials. The total number of papyri concerning Palestine is very small compared with the immense number belonging to the Zenon archives as a whole—in all, some forty notes, accounts, letters, and memoranda out of a grand total of approximately twelve hundred. Nevertheless, their value for the historical study of

Palestine in the third century is very great, as this period—from 300 to 220 or thereabouts—is otherwise completely lacking in sources.[1]

In addition to the Zenon papyri we now have another important papyrus published in 1936 from the great collection of papyri at Vienna; it contains two orders of King Ptolemy Philadelphus: one for the registration of flocks and herds in Ptolemaic Syria, the other settling the question of slaves (or, more correctly, of free men and women who had been unlawfully enslaved) in the same country. On several points this Vienna papyrus fills out our information derived from the Zenon papyri.[2]

Southern Syria, when it was in the hands of the Ptolemies, was known in the official language of the Egyptian offices as "Syria and Phoenicia," and popularly simply as "Syria."[3] The Zenon papyri enable us to determine the frontiers of the country, if not with strict precision, at least on general lines. Three points mentioned in the Zenon archives fix the northern frontier between Ptolemaic and Seleucid Syria; these are the city of Tripolis (*PSI* 495); the Plain of Masyas, that is, the valley between the Lebanon and the Anti-Lebanon (*PCZ* 59093); and Damascus (*PCZ* 59006). The boundary itself is not precisely known. According to Strabo (XVI.756), Arethusa was the frontier between Seleucid and Phoenician Syria in the Roman period. This town stood several kilo-

1. The Zenon papyri have so far appeared in the following publications: *Pubblicazioni della Società Italiana (PSI)*, IV–VII; C. C. Edgar *Zenon Papyri* (Catal. général des antiquités égypt. du Musée de Caire = *PCZ*), I–V; C. C. Edgar, *Zenon Papyri in the University of Michigan Collection* (P. Zen. Mich.); Westermann and others, *Zenon Papyri*, Columbia Univ. Press (P. Col. Zen.), I–II. The following books may be mentioned among the considerable literature devoted to the Zenon archives: Rostovtzeff, *A Large Estate in Egypt in the Third Century*, B.C. (1922); Viereck, *Philadelpheia* (1928); Edgar, *P. Zen. Mich.*, Introduction; Cl. Préaux, *Les Grecs en Egypte d'après les archives de Zénon* (1947). On Palestine in the Zenon papyri, see my article "Palestine in the Light of the Zenon Papyri," *Tarbitz* (Heb.), IV (1933): 226ff., 354ff.; cf. idem, "Palestine under the Ptolemies," *Mizraim* (Heb.), IV–V (1937): 9ff.; O. McLean Harper, Jr., "A Study in the Commercial Relations between Egypt and Syria in the Third Century B.C.," *AJP* 49 (1928): 1ff.

2. This papyrus (P. Rainer inv. 24552 gr.) was first published by Liebesny in the papyrogical journal *Aegyptus* 16 (1936): 257ff.; see now *SB* 8008. The papyrus originates from the twenty-fourth or twenty-fifth year of Ptolemy II Philadelphus, that is, 261 B.C.E. See on this papyrus, M. Rostovtzeff, *Social and Economic History of the Hellenistic World* 1:340ff.

3. The official name "Syria and Phoenicia" is mentioned three times in *SB* 8008 (lines 33 and 51, and the fragment b + c); cf. also Ezra III (= Ezra I in the Septaugint, 6.3; 6.7; 6.27), and the Aristeas letter, 22. The popular use of the name "Syria" instead of "Syria and Phoenicia" is very usual in the papyri of Zenon; cf.*P. Zen. Mich.*, 2; *PCZ* 59012, 59093; cf. also *CPJ* 1, p.5 n.13.

meters north of Tripolis; possibly therefore the frontier passed by here in the Hellenistic period also. From Arethusa it crossed obliquely in a southeasterly direction to Baalbek, thence to Damascus, and on to the desert.[4]

As regards the eastern frontier, there is no doubt that the whole of Transjordan as far as the desert was in Ptolemaic hands. The papyri of Zenon refer to Hauran (*PSI* 406; *PCZ* 59008), Ammon (*CPJ* 1) and to the Nabataeans (*PSI* 406), that is, to all the central and southern part of Transjordan; but it is clear, if the Ptolemies held Damascus on the one side and Hauran on the other, that they also ruled Trachonitis and Batanea.[5] Concerning the administrative divisions, we learn from the Vienna papyrus that the country was divided into hyparchies; the smallest administrative unit was the village, as in Egypt.[6] The royal concern for the Syrian province was expressed in the publication of several orders, regulations, statutes and rescripts which are all referred to in the Vienna papyrus, hence it is clear that the government of Alexandria paid special attention to the welfare and economic development of Syria.[7]

We do not know whether Ptolemaic Syria was organized as a proper "province," to use the term in its Roman sense—that is, whether it was under a special governor and lived under laws peculiar to itself, for such a governor is not mentioned in our sources. According to the account in the Zenon papyri, the contacts between Alexandria and Palestine were so lively and direct that the post of a governor as intermediary seems to have been unnecessary.[8] The great interest shown by Apollonius in the

4. The question of the frontier between Ptolemaic and Seleucid Syria is discussed in detail by Kahrstedt, *Syrische Territorien in hellenistischer Zeit (1926)*, 22ff., but most of his suppositions are unacceptable; see my above-mentioned article in *Mizraim*, 32ff.; cf. W. Otto, "Beiträge z. Seleukidengesch. des III Jahr. v. Chr.," *ABAW* 34/1.

5. On the eastern frontier of Ptolemaic Syria, especially the attachment of Damascus to the Seleucid kingdom, see my above-mentioned article in *Tarbitz*, IV.360; *Mizraim*, 34ff.

6. Hyparchia: *SB* 8008, lines 1, 38; villages: ibid., 18, 19; cf. *CPJ* 6.

7. Orders (προστάγματα): *SB* 8008, lines 3, 8, 33, 38; regulations (διαγράματα): ibid., 6ff., 26, 30, 31; laws: ibid.; (ἐν τῶι νόμωι τῶι ἐπὶ τῆς μισθώσεως): letters: ibid., 25 (ἐν τῇ παρὰ τοῦ βασιλέως ἐπιστολῇ). Possibly part of the above legislative activity was directed not to Syria alone; but we hear of it, at any rate, only in that connection.

8. Cf. *Tarbitz*, V. 38; *Mizraim*, 38ff.; Rostovtzeff (*Social and Economic History* 1:344) and Bengtson (*Die Strategie in der hellenistischen Zeit*, 166ff.) assume that the king was represented in Syria and Phoenicia by a *strategos*, but this assumption is hard to prove. It is indeed true that in other provinces (such as Thrace and Cyprus) there were *strategoi* who were deputies of Ptolemy (cf. Cohen, *De magistratibus Aegyptiis*

Syrian countries makes one think that Ptolemaic Syria was under the special supervision of the *dioiketes* at Alexandria. On the other hand, there was also a special *dioiketes* in Syria, as we learn from the Vienna papyrus, and he was perhaps the most important official in the country. In every hyparchy there resided on *oikonomos*, a special official in charge of economic life; moreover, we hear of a very large number of officials, high and low, who attended chiefly to matters of administration and economy.[9]

We can judge the number of government officials in Palestine from one of the Zenon papyri, which contains drafts of five letters sent by Zenon to the officials of Marissa in Idumea. In all five Zenon refers to the same matter: when he was in Marissa he had purchased young slaves who had escaped from him and returned to their former masters. The masters now demand five hundred drachmae compensation for the return of the slaves to Zenon, who therefore applies to the various officials at Marissa requesting them to aid his emissary to recover them. Two of the letters are very politely written, being sent evidently to the head of the civil administration and to the city police chief respectively. In two more of the letters Zenon requests the officials (whom he apparently knew personally) to use their good offices with other officials not to impose "liturgical" labor on his emissary as this would interfere with his search for the slaves.[10]

We have here, therefore, a miniature of the Egyptian officialdom, and

---

externas Lagidarum regni provincias administranitibus, 2ff., 7ff.); but these were distant provinces demanding the concentration of power in the hands of one high official, while Syria could easily be managed directly from Alexandria. As for the *strategoi* mentioned by Polybius during the war between Antiochus III and the Ptolemies, these may not have been permanent officials at all, but military commanders to whom authority had been delegated in a time of emergency. Polybius is here using the administrative terminology of the Seleucid Empire, as may be deduced from the title τεταγμένος ἐπὶ Κοίλης Συρίας (V.40.I), which would have been impossible under the Ptolemies, and this casts doubt on his acquaintance with the Ptolemaic provinces in general. I would therefore leave the question open for the time being.

9. The Syrian *dioiketes*: SB 8008, line 55 (the subject is public sales held ὑπὸ τοῦ διοικοῦντος τὰς κατὰ Συρίαν καὶ Φοινίκην προσόδους). The *oikonomoi*, ibid., 1, 37; the *komarchs* (village headmen): ibid., 18. The Zenon papyri mention several government officials by their private names but do not give their titles. Among these officials may be mentioned Menekles (perhaps the chief of the customs office at Tyre), Alexis (perhaps the police chief at Jaffa), Orias and (Alexan)dros (the latter apparently a village headman, the former perhaps a higher official in the *hyparchy*); see PCZ 59018, 59077, 59093. Among the officials engaged in economic affairs we know of "Diodorus in charge of the incense trade" at Gaza (PSJ 628).

10. PCZ 59015 verso. Cf. *Tarbitz*, IV.238; *Mizraim*, 40ff.

it may be legitimate to suppose that they had transferred to Palestine the whole Egyptian bureaucracy with all the defects which we know so well from the papyri of that country. This had brought not only the defects, however; we also detect among the Ptolemaic officials of Palestine the great diligence of the Ptolemaic government offices, the same enforcement of the law of the state in the remotest corners, the same strict official surveillance over the life of the private individual. Thus, for example, the Vienna papyrus mentions certain dates by which people concerned must fulfill government demands, the fines imposed on offenders, annual registrations of property (in one case—of sheep and cattle), and the like.[11] Anyone who is acquainted with the elements of the Ptolemaic administration of Egypt will have no difficulty in recognizing the same method and the same practices now transferred almost without change to the province of Syria.[12]

A special position was held in Syria by the agents of the finance minister Apollonius. They did not belong to the regular government officialdom, but acted as special emissaries of Apollonius and called themselves "the people of Apollonius the *Dioiketes*."[13] These agents were scattered over the whole country and were especially active in the coastal cities of Gaza, Jaffa, Acco, Sidon, and Beirut. There they supervised the trade in grain and olive oil, dispatched ships laden with merchandise to Pelusium, and also had to carry out all the private orders of the minister of finance, buying slaves for him and sending him "gifts." Possibly not all Appollonius's agents did their duty honestly and legally; nevertheless, it cannot be denied that their activity was extensive and productive, if judged from the point of view of the Egyptian authority: with their help was organized the commercial connection between the two countries so profitable to the Alexandrian government.

11. Registration of property must be carried out in every *hyparchy* during the sixty days following the publication of the order; in case of nonobedience to the order, the offender will be fined in accordance with regulations: *SB* 8008, 1ff.; registration of flocks and herds liable to tax or exempt from it: ibid., 17ff.; such registrations to be carried out annually: ibid., 23; declarations on acquisition of slaves within twenty days: ibid., 33ff.; fines imposed on those not declaring their slaves: ibid., 39ff.

12. On the Ptolemaic administrative organization in Egypt, see Bouché-Leclercq (1906), 3:123ff.; Jouguet, *L'Impérialisme macédonien et l'hellénisation de l'Orient* (1926), 332ff.; Bevan, *A History of Egypt under the Ptolemaic Dynasty* (1927), 132ff.; Rostovtzeff, *CAH* 7:116ff.

13. *CPJ* 1, line 21: τῶν περὶ Ἀπολλώνιον τὸν διοικητήν.

There are grounds for thinking that the year 259, the year in which Zenon visited Palestine, was that in which Apollonius decided to turn his attention to the Syrian countries in particular: he sent a large group of his agents (perhaps under Zenon's management) to tour the country, to examine its economic situation and to set up a liaison between it and Egypt. These agents made numerous journeys throughout the country and were joined both by resident Greeks and by natives, till the group became a caravan of some hundred or more people which traversed the whole land of Palestine, including Transjordan, creating contacts with the inhabitants in every locality. In subsequent years we find many of Apollonius's agents who had been members of this large convoy, permanently settled in the country's large towns, such as Jaffa, or carrying on the affairs of Apollonius's estate at Bet-Anat and at other places. The long lists of the travelers' names preserved in Zenon's archives are reliable evidence of the activity of Apollonius in the year 259.[14]

The unstable equilibrium of Palestine's political situation faced the Egyptian kings with the grave problem of the country's defense; it should not be forgotten that from a military point of view southern Syria served as the first line of defense to Egypt itself; from the Zenon papyri we learn the methods employed by the Ptolemies to attain this object, namely, the founding of *cleruchies* and the stationing of garrisons in the Syrian cities. In one of the papyri (*PSI* 495) troops are referred to at Tripolis, evidently the Ptolemaic garrison protecting the northern frontier of Ptolemaic Syria. The mobile group of Apollonius's agents

---

14. See my article in *Mizraim*, 57ff., on the large caravan of Apollonius's agents in 259; I have there investigated the composition of the group of travelers, whose sixty-six members, all of Greek origin, are known to us by their personal names. As the activity of Apollonius's agents in Syria had two aspects—their service for the state and their private service for the finance minister, it is very hard to establish in every instance what was the purpose of their activity—for the benefit of the state or for the private benefit of the *dioiketes*. Cf. *Mizraim*, 30ff. Sometimes Apollonius's agents used their power and influence to carry out activity on their own initiative, for their own private advantage; thus, for example, one of the agents wanted to bring slaves out of Syria and sell them abroad (*PCZ* 59093), which was illegal (cf. *Mizraim*, 68, also *Tarbitz*, IV. 244). The hero of *PSI* 616 is also under grave suspicion of carrying out illegal transactions. This behavior on the part of Apollonius's agents caused Rostovtzeff to pass a negative verdict on their operations in Syria (cf. *Large Estate*, 34). However, crimes and frauds were the deeds of isolated individuals only, and they were not so numerous as to justify the condemnation of the acts of all the *dioiketes's* agents. Their wide function as organizers of trade relations between Syria and Egypt is beyond all doubt.

was joined by several high-ranking officers whose military titles evidence that they belonged to the garrisons of fortresses.[15] The Vienna papyrus speaks of "the soldiers and other settlers in Syria and Phoenicia" who had taken wives from among the local women;[16] these mixed marriages shows that the king's reference was not to troops who were visiting the country for a short time, but to garrison troops who were quartered in Syria permanently.

The most interesting information preserved by the Zenon papyri concerns the *cleruchy* of the Ptolemaic troops in Transjordan. Papyrus *CPJ* 1 (*PCZ* 59003) contains a deed of sale passing between a Greek, a native of Cnidos in Caria, and Zenon; the Greek describes himself as "one of Tobiah's people," and the name of the place where the deed has been drawn up is "the citadel of the Land of the Ammonites." The contract is signed by six witnesses, two of them "*cleruchs* of the cavalry of Tobiah," and four members of Zenon's retinue ("of the people of Apollonius the *Dioiketes*"). One other person signed the deed as guarantor; he too was one of Tobiah's *cleruchs*. This papyrus is evidence that the Ptolemies had also transferred to Palestine their practice of distributing land-holdings to their troops and of settling them in *cleruchies*. The aim of the founding of the *cleruchy* in Transjordan was the defense of the country against the attacks of Bedouin from the desert; the citadel mentioned in the papyrus was the center of the *cleruchy*, and the troops who had settled there belonged in part to the cavalry and in part to the infantry.[17]

One detail in the above papyrus demands special emphasis: at the head of the *cleruchy* stands not a Greek or Macedonian officer, but a local native prince, Tobiah. This man is mentioned in several other

15. In *PCZ* 59004 and 59006, the following posts are referred to: *hegemon* (evidently garrison commandant), *akrophylax* (chief of the citadel), *phylakarches* (chief of police), *archyperetes* (perhaps an official in charge of military pay). On these posts cf. *Mizraim*, 37ff.

16. *SB* 8008, 1.49ff.: τῶν δὲ στρατευομένων καὶ τῶν ἄλλων τῶν κατοικούντων ἐν Συρίαι καὶ Φοινίκηι.

17. Tobiah's fortress is evidently identical with the place in Transjordan known today as 'Arak el-Emir; on the remains of a large building near this place the name of Tobiah is incised twice. Whether the head of the Ptolemaic *cleruchy* is here meant, or Hyrcanus "son of Tobiah," his grandson, or one of Tobiah's ancestors (all of these opinions have been expressed in modern literature), it is clear that we have here the remains of the ancient palace which was the family seat. For the topographical questions and an account of the ruins, cf. M. C. Butler, *The Princeton Univ. Arch. Exped. to Syria in 1904–05*, Div. II, Sect. A, 1ff.: Dalman, *Palästina Jhrb.* (1920): 33ff.; Watzinger, *Die Denkmäler Palästinas* 2 (1935): 13ff.; Vincent, *JPOS* 3, 55ff.

papyri: he writes letters to Apollonius and to King Ptolemy Philadelphus himself and sends them gifts—to the king, rare animals (perhaps for the zoological garden of Philadelphus at Alexandria) and to Apollonius, four young slaves accompanied by a eunuch (*CPJ* 4–5). In one of the papyri Tobiah's residence (apparently the above-mentioned *cleruchy*, including the citadel) is described as "Tobiah's land"; this name evidences that Tobiah was a wealthy sheikh known throughout the region.[18] It is not difficult to discover his origin: he was without doubt one of the descendants of "Tobiah the Ammonite slave" mentioned several times in Nehemiah as one of the opponents of the Jewish national policy of Nehemiah; and his genealogy can be scrutinized in even more than ancient times.[19] Nor is there any doubt but that this

18. The "land of Tobiah" is mentioned in an unpublished papyrus of the Zenon archives: *P. Lon. inv.* 2358(A). In this papyrus a group of travelers is described which visited two places on the same day, namely Abila and Sourabitt(ois), arriving the following day in "the territory of Tobiah." Abila and Sourabitt are also mentioned in *PCZ* 59004: Abila is "Abel Ha-Shittim in the steppes of Moab" of Num. 33:49, opposite Jericho; the second place (? = Zur bet Tobiah) is probably in Wadi es-Sir near 'Arak el-Emir. On the list in *PCZ* 59004 (= *CPJ* 2a) see Abel's article in *RB* 32 (1923), 409ff., and Alt's remarks in *Arch. F. Pap.* 7:293. Abel has identified Abila with Abila of the Decapolis, and "Bet Zur . . ." with Imm es-Surab. These conjectures have been disproved by the above London papyrus. The question as to whether the "territory of Tobiah" is to be identified with the *Eretz Tov* mentioned in 1 Macc. 5:13 (cf. 2 Macc. 12:17) as Klein and others think (*Jew. Pal. Expl. Soc. Bull.* [Heb.], 3:115) is not easily soluble, as *Eretz Tov* is mentioned elsewhere in the Bible: Judges 11:3–5; 2 Sam. 10:6–8. Cf. Abel, *Les Livres des Maccabées* (1949), 93.

19. On the origin of the Tobiah family see Maisler's article, "The House of Tobiah," *Tarbitz* (Heb.), XII.109ff. (cf. idem, *Eretz Israel* 4:249ff.). Maisler ascribes to the family not only "Tobiah the Ammonite" of the time of Nehemiah, but also the Tobiah mentioned in the year 519 (approximately) in Zechariah (6:9ff.) as one of the heads of the people, and also Tobiah the contemporary of Zedekiah, whose name was discovered among the Lachisch documents. The results of Maisler's study seem reasonable. We have before us, then, a very ancient family whose roots go back to the period of the kings. This study has solved the problem which long engaged scholars: were the Tobiads Ammonites who had joined the Jews, or were they Israelites who had settled among the Ammonites? Nehemiah's evidence could be used in favor of the first possibility, since he not only consistently calls Tobiah an "Ammonite," but aims against him the passage that "an Ammonite and a Moabite shall not enter the congregation of the Lord" (Deut. 23:4). However, hard and fast conclusions are not to be drawn from Nehemiah's words, since the latter thoroughly detested Tobiah, and may therefore have deliberately confounded his geographical with his national origin in order to keep him away from Jerusalem as one alien to the Jews. Maisler's research has shown that the Tobiads were already a well-connected Israelite family in the days of the kings, and went into exile in Babylon with the rest of the Jerusalem aristocracy. (They are referred to in cuneiform texts of the time of Darius II at Nippur; see Maisler, "House of Tobiah," 128.) As to the

Tobiah was the father of Joseph son of Tobiah, the famous tax-gatherer, who played such an important role in Jewish society in the third century.

We therefore have before us a unique political phenomenon: the appointment of a local sheikh, a man of great influence among the local population, to a high rank in the Ptolemaic army. The Ptolemies in Egypt were careful not to assign high posts to native Egyptians, and until the middle of the second century we do not find Egyptians in key positions in the Ptolemaic army. But in Palestine the Ptolemies had to take account of local conditions; their rule of the country could not be placed on a firm footing without gaining the sympathies of people of influence there. It was very important in the eyes of the Egyptian government to win to its side powerful princes such as Tobiah and to make them its allies in case of war against the kings of Syria. Tobiah, in fact, did not disappoint the hopes reposed in him by the kings of Egypt: his loyalty to the Ptolemies was transmitted to his son Joseph, who throughout his life kept a careful eye on Jewish loyalty to the Ptolemies. . . .[20]

The residence of the Tobiads and the family's origin have been discussed (pp. 84–85), and something may be added on the latter subject. From the Book of Nehemiah it may be deduced that Tobiah "the Ammonite" was no stranger in Jerusalem, but stood in frequent contact with the prominent men of Judea, being the son-in-law of one of them. His son Jonathan, moreover, married a daughter of one of Jerusalem's prominent men (Neh. 6:18). He also had access to the Temple, since Elyashiv the Priest made a special chamber in the Temple court for him (Neh. 13:4–8). His name, Tobiah, and that of his son, Jonathan (Yeho-natan), are sufficient evidence that he belonged to the cult of the Jewish God in Jerusalem. All these facts justify the question, whether Tobiah was not of priestly descent: his links with the priesthood are beyond doubt, for Elyashiv the Priest was his relative (Neh.

family estates in Transjordan, these may have come into their hands after they had returned from Babylon, or possibly, as Maisler supposes, the Tobiads had ruled those parts from the days of the First Temple, or even before the conquest of Transjordan by Tiglathpileser III (in the eighth century B.C.E.); cf. *Eretz Israel* 4:249ff.

20. The literature on the Tobiads written since the publication of the Zenon papyri is very extensive. Cf. Vincent, *RB* 29 (1920): 161ff.; Wilcken, *Arch. f. Pap.* 6, 449ff.; Gressmann, *SBAW* 39 (1921): 663ff.; Ed. Meyer, *Ursprung u. Anfänge d. Christ* (1921), 2:128ff., 462; Rostovtzeff, *Social and Economic History* 1:111, 3:1746 (Index); Momigliano, *Atti della Reale Accad. d. scienza di Torino* 67 (1931–32): 165ff.; *CPJ* I.115ff.

13:4–8) and we shall see below that Joseph son of Tobiah was the nephew of Onias II, the High Priest. In view of the fact that the leaders and representatives of the nation to the foreign authorities belonged at this period to the priests, it may be conjectured that the brilliant career of Joseph son of Tobiah at the royal court of Egypt was possible chiefly because he belonged to the ruling group, the priests. Tobiah the contemporary of Zerubbabel—one of the family's forebears, if Maisler's conjecture is correct—may have been a priest, since he is mentioned together with Jedaiah, one of the prominent priests of the time.[21] The silence of the sources, however, does not permit definite conclusions on this question.

In his *Antiquities* Josephus relates the biographies of Joseph and his son Hyrcanus in great detail.[22] Not every detail need be dwelt on; scholars have more than once pointed out the legendary aspect of the narrative and the untrustworthiness of several features of it. Nevertheless we need not follow Wellhausen in rejecting the historical value of the story completely,[23] and if we put aside the fabulous element in Josephus's narrative, a short account remains which is more or less consonant with historical reality. Under King Ptolemy of Egypt (we shall see below which Ptolemy Josephus meant) the High Priest Onias II refused to deliver the large tribute which he paid annually to the Egyptian sovereign. The king, angered, sent his envoy to Jerusalem with a severe message and the threat that, if Onias did not pay, he would divide Jewish territory into cleruchies and send troops to Jerusalem as military settlers. Despite these threats Onias refused to yield and maintained his former decision.

Then arose Joseph, the youthful son of Tobiah and of Onias's sister, called the people together to an assembly in the Temple, and proposed himself as emissary to the king to effect a compromise in the dispute. The people agreed to his proposal, and after he had honored the Egyptian envoy with fine gifts and borrowed money for the journey from friends in Samaria, he went down to Egypt, appearing there before the king as chief (*prostates*) of the Jews. He succeeded not only in softening the king's wrath, but also in negotiating a successful deal in his own favor, by leasing from Ptolemy the taxes imposed by the king

21. Maisler, "House of Tobiah," 116.
22. *Ant.* XII.154–222, 224, 228–36.
23. See Wellhausen, *Israelitische und jüdische Gesch.* (7th ed.), 231.

on Syria; from this time his wealth increased steadily, till he became one of the richest men of his generation. He acted as tax-gatherer for twenty-two years, and bequeathed his wealth to his numerous sons.

Josephus's story of Joseph the son of Tobiah dovetails into his narrative of Hyrcanus son of Joseph. If we divest this story also of its legendary elements, we get an historical picture whose essence is as follows: Hyrcanus was clever and energetic, loved by his father and envied by his brothers, and jealousy led to hatred. When on one occasion Hyrcanus was sent by his aged father to Egypt to congratulate the king on the birth of a son, he was able to gain the king's favor, but in so doing spent much money from his father's funds in Egypt, so that on his return to Jerusalem a quarrel broke out between him and his father and brothers, which compelled him to seek refuge across the Jordan. There he built a strong fortress, which served also as a resort for his many pleasures, and passed the time fighting the Arabs. These wars were not to the liking of the Syrian government, although under Seleucus IV it did nothing to prevent them; but after the accession of Antiochus Epiphanes, Hyrcanus saw that he could not stand up to the new king and committed suicide. His entire property passed to Antiochus. . . .

We may now pass to the internal analysis of the historical material preserved in Josephus's narrative. This is a legend, and we may ask with some surprise, what was it that caused the transformation of the life of Joseph the Tobiad into a hero tale? He was neither a general nor a great statesman, much less a man of intellect; yet his name has survived in Jewish history, in contrast to several important men who headed public life in Judea, whose names are lost to us for good, and even the High Priests of the period have left no clear memory. This curious fact can be rightly interpreted only on the assumption that Joseph introduced new principles into the Jewish society of his time. What were they and what was the innovation made by Joseph in the Land of Judea?

To answer this question it is essential to survey Joseph's entire career. His father Tobiah was perhaps the first of the Tobiads not to see himself confined to the narrow frontiers of his estate in Transjordan and to dream of a more important political role. As a member of a noble house, he wedded the High Priest's daughter and so obtained a foothold in Jerusalem, coming into contact with the Ptolemaic administration and acquiring recognition as its military representative in Transjordan. He was bound by ties of business and perhaps friendship with Apollonius, the all-powerful finance minister of Philadelphus. His son

Joseph knew well how to exploit his father's connections and, as the High Priest's nephew, was one of the respected residents of Jerusalem; the estate where he was born and which had apparently been acquired by his father, was near the city.[24] Yet it is to be doubted whether this family, whose origin was linked with Transjordan, found it easy to acquire the entire ancient tradition of the Jews of Jerusalem. Josephus relates that, before his journey to Alexandria, Joseph borrowed money from his "friends in Samaria" (*Ant.* XII.168), and anyone knowing the eternal hostility and detestation prevailing since Nehemiah's day between the Jewish community of Jerusalem and the Samaritans will quickly grasp that no loyal and patriotic Jew could have had "friends" at Samaria.[25] As noted, the cultural atmosphere in Tobiah's home was "Greek," and this atmosphere Joseph had breathed from his childhood on.

From the beginning of his career Joseph appears as an "international" figure standing above the "petty" interests of his native country. This "internationalism" was based mainly on money. Just as he had friends at Samaria ready to grant him loans in the hour of need, so he stood in communication with powerful people at the court of Alexandria who were also prepared to aid him (*Ant.* XII.180, 185), and these connections were especially important to him, since here was the financial center of the world and here the supreme administration of Palestine was focused. His journey to Alexandria after the Onias affair may not have been his first visit, and possibly from his youth on he had discharged a certain fiscal function as representative of the Ptolemaic government in Jerusalem, initially perhaps merely as his father's assistant. This would enable us to understand his political position vis-à-vis Onias: as an Egyptian official Joseph was closely bound to Egypt, for there lay all his prospects of future success. His relatives supported him and aided him to strengthen his position: Josephus tells us that when Onias refused to pay tribute to Ptolemy, Joseph was not in Jerusalem; but that his mother, Onias's sister, immediately informed him of the matter as if to warn him that his affairs were in danger. He at once returned to Jerusalem, frustrated Onias's intention and restored the

---

24. Joseph was born in the village of Phichola (*Ant.* XII.160), whose location is unknown. According to Maisler's conjecture ("House of Tobiah," 109 n.4) this may be Wadi Fukhin near Bethlehem.

25. Cf. Ben Sira, L.26: "That foolish nation that dwelleth in Sichem." It were well to observe that, some time before Joseph's appearance, the Samaritans had attacked the Jews and ravaged Judea (*Ant.* XII.156).

people to its former loyalty to Egypt. This was the beginning of his career. He appeared before Ptolemy as *prostates* of the Jews. To our regret we have no clear information on the character of this position; as we have seen the post of the *prostasia* was in the hands of the High Priest at the beginning of the Hellenistic period, on the evidence of Hecateus, and evidently carried with it considerable profits. Joseph accused Onias of retaining the *prostasia* out of greed for gain (*Ant.* XII.162); it is therefore to be assumed that the tax collection in Judea was concentrated wholly or partly in the hands of the *prostates*, who could hardly have enjoyed any other opportunity of enriching himself from his position.[26] It is at any rate clear that the post of *prostates* was of high financial and administrative character, apparently the highest in Judea, and it now passed to Joseph. Thus occurred the first breach in the edifice of the theocracy of Jerusalem: the responsibility for the levying of taxes and their transmission to the king was removed from the High Priest and handed to a professional financier.

Joseph the son of Tobiah became, in Hellenistic terminology, the *dioiketes* of the High Priest; but the responsible tax-collector was also liable for the country's allegiance to the government, hence he was not just a financial official but the people's political representative to the king. The manner of Josephus's account of the transfer of power from Onias to Joseph is quite idyllic: Onias resigning his post voluntarily, as it were, the people empowering Joseph to appear before the king as its delegate or *prostates*. It is improbable that Joseph's victory was so easily won; there was doubtless a conflict between the parties at Jerusalem before the Jews agreed to hand over power to a *novus homo* and to alter the ancient political tradition in such an offhanded manner. The fact was, at any rate, that there now arose, alongside the traditional theocratic authority, a new power based on the personal financial skill and experience of a private individual who was closely bound up with the broad international field.

This field was more important to Joseph than the tiny land of Judea. Hence his second act, namely, to lease from the king the collection of

26. Josephus relates that the sum of money amounted to twenty talents (*Ant.* XII.158). This sum is too small to satisfy the assumption that this was all the Jews paid to Egypt. According to Josephus (ibid.) the high priests paid this tax from their private property; it is possible therefore that these twenty talents did not belong to the regular taxes of the land of Judea, but were a special tax paid by the high priests with which they purchased the *prostasia*. As for the general taxes, the sum may have been three hundred talents (Bickerman, *Inst. des Sél.*, 108), although the passages cited to support this supposition (2 Macc. 4:8; 24; 1 Macc. 11:28; Sulp. Sev. II.17.5) are open to several different interpretations.

the taxes "from all Coele-Syria, Phoenicia, Judea and Samaria" (*Ant.* XII.175).[27] This activity had no bearing on the internal development of Judea; it was undertaken on his own initiative. Josephus's story of the negotiations between Joseph and the king at Alexandria is full of legendary traits, although its core is in harmony with historical reality, for the annual leasing of the taxes was a permanent practice in Egypt, and there are grounds for thinking that those abroad were also leased by the kings to private individuals, as Josephus relates.[28]

As *prostates* of the Jews, Joseph would certainly have appeared from time to time at Alexandria to renew his lease on the taxes of Judea, and simultaneously would have appeared the representatives of the Greek cities, each of whom leased the taxes of his own town. Joseph's financial ability apparently was much superior to that of the Syrians; at any rate the program of financial reform which he proposed to the king was his own invention, and was simple: why should the king negotiate with various people, work out the conditions of lease and demand a guarantee from each one? Let him hand over the lease of the whole of the province of Syria to one man, and not only would the royal treasury not suffer from the change, but would profit from it. At the same meeting Joseph proposed himself for the task and promised to remit to the king double the sum he had received till then.[29] The king agreed to his proposal, and thus a fundamental change took place in the system of leasing the taxes of Ptolemaic Syria.

No other Jew had ever attained so high a rank; and clearly his authority grew also in the eyes of his compatriots, before whom he now stood as a man successful in a peculiar field, possessing a unique

27. The geographical designation is not appropriate to the administrative terminology current in the Ptolemaic offices. The official name here ought to be "Syria and Phoenicia" (cf. above, p. 79). Josephus here links the terminology of the Seleucid offices (Coele-Syria and Phoenicia) to the traditional Jewish division of Palestine into Judea and Samaria.

28. We find authority for this conjecture in a papyrus of the year 201 B.C.E. (*P. Tebt.* 8 = *W. Chrest.* 2), which speaks of the sale of the taxes of the country of Lycia, then under Ptolemaic rule. Cf. on the method of auctioning the taxes in Ptolemaic Egypt generally, Rostovtzeff, *CAH* 7:129ff.; *Social and Economic History*, 328ff.; C. Préaux, *L'économie royale des Lagides*, 450ff.

29. The figures given by Josephus cannot stand up to criticism: the countries of Ptolemaic Syria paid, allegedly, 8,000 talents (*Ant.* XII.175), and Joseph doubled this huge sum. We know that the fifth Satrapy of Darius—Ever-Nahara—which extended from the frontiers of Cilicia to Egypt, paid only 350 talents (Herod. III.91); the incomes from all the lands ruled by Antigonus amounted to 11,000 talents (Diod. XIX.56.5) and those from Ptolemaic Egypt under Philadelphus, to 14,800 talents (Jerome *Comment. ad Daniel* XI.5; cf. Cl. Préaux, *L'economie royale des Lagides*, 424).

importance; they could be proud of him. Not so the Syrians and the citizens of Greek cities, who were compelled to notice that a stranger was performing an important function in their internal life. Attempts were made to resist him, and the cities of Ascalon and Scythopolis refused to pay the taxes which he imposed. But as a government tax-gatherer Joseph was a powerful person, supported by the army of Ptolemy. He punished both towns severely and executed some of their most respected citizens; his action was confirmed by the king.[30] After this display of force the Syrian towns submitted to Joseph; nor do we hear of any further rebellion or insubordination.

The principles introduced by Joseph the Tobiad into Judea are now clear. They were the principles of the Hellenistic epoch as a whole, dominated by the striving of the strong personality to make its way in life. Joseph's character manifests those basic traits so typical of a number of Greeks of the period: immense willpower, rapidity of action, self-confidence, and, resulting from them, undisguised contempt for ancestral tradition. Through quiet unchanging Jerusalem new winds were suddenly blowing, as if a window had been suddenly thrown open to reveal all the wealth and splendor of the wide world, a world where power and money reigned supreme, annulling religious, national, and moral tradition. Samaritans might be negotiated with if profits were to be gained from the business; it was permissible to live at the king's court, to eat forbidden food at his table, and to pursue Greek dancing girls, if thereby a man could gain entry to the society necessary to his career; it was ethical to attack peaceful cities and to slay their citizens, if it was likely to strengthen a man's position as royal official. But all these things which were "permitted" in the Greek world were in complete contradiction to the spirit of Jewish tradition.[31] A Jew of the

30. Josephus reports this confirmation in very naive language: The king permitted Joseph "to do everything his heart desired" (*Ant.* XII.182). If we credit Josephus's story in all its minor details, we shall have to believe that the entire control of the economic and administrative affairs of Syria as known from the decrees of Philadelphus (*SB* 8008) was suspended under Euergetes. This is very hard to believe, although it is apparently a fact that Euergetes introduced into Syria a more concentrated method of tax collecting, which was also stricter, and that Joseph played the most prominent part in this reform.

31. The following are the words of a traditional writer on the subject of forbidden foods: "And Daniel purposed in his heart that he would not defile himself with the portion of the king's meat, nor with the wine which he drank" (Dan.1:8–9). Without going into the complicated question, when the first six chapters of the Book of Daniel were written (cf., for example, M. A. Beek's *Das Danielbuch* [1935], 7ff.), I would merely remark that verses 1:8ff. sound like a direct reply to the antitraditional behavior of Joseph the Tobiad at the Egyptian royal court.

type of Joseph the Tobiad had no alternative but to quit the narrow framework of Jewish tradition or even to encounter it in head-on collision, and although we hear nothing of such a clash, the fact that from Joseph's family originated the "sons of Tobiah," the politicians who under Antiochus Epiphanes headed the Hellenistic movement in Jerusalem, itself suffices to explain in which direction the sympathies of Joseph and the members of his family inclined.

One of his sons was Hyrcanus, whose life also became a legend, and here too the question is apposite: why? It is extremely difficult to discover the answer, as the legendary in Josephus has blurred Hyrcanus's real life-story by its false details. The only way is to analyze the story and to seek the historical nucleus hidden in it, commencing with his journey to Egypt.

Why did he go to Egypt and what did he do there? In the story as related by Josephus details are given, most of which are incredible. Moreover, the narrative seems to stop in the middle and its point becomes incomprehensible. Hyrcanus is a clever and capable young man, loved by his father in preference to his other sons; and for this reason his brothers are jealous of him. His father sends him to Egypt, where he wastes his father's money, a thousand silver talents, amounting to a third of Joseph's total capital, in order to bestow upon the king and queen rare and beautiful gifts unusual in the royal court. This waste transforms his father's love into hatred. When the king asks Hyrcanus what gift he desires to receive from him, Hyrcanus replies that he asks no gift, but that the king should speak well of him in his letters to his father and brothers. The king does as he asks, but in vain; the brothers attack Hyrcanus on the road, while at Jerusalem both the brothers and father oppose him and prevent him from entering the city. What does all this mean? Why were Hyrcanus's gifts to the king so much more valuable than the other gifts on the same occasion? (Cf. *Ant.* XII.215ff.)

As the favorite son of Joseph, Hyrcanus could be confident of a favorable reception at the royal court even without presenting the king with exceptional gifts. To obtain this great sum he had thrown Arion, Joseph's agent in Egypt, into prison, and he knew that such an act, added to the waste of money, would bring upon him his father's wrath. If we accept the version of the story as it stands, we shall have to confess that Hyrcanus's doings in Egypt display no wisdom whatever and that there are no grounds for making him the hero of the tale. But the very fact that he became this, and that everything Josephus tells of his childhood cleverness (*Ant.* XII.190ff.) prepares the reader for some derring-do or other in Egypt, shows us that some unknown factor here lies concealed in that we must read between the lines in order to understand the motive of Hyrcanus's action. That he did what he did without a definite aim is inconceivable, and I think that this aim was to depose his father from his position as tax-collector and to purchase it for himself (or at least to obtain the king's promise that the post would be given to him after his father's death). His reasons were sufficiently clear. Hyrcanus was the youngest in the family, and his enemies spoke of improprieties connected with his birth.[32] It was therefore well known that not he but his elder brothers would inherit Joseph's immense property; and being a clever and energetic person, he determined to purchase his father's position, in order to prevent his brothers from holding it after his father's death.

This supposition satisfactorily explains the obscurer details of Josephus's narrative. The expensive presents were not simply prodigality, but a means of purchasing the king's consent and of influencing him to grant Hyrcanus's requests. He also gave presents to the courtiers, whose sympathy had to be acquired, especially as they constituted a great danger to him, since his brothers had sent them letters requesting them to slay him (*Ant.* XII.218). This formidable hostility on the part of the brothers receives its logical interpretation, since they detested Hyrcanus not for his superior wits, as the story explains (*Ant.* XII.190), but because they noted his success at the royal court and feared it. They also won old Joseph to their side; but it is interesting that he did not venture to pour his wrath on Hyrcanus openly "for he feared the king" (*Ant.* XII.221). These words show that Hyrcanus had gained his objective and obtained from the king what he had asked. We do not know if he really purchased his father's position in his lifetime, or only obtained the king's permission that it should be given to him after Joseph's death, and the matter is not particularly important. The main point is that Hyrcanus had closed the door to his brothers, had secured for himself the collection of the taxes, and had thus become an Egyptian

---

32. Josephus (*Ant.* XII.186) relates that when Joseph was in Egypt, he fell in love with a dancing girl and wished to possess her. He asked his brother to aid him; but the latter tricked him by sending him his own daughter by night in place of the dancing girl, in order to keep Joseph from sinning. After the event, Joseph's brother told him of the whole affair, and Joseph, who had been apprehensive of the king's anger because of the dancing girl, was overjoyed that all had ended well and took the niece in question in marriage, it being she who bore him Hyrcanus. All this may have been true, but it is also credible that Hyrcanus was really the son of a gentile woman, and that the aforementioned events were related fictitiously in order to conceal his illegitimate origin and to make him a genuine legitimate son of Joseph.

official. According to his request, the king addressed to his father, brothers and the high officers[33] official letters whose text has not survived, but in which the king doubtless praised Hyrcanus fulsomely and indicated his new standing in the state.

It is therefore no wonder that Hyrcanus's brothers attacked their younger brother and attempted to murder him; they were unsuccessful and two of them fell before his sword. But Hyrcanus himself was not strong enough to hold his own at Jerusalem and was compelled to cross to Transjordan, where his father had long had his estate. "There," writes Josephus (*Ant.* XII.222), "he dwelt and levied taxes upon the barbarians," that is, he at once set about employing the rights which he had obtained in Egypt, and continued to discharge in Transjordan the function which till then had belonged to his father Joseph. It is hard to establish whether he succeeded in utilizing his privilege in the other lands of Syria, since the story says nothing on that score. Political events may have prevented him from so doing, for in 198 came the great upheaval in the life of the country: Syria passed into Seleucid hands, and the whole political situation changed completely.

After his father's death, Hyrcanus returned and attempted to penetrate Jerusalem, but his brothers barred his way and the struggle broke out anew (*Ant.* XII.228ff.). As far as can be judged from Josephus's brief account, it now exceeded the bounds of a family quarrel and took on political garb; the whole people was divided into two camps, the majority siding with the elder brothers, while Simon the High Priest also supported them. The interest taken by the people and the chief of the Jewish community in this struggle proves that important political issues hung on its outcome. Unfortunately we do not know precisely when the conflict blazed up between Hyrcanus and his brothers; but it is reasonable to believe that it occurred some time before the country was conquered by Antiochus III or even at the time of the conquest itself. The pro-Seleucid orientation of the High Priest Simon is already known to us; we learn that the elder sons of Joseph also belonged to the same party. It is to be assumed that Hyrcanus's success in Egypt had

---

33. The king wrote πᾶσι τοῖς ἡγεμόσιν αὐτοῦ καὶ ἐπιτρόποις. This terminology is not Ptolemaic, but more in harmony with the Roman period: the title *hegemon* was the term with which the Prefect of Egypt was addressed, and the *epitropos* was the Roman "procurator." In the Ptolemaic period *hegemon* was a military rank, and the title *epitropos* is not found at all. May it then be concluded that Josephus used the story of the House of Tobiah in its last edition made during the Roman period? Or did he himself substitute the Ptolemaic titles, which were no longer current, by Roman titles to which he was more accustomed?

bedeviled the good relations between Joseph's elder sons and the Ptolemies, and the former hoped to obtain from the king of Syria those privileges that their father Joseph had once obtained from the kings of Egypt. Hyrcanus, on the contrary, as an Egyptian official, supported the Ptolemies and did all he could to strengthen their government in the country, or (if the quarrel broke out after the year 200) to restore Palestine to Egyptian rule. Whichever was the case, Hyrcanus's attempt failed and he was forced to return to Transjordan.

There he resided till his death. Josephus gives a brief account of his activity in Jordan: he fought successfully against the Arabs, slaying and capturing many of them and building himself a fortress not far from Heshbon, at a place called Tyros, Tzur, or Tirah. He adorned this castle with marble blocks and with paintings of various animals; in it he built chambers for banquets, installed water pipes, planted groves about it, and so forth.[34] He ruled seven years in those regions; and he put an end to his own life on the appearance of Antiochus Epiphanes, fearing "to be punished by the king for what he had done against the Arabs." All this information shows that Hyrcanus did not reside in Transjordan as a simple landowner, but as a politically independent prince. His wars against the Arabs, the building of the fortress, the edifice's wealth and magnificence, clearly prove that Hyrcanus was a petty king, and there is no doubt that he wielded great influence across the Jordan. We are not in a position to determine whether he stood in contact with the kings of Egypt; it is possible that his previous relations with the Ptolemies did not cease at this period, although he could no longer discharge an official function for the Egyptian government. For seven years Hyrcanus ruled his small state,[35] which might have developed and performed an important task for the Jews, had not the course of world history led to its destruction. An independent Transjordanian state did not suit the views of Antiochus Epiphanes, least of all when he was plotting to make war on Egypt, and any independent political power constituted a danger to his plans. We have no notion what occurred between Antiochus and

34. On 'Arak el-Emir and the residence of Hyrcanus, see p. 84 n. 17. Representations of an eagle and a lion are still preserved on the walls of the fortress. See Butler, *Princeton Expedition*, IIA, i, p. 21, fig. 12; ibid., II, pl. i.

35. Josephus's words: "He ruled seven years in those places" (*Ant.* XII.234) immediately follow the account of the building of the fortress "not far from Heshbon." It is clear that by the words "those places" not the whole of Transjordan is meant but the district around the fortress only, that is, the small state which Hyrcanus established and ruled for seven successive years. He spent in all twenty-five years in Transjordan.

Hyrcanus, whether the latter attempted to fight the king and suffered military defeat, or whether he saw beforehand that no such attempt could succeed and decided to accept his fate. He committed suicide and with him his little kingdom came to an end.

Although Hyrcanus spent some twenty-five years over the Jordan, he did not give up his desire to return to Jerusalem, and there are grounds for supposing that he had lived there for some time and had acquired friends in the city. The author of 2 Maccabees has preserved a very important piece of information, to the effect that when Heliodorus, the minister of Seleucus IV, came to Jerusalem to confiscate the Temple funds, money belonging to "Hyrcanus son of Tobiah" was lying in the Temple treasury (2 Macc. 3:11).[36] At this time Onias III was High Priest in Jerusalem, and in conversation with Heliodorus he alluded to Hyrcanus, designating him as "a man of very important standing" (ibid.). Had Onias been one of Hyrcanus's opponents, as the High Priest Simon, his predecessor, had been, he certainly would not have referred to Hyrcanus with such respect; hence we learn that Onias was his friend. Nor is this surprising, if we consider that Onias was opposed to Tobiah's sons, that is, Hyrcanus's brothers. The fact that Hyrcanus's money was lying in the Temple treasury proves that he had confidence in those at the head of the Temple, and particularly in the High Priest Onias. It may well be therefore that he was in the habit of coming to Jerusalem personally and of meeting his friends there; and it may be believed that these meetings also possessed a political significance, since Hyrcanus, who was a supporter of Egypt, certainly would not have regarded the Syrian sovereign with favor and would have dreamed of the restoration of Palestine to the Ptolemies.

Hyrcanus, like his father Joseph, appears as a characteristic personality of the Hellenistic period, symbolizing the strong, self-reliant man. His aspirations, however, differed from those of his father, for Joseph was chiefly a financier and, if he also discharged a political function by the way, this was only insofar as this function helped him to establish his private position. Hyrcanus, on the other hand, was a politician, maintaining an opinion and a permanent stand on questions

---

36. "Ben Tobiah" is here Hyrcanus's surname; all his brothers were known as "B'nei Tobiah," although they were actually sons of Joseph ben Tobiah. Those scholars may be right who have supposed that Hyrcanus's Hebrew name was Tobiah, so that we ought to read ʿΥρκανοῦ τοῦ καὶ Τωβίου, "Hyrcanus also called Tobiah." The custom of calling the grandson after the grandfather was common among the Jews.

of state, and in different circumstances might have become renowned as a great statesman. But it was his tragic lot to fight a losing battle from the start. He charted his political path on devotion to Egypt, which was at that time a broken reed not to be leaned on. A career in Jerusalem was closed to him from the outset, and there, under the protection of the Seleucids, his brothers kept wary watch. Against them he fought all his life without avail, for he lacked the support of the people, who apparently did not see in him a national leader. He thereupon followed the example of many Hellenistic princes and established his own state. But if his relation to Egypt was outdated, the establishment of an independent state between Syria and Egypt was premature, anticipating the historical development of the Jewish people and of Palestine by some fifty years. Here too he was fighting a losing battle. He was unsupported, and his great energy, which found no worth cause in politics, was wasted; Hyrcanus exhausted his powers in drinking bouts and pleasures, resembling several Hellenistic princes and kings in this respect as well. It is easy to imagine him overcome by despair; he died in solitude, and his tragic end was a sad but logical termination of his unsuccessful life story.[37]

What was the attitude of Joseph the Tobiad and his son Hyrcanus to that same striving to Hellenization which in course of time, under Antiochus Epiphanes, came to occupy to important a place in the life of the population of Jerusalem? There can be no doubt that Hellenism was not alien to them; but they cannot be reckoned among the deliberate Hellenizers who sought Hellenism through a thoroughly prepared and premeditated program. Their Hellenism was the outcome of imitation; they were the first Jews to maintain frequent contact with the Greeks,

---

37. Hyrcanus's personality has always attracted scholars. Our few sources are such as to arouse historical curiosity without furnishing the material to satisfy it. Hence the endeavors of inquirers to extend our knowledge by diverse conjectures. Klausner (*Ha-shiloah*, XLII Heb.; *History* 2:230) saw in Hyrcanus the author of the Book of Ecclesiastes (a hint of a similar view may also be found in Renan, *Hist. du peuple d'Israel* 4:275). According to Gressmann, Hyrcanus regarded himself as a messiah, and his tragic end formed the basis of the legend of "the Messiah son of Joseph" (Gressmann, *SBAW* 39 [1921]: 668). A realistic historical approach free of far-reaching conjecture is found in Momigliano, "I Tobiadi nella prehistoria del moto maccabaico," *Atti d. reale Accad. di scienze di Torino* 67 (1931–32): 170ff. In the writer's view, a closer understanding of Hyrcanus's personal life could be obtained if those who seek it were to pay attention to the lives of the Greeks of the period, instead of restricting themselves to the narrow confines of Jewry. The lives of Eumenes, Demetrius, and Pyrrhus as told by Plutarch may perhaps help us to understand Hyrcanus's psychology and character.

and the life which they witnessed in Alexandria influenced them chiefly in externals. Some details of the lives of Joseph and Hyrcanus indicate that they were not strict in the maintenance of practical Jewish observances, since they ate at the king's table and took part in the drinking parties of the Alexandrian court; Hyrcanus, moreover, adorned his fortress with the pictures of animals.

Contact with the Greeks brought them wealth and the opportunity of playing an important part in the life of their land; they had no grounds for a negative attitude to the Greeks and doubtless saw no need for such an attitude, since in the time of Joseph the question of Hellenizaton was not yet the acute question which it became under Antiochus Epiphanes. We may therefore suppose—and lack of information permits no more than conjecture—that Joseph and Hyrcanus adopted Greek habits in daily life, learned Greek, gave their children Greek names, and so on. It was not, of course, Greek philosophy or art which they picked up in Alexandria; the anecdote of Joseph and an Egyptian dancing girl (see n.32, above) shows convincingly that they were influenced mainly by the external aspects of Hellenism, by its physical rather than by its intellectual freedom. But it is a well known rule in the lives of peoples, that the culture of a more civilized nation influences its backward neighbor first of all by its externals, which are sometimes not worthy of the name of culture; understanding of the internal aspects comes later—if at all.

Hellenization

Morton Smith

5

Hellenization (1971)

> The question of Hellenization has been omnipresent in the preceding chapters. Each of the major discoveries treated above has been described and analyzed against the background of the conquests of Alexander the Great and their implications for the understanding of Judaism in Palestine during the fourth and third centuries B.C.E. Yet a great amount of research, literary and archeological, gradually has made us aware that the strict division between the periods of Persian and Hellenistic administration, while accurate politically, has surprisingly less significance in terms of religious or cultural history.
>
> Morton Smith's wide-ranging discussion attempts both to chart the course and extent of Greek influence in Palestine before the arrival of Alexander and to invest the phenomenon of Hellenization with a new precision and significance. He assesses the Greek influence in Palestine prior to Alexander and clearly sets forth the chief instruments by which Hellenistic influence was ever enhanced in the Ptolemaic period. Greek troops settled in the country, and Greek cities were founded. What did these events mean? Smith investigates the varied aspects of political and social Hellenization in order to chart their broader implications for cultural and religious history.

THE FOUR hundred and twenty years between Nebuchadnezzar's destruction of Jerusalem (587) and the outbreak of the Maccabean revolt (167) saw an immense cultural change, not only in Palestine, but throughout the Near East. This change is usually described as "hellenization." The term is unfortunate, since it suggests that the change was due entirely to imitation of Greek ways. That was not the case, but much of the change was due to Greek influence and the dominant elements in some aspects of the resultant culture—notably in language, in design and decoration, in business, in scholarship, and in technology—were Greek. Therefore we shall begin our study of the hellenization of Palestine with an account of the ways in which Greek influence was exercised in the country.

Trade between Palestine and Greek lands began in remote antiquity and was considerable in the late bronze age.[1] The invasions at the end of the second millennium doubtless interfered with it, but did not wholly interrupt it.[2] Among the invaders, the Philistines were themselves a seagoing people in touch with the Greeks.[3] Gaza is persistently associated by legend with Crete, and there is linguistic and archeological evidence to support the legend.[4]

Throughout the first millennium B.C. trade was supplemented by the continuous emigration of Greeks and other Aegean peoples to serve as mercenaries in the pay of near eastern rulers. David's mercenaries "the Cherethites and the Pelethites" have been conjecturally identified as "the Cretans and the Philistines" and the conjecture is not implausible.[5] The Carian (or Cretan?) mercenaries of Athalia put Joash on the throne about 840,[6] and two centuries later Greek adventurers probably played a considerable part in Egyptian resistance to Assyria.[7] A legend in Herodotus reports that the Egyptian king Psammetichus I, in the second half of the seventh century, owed his conquest of the country to his alliance with them.[8] There were undoubtedly many Greeks in the army

---

1. W. F. Albright, *The Archaeology of Palestine* (Harmondsworth, 1949), 99–100.

2. *Iliad* 23.743, etc. D. Auscher, "Les Relations entre la Grèce et la Palestine avant la conquête d'Alexandre," *VT* 17 (1967): 8ff.; but cf. S. Weinberg, *Post-Exilic Palestine* (Jerusalem, 1969), 11ff.

3. M. Dothan, "Excavations at Azor, 1960," *IEJ* 11 (1961): 173ff.; A. Biran, "Archaeological Activities, 1968," *CNI* 20 (1969): 50; J. Waldman, "Philistine Tombs at Tell Fara and Their Aegean Prototypes," *AJA* 70 (1966): 335ff.

4. S. Cook, *The Religion of Ancient Israel in the Light of Archaeology* (London, 1930), 180–86; G. Hill, "Some Palestinian Cults in the Greco-Roman Age," *Proceedings of the British Academy* (1911–12): 427.

5. Cook, *Religion;* 2 Sam. 8:18; 15:18; 20:7, 23; 1 Kings 1:38, 44; Greenfield, "Cherethites and Pelethites," *IDB* 1:557. (I am indebted to Prof. M. Greenberg for the information that the Greek in *ANET* 286–87—at Ascalon in the time of Hezekiah—was produced by the translator's mistaking a proper name for a gentilic.)

6. 2 Kings 11:4–5; cf. Greenfield, "Cherethites."

7. H. W. Parke, *Greek Mercenary Soldiers* (Oxford, 1933), 4–5.

8. Herodotus II.152.

with which Necho, the son of Psammetichus, defeated and killed King Josiah of Judah in 609. (Josiah's death put an end to the deuteronomic reform. And Josiah himself had some Greek mercenaries. There were "Kittim" in the Judean fortress at Arad in Josiah's time, and seventh-century Greek pottery has been found in the central Negeb.)[9] Necho celebrated his victories by sending an offering to the temple of Apollo in the territory of Miletus.[10] Necho's grandson, Apries, who tried to relieve the siege of Jerusalem by sending an army into Palestine in 588,[11] had some thirty thousand Greeks in his service, if Herodotus (II.163) is to be believed. The Jews who fled from Palestine to Egypt after the fall of Jerusalem, therefore, fled to a land where Greek influence was long established and of great importance. Moreover, in one particular town to which they fled (Tahpanhes) the Pharaoh Psammetichus had established a settlement of Greek mercenaries.[12] Nor was Greek influence absent from Mesopotamia. Nebuchadnezzar, too, had Greek mercenaries in his army, one of them the brother of the poet Alcaeus, who returned to tell of the fall of Ascalon, of which the capture by Nebuchadnezzar in 604 was also celebrated by Jeremiah.[13] A Babylonian text recording a payment of oil to Jehoiakin, "the son of the King of Judah," records similar payments to seven Greek carpenters.[14]

With the Persian conquest, Palestine became part of an empire which included Greek territories in Asia Minor and raised its army by conscription from its territories. Greek conscripts certainly played a large

---

9. Y. Aharoni, "Arad: Its Inscriptions and Temple," *BA* 31 (1968): 14. H. Tadmor, "Philistia under Assyrian Rule," *BA* 29 (1966): 102 n.59, conjectures that the plentiful East Greek pottery at Mesad Hashavyahu, from the late seventh century, may have been left there by Greek or Cretan soldiers in Josiah's employ. For seventh-century and earlier Greek and Cypriote pottery at other sites see Auscher, "Relations," 14; M. Kokhavi, "Notes," *IEJ* 17 (1967): 273; A. Biran and R. Gophna, "Tell Halif," *RB* 74 (1967): 77; but cf. Weinberg, *Post-Exilic Palestine*, 12–13.

10. Herodotus II.159.

11. Jer. 37:1–8. 2 Kings 24:7 is probably mistaken.

12. E. Bickerman, *From Ezra to the Last of the Maccabees* (New York, 1962), 32. Tahpanhes is Daphnae, later well known as a center of Greek mercenaries. Greek pottery there dates from the seventh century B.C., Weinberg, *Post-Exilic Palestine*, 16–17.

13. Alcaeus Z.27 and B.16 in E. Lobel and D. Page, *Poetarum Lesbiorum Fragmenta* (Oxford, 1955); Jer. 47:5ff.; J. Quinn, "Alcaeus 48 (B16) and the Fall of Ascalon," *BASOR* 164 (1961): 48; cf., however, E. Auerbach, "Der Wechsel des Jahres-Anfangs in Juda," *VT* 9 (1959): 113ff.

14. *ANET* 308–9.

part in the Persian army.[15] Some were probably stationed in Palestine, since Palestine was important in Persian military history.[16] The country became the line of communications for the Persians when they conquered Egypt (525–521) and, thereafter, whenever they had to suppress revolts there (520?, 486–484, 460–449, 445?, 414–404).[17] In spite of the Persian conquest Greek influence remained strong in Egypt and Greek traders, mercenaries, and tourists were common there.[18] The revolt of 460–449 was supported by the Athenians who were for some time masters of the country and held out for six years; the minimal figure for their expeditionary force in Egypt is eight thousand; the maximal, fifty thousand.[19] They were also fighting on the Palestine-Syrian coast; it has even been suggested, albeit on dubious evidence, that they seized Dora, about sixty miles northwest of Jerusalem, as a base for their operations.[20] Though eventually defeated, the Athenians continued to have important connections with Egypt and probably supported Egyptian rebels again in the 440s.[21] The Persians finally lost Egypt in 404–401;[22] thereafter, Palestine was frontier territory and was garrisoned accordingly.[23] The remains of a string of Persian forts run for some fifteen miles across country south of Gaza.[24] The Persian garrison at Gaza was strong enough and loyal enough to hold up Alexander by three months of suicidal resistance.[25] But Palestine was not only a frontier district for the Persians; it was also their base for repeated

15. A. Olmstead, *A History of Persian Empire* (Chicago, 1948), 237ff., esp. 242. Greek conscripts were used by Cambyses in his attack on Egypt in 525: Herodotus II.1.

16. The date of the Persian takeover is uncertain.

17. On the Elamite version of the Behistun inscription see F. Kienitz, *Die politische Geschichte Ägyptens vom 7. bis zum 4. Jahrhundert* (Berlin, 1953), 60 n.4; for the rest of the chronology, E. Drioton and J. Vandier, *L'Egypte* (Paris, 1952), 603–5 and notes.

18. Herodotus III.139, but Herodotus's statement seems to be contradicted by the pottery finds; cf. Weinberg, *Post-Exilic Palestine*, 15–17.

19. Thucydides I.104–10 and A. Gomme's notes, which cite the other sources.

20. F. Heichelheim, "Ezra's Palestine and Periclean Athens," *ZRG* 3 (1951): 251ff.; see, however, the discussion by Jacoby, *F.Gr.H.*, nn. on no. 342 F 1.

21. Drioton and Vandier, *L'Egypte*, 605.

22. Following H. Hall, "Egypt to the Coming of Alexander," *CAH* 6:137ff.; W. Tarn, "Persia from Xerxes to Alexander," *CAH* 6:1ff. The trouble in 414–408 is known from the Elephantine papyri, as is the continuance of Persian rule until 401. E. Kraeling, *Brooklyn Pap.*, 112.

23. M. Noth, *Geschichte*, 287, 311.

24. K. Galling, "Denkmäler zur Geschichte Syriens und Palästinas," *PJB* 34 (1938): 79, which refers to many other Persian remains in the vicinity.

25. Arrian *Anabasis* II.25.4ff.

attempts to reconquer Egypt (385–383, 374–370, 357 [?],[26] 350), which succeeded only in 343.

About 420 the Persians began the practice of employing Greek mercenaries, as well as Greek conscripts.[27] These mercenary forces soon became large. During the years from 379 to 374, some twelve thousand mercenaries (at least)[28] were collected in Galilee, in preparation for the campaign against Egypt. The campaign, based on Akko, dragged on for several years, then failed, and the Greek forces were left in Akko under the command of a Greek general.[29] Egypt, at the same time, was using large numbers of Greeks in its forces. In 360 the Spartan king Agesilaus, with a thousand Spartans, ten thousand other Greek mercenaries, and a supporting Greek fleet, took part in a Greco-Egyptian occupation of Palestine.[30] Jerusalem probably participated in this revolt, since it seems to have issued silver coinage in the name of its own territory and authorities; in the Achaemenid empire such coinage was normally issued only by Persian authorities and autonomous cities.[31] Sometime within the next ten or fifteen years both Jerusalem and Jericho were taken and punished by Artaxerxes III,[32] whose forces probably included a large Greek contingent—at his conquest of Egypt in 343 he had 1,000 Thebans, 3,000 Argives, and 6,000 Asian Greeks, besides 4,000 Greeks of unspecified origin.[33]

Along with this military penetration by Greek forces went economic and cultural penetration by Greek traders, Greek merchandise, and Greek ways. Palestine was crisscrossed by trade routes—not only those from Egypt to Phoenicia, Syria, and Babylonia, but also those from

26. Compare Hall, "Egypt," 152, with Tarn, "Persia," 21ff. Olmstead, *Persian Empire*, thinks attacks were made on both dates.

27. Tarn, "Persia," 3. Xenophon *Cyropaedia* VIII.8.26 (probably propaganda, but not wholly baseless).

28. So Nepos *Iphicrates* 2.4; Diodorus XV.41 says 20,000.

29. A. Jones, *The Cities of the Eastern Roman Provinces* (Oxford, 1937), 231; Parke, *Greek Soldiers*, 106–7.

30. Diodorus XV.92.2; Nepos *Chabrias* 2.3; Plutarch *Agesilaus* 36ff.

31. A. Reifenberg, *Ancient Jewish Coins* (Jerusalem, 1947), nos. 1–3 and pp. 8–9; cf., however, Auscher, "Relations," 22ff.; and E. Bickerman, review of E. Goodenough, *Jewish Symbols in the Graeco-Roman Period*, I–IV, *L'Antiquité Classique* 25 (1956): 246.

32. E. Schürer, *Geschichte des jüdischen Volkes* (Leipzig, 1901–11), 3:7–8. Bickerman, *Ezra*, 11–12 and n.8, connects the capture with that of Sidon reflected in the Babylonian docket translated in S. Smith, *Babylonian Historical Texts* (London, 1924), 148–49.

33. Diodorus XVI.44.1–4 interpreted as by Tarn, "Persia," 22–23.

Damascus, Gerrha on the Persian Gulf, and South Arabia, to the coastal ports of the Mediterranean. Travel was slow and any town or village along the way might serve as an overnight stopping place. The land through which these routes ran could hardly preserve an uncontaminated population or an isolated cultural tradition.

The penetration of the country by foreign elements is demonstrated by the archeological evidence, which shows that there were Greek settlements along the coast in the late seventh century,[34] and even the small towns of the central part of the country had trading connections with Greece in the seventh century.[35] Such connections became frequent in the sixth century.[36] Summarizing the finds at Beth Zur—a few miles south of Jerusalem—Sellers writes: "Culturally, from the early part of the fifth century on, Palestine was dominated by Greece. The few objects showing Persian influence are almost negligible. There is no change in pottery forms or other objects at the coming of Alexander. That conqueror did not introduce Greek culture into Palestine . . . he found . . . it there."[37] That Beth Zur was not exceptional has been shown by Rostovtzeff's survey of the evidence from the whole Near East, which led him to conclude that the demand for Greek wares in Palestine, Phoenicia, and Syria reached a peak in the fifth century B.C. Thereafter, local manufacturers in these countries took to producing goods of hellenistic style, and the imports from Greece declined until, after Alexander's conquest, the large-scale settlement of Greeks throughout the area led to a renewed demand for genuine Greek merchandise.[38]

34. Mesad Hashavyahu near Yavneh, an East Greek settlement begun about 640. See J. Naveh, "The Excavations at Mesad Hashavyahu," *IEJ* 12 (1969): 89ff.

35. E.g., Tell Mahlata, SE of Arad, Kokhavi, "Notes," 273. En Gedi, B. Mazar, T. Dothan, and I. Dunayevsky, *En Gedi* (Jerusalem, 1966), 30–31; cf. Weinberg, *Post-Exilic Palestine*, 12; and E. Stern, "Eretz-Israel in the Persian Period" (in Hebrew), *Qadmoniot* 2 (1969): 118–19.

36. Tell en-Nasbeh, a few kilometers NW of Jerusalem, Albright, *Archaeology of Palestine*, 143. Samaria, G. Reisner et al., *Harvard Excavations at Samaria* (Cambridge, 1914), 62. Shechem, G. Wright, "The First Campaign at Tel Balatah (Shechem)," *BASOR* 144 (1956): 19–20; idem, *Shechem* (New York, 1965), 167ff. En Gedi, see preceding n. Elsewhere, M. Rostovtzeff, *Social and Economic History of the Hellenistic World* (Oxford, 1941), 1325 n.17.

37. O. Sellers, *The Citadel of Beth Zur* (Philadelphia, 1953), 41. Weinberg, *Post-Exilic Palestine*, 13, thinks Greek trade did not become substantial until the second half of the century.

38. Rostovtzeff, *Social and Economic History*, 94, 104–5, 130ff., 158–59, 160 n.33.

Where Greek merchandise went, Greek merchants followed. Some were resident in Akko in the days of Demosthenes (384–322),[39] and Joel, perhaps a contemporary of Demosthenes, complains of the frequency of foreigners passing through Jerusalem (4:17b). Probably for their trade, but also for domestic use, the authorities of Jerusalem (?) began in the fifth century to issue coins modeled on hellenistic and Greek types.[40] Issuance was continued in the fourth century.[41] It is now generally recognized "that Alexander chose the Attic standard [of currency] not only in view of its popularity in the Aegean world, but also because it was widely used alongside of the Persian in the Persian Empire, especially in Palestine."[42]

Pottery and coinage were not the only means by which Greek iconography was introduced to the country. Along with coins went seals. A representative group from the Persian period, in the Palestine Archaeological Museum, Jerusalem, includes three representations of Heracles, one of a dancing satyr, two of males "half-running" in Greek archaic style (one of them winged), and one of a Persian holding a phallus (Gallery Book: "an object like a stick").[43] Commenting on the bullae and signets from Wadi Daliyeh, Cross writes: "One is particularly struck with the vivacity of Attic Greek influences in the glyptic art of Samaria in the era before the coming of Alexander."[44] Besides such glyptic representations, Greek statuettes of deities were popular. The same museum displays, from the sixth and early fifth centuries, a seated goddess of Greek style (Demeter?), a head of Athena, a reclining male holding a rhyton (like the representations of the heroized dead on Greek tomb reliefs), two heads of Heracles, a mask of Kore (Rhodian), two "Astarte" figurines showing Greek influence, two "mother goddesses" (pregnant woman, Cypriot-Egyptian), and an Isis with Horus

39. V. A. Tcherikover, *Hellenistic Civilization and the Jews* (Philadelphia, 1959), 91–92; Isaeus IV.7–8.

40. E. Bickerman, "The Historical Foundations of the Postbiblical Judaism," in *The Jews*, ed. L. Finkelstein (New York, 1949), l:75; A. Reifenberg, "A Hebrew Shekel of the Fifth Century B.C.," *PEQ* 75 (1943): 100ff.; D. Schlumberger, *L'Argent Grec dans l'Empire Achéménide* (Paris, 1953), 22–24; Auscher, "Relations," 22ff.

41. E. Goodenough, *Jewish Symbols in the Greco-Roman Period* (New York, 1953–68), 3:668–70.

42. Rostovtzeff, *Social and Economic History*, 1338 n.6, approving the suggestion of Sellers and Albright. Schlumberger, *Argent*, 27.

43. Palestine Archaeological Museum, *Gallery Book* (Jerusalem, 1961); idem, *Persian, Hellenistic, Roman, Byzantine Periods* (Jerusalem, 1943), nos. 759–63, 770, 728.

44. F. Cross, "The Discovery of the Samaria Papyri," *BA* 26 (1963): 115.

who holds a stalk of wheat reminiscent of Eleusinian symbolism.[45] These figurines come not only from the coastal area (Athlit, Tell es-Safi) but also from inland sites (Lachish, Megiddo, Beth Shan). A number of them show Greek influence mediated through or combined with traits from near eastern countries; of this we shall speak later.

After Alexander's conquest in 332, both military and economic penetration were intensified. As an example of military penetration, consider the history of Jerusalem. The city must have made its submission to some body of Alexander's forces and have been occupied by them for a short time, at least.[46] After Alexander's death in 323, his empire was carved up by his generals, and Ptolemy, who got Egypt, acquired Palestine. His descendants held it until 198. In the Ptolemaic period Jerusalem was captured ten or twelve times,[47] and was often occupied for considerable periods by Greek garrisons. In particular, it almost certainly had a garrison in the years from 320 to 290: Josephus speaks of Ptolemy I as governing the city harshly, which supposes some body of troops to enforce his decrees.[48] Other garrisons in 218 and 199 are mentioned.[49] A garrison was there in the time of Antiochus Epiphanes—sometime after 175—*before* the troubles leading to the Maccabean revolt began.[50] Further, the city was presumably an important base for the Ptolemaic forces—and therefore garrisoned by them—during their chronic war with their northern neighbors, the Seleucids, a war which raged intermittently from 280 to 241.[51] Launey, from exhaustive studies of hellenistic military methods, has concluded that "the presence of a garrison composed of aliens is a characteristic and quasi-

45. Palestine Archaeological Museum, *Gallery Book*, 685, 694, 696, 697, and 712, 703, 710–11, 713–14, 705.

46. Josephus *Ant.* XI.321ff. reflects, if anything, a meeting of Simeon the Righteous and Antiochus III, G. Moore, "Simeon the Righteous," in *Jewish Studies in Memory of I. Abrahams* (New York, 1927), 357.

47. By Perdiccas in 321, Ptolemy in 320, Antigonus in 315, Ptolemy and again Antigonus in 312, Ptolemy in 302, perhaps the Seleucids and again the Ptolemies in the succeeding ten years, certainly Antiochus in 218, Ptolemy IV Philapator in 217, Antiochus in 201, Scopas in 199, and Antiochus in 198 (Tcherikover, *Hellenistic Civilization*, compared with F. M. Abel, *Histoire de la Palestine* [Paris, 1952], 1:25–87; and W. Tarn, "The Struggle of Egypt against Syria and Macedon," *CAH* 7:699ff.).

48. Josephus *Ant.* XII.4.

49. Ibid. XII.133; Abel, *Histoire* 1:82–83, 86.

50. 2 Macc. 4:27ff.

51. Josephus *C. Ap.* II.48. Tcherikover, *Hellenistic Civilization*, 106, thinks the Decapolis was built up as a string of fortresses against the Seleucids. Rostovtzeff, *Social and Economic History*, 346ff., extends this theory to the cities of the Palestinian coast and Idumea, as secondary and tertiary lines of defense.

permanent trait of hellenistic cities," not only of those in Asia Minor, Syria, Palestine, and Egypt (where he takes the presence of a part of the royal army as "normal"), but even of the cities in Greece—and from the histories of these he demonstrates his rule.[52]

The breakdown of established standards which accompanies military occupation by aliens need hardly be mentioned. It seems worthwhile, however, to emphasize that armies traveled—on land—almost entirely by foot, and consequently spread all over the country, and were in intimate contact with the population. This was inevitable, for even friendly armies had to live off the country—like friendly swarms of locusts.[53] Launey remarks the frequency with which soldiers acquired civic rights in the area where they were stationed, the custom of camping and even wintering in the countryside, which brought the armies in close touch with the rural population, and the custom by which both passing armies and permanent garrisons billeted their soldiers in civilian families.[54] A general of Antiochus III shortly after 200 protests the billeting of royal troops in his villages in Galilee by Ptolemy, son of Thraseas, and also complains of the damage done by transient troops who stopped to rest in the villages.[55]

Further, the hellenistic army was not an exclusively military group. Rather—especially in the Seleucid Empire—it was an international organization, composed of troops from all peoples, centered around a Greco-Macedonian core and commanded in Greek. These troops formed an economic and social center, followed by purchasers (of booty, slaves, etc.) and vendors and money-changers and women and their children and servants and slaves and miscellaneous hangers-on. An army was a nomadic city, constantly interchanging its population with that of the countries through which it traveled, receiving both individuals and groups as accretions, and giving back both individual deserters and whole colonies, which were detached from it to form or reform cities in strategic points.[56] In the 260 years from Alexander's death to the conquest of Jerusalem by the Roman general Pompey, there were at least two hundred campaigns fought in or across Pale-

52. M. Launey, *Recherches sur les armées hellénistiques* (Paris, 1949–50), 633–34.
53. Rostovtzeff, *Social and Economic History*, 137; Ghirshman, *Iran* (Harmondsworth, 1954), 193.
54. Launey, *Recherches*, 642–75, 690–700.
55. Y. Landau, "A Greek Inscription Found near Hefzibah," *IEJ* 16 (1966): 61.
56. Abel, *Histoire* 1:40; Rostovtzeff, *Social and Economic History*, 130, 143ff., 262–63.

stine.[57] This military history alone shows that no part of the country can have escaped Greek influence.

But this military history was now supplemented by the Greek[58]

57. I. Abrahams, *Campaigns in Palestine from Alexander the Great* (London, 1927), is inadequate. From Abel, *Histoire;* A. Bouché-Leclercq, *Histoire des Séleucides* (Paris, 1913–14); Tarn, "Struggle"; and Tcherikover, *Hellenistic Civilization,* I have compiled the following list of wars or military leaders responsible for operations in or through Palestine in (approximately) the years specified. (The Maccabees are included when they fought outside Jewish territory.) An average of at least two campaigns (one for each army) must be allowed for each year of operations. The dating of the Syrian wars differs from author to author; to those entries, therefore, I have added in parentheses the dates given by H. Bengtson, *Griechische Geschichte* (Munich, 1960), 571–72.

321 Perdiccas	164 Lysias	in Acre)
320 Ptolemy	163 Judas in Trans-Jordan	108 Hyrcanus in Samaria
315 Antigonus	163 Judas in the Hauran	107 Hyrcanus in
312 Ptolemy	163 Simon in Galilee	Scythopolis, etc.
312 Antigonus	162 Lysias	104 Aristobulus I in
302 Ptolemy	161 Bacchides	Galilee
301 (?) Seleucus	160 Nicanor	104 Antigonus in Galilee
296 Demetrius	160 Bacchides (occupied	103 Jannaeus in Acre
288 (?) Ptolemy	to 157)	103 Ptolemy Lathyrus
280–272 First Syrian War	152 Alexander Balas	102 Ptolemy Lathyrus
28(280–279 and 274–	150 Ptolemy VI	102 Cleopatra III
271)	147 Apollonius	101–93 Jannaeus in
260–255 Second Syrian	147 Jonathan in the plain	Trans-Jordan
War (260–253)	146 Ptolemy VI	93–88 Jannaeus
252–241 Third Syrian	145 Demetrius II	throughout Palestine
War (246–241)	144 Jonathan in Syria	88 Demetrius III
219 Antiochus III	144 Simon in the plain	86 Antiochus XII
218 Antiochus III	143 Tryphon	84 Aretas III
218 Ptolemy IV	142 Tryphon	83–80 Jannaeus in the
201 Antiochus III	142 Simon in the plain	plain
199 Scopas	138 Antiochus Sidetes	80–76 Jannaeus in Trans-
198 Antiochus III	137–135 Kendebaios	Jordan
169 Antiochus Epiphanes	134–132 Antiochus	74 Aristobulus II in
168 Antiochus Epiphanes	Sidetes	Damascus
(bis)	128 Hyrcanus in Trans-	70 Tigranes
167 Apollonius	Jordan	68–63 Aristobulus II vs.
166 Apollonius	128 Demetrius II	Hyrcanus II and
166 Seron	128 Cleopatra Thea	Nabateans
165 Ptolemy Macron	(residence henceforth	

58. A. Schlatter, *Geschichte Israels* (Stuttgart, 1925), 383 n.7, lists a dozen obscure places with Persian names as evidence for Persian foundation of towns in Palestine, but of these, the only one about whose settlement anything is known is a colony of Babylonian Jews established by Herod (Josephus *Vita* 11.54ff.; see Thackeray's note

policies of military colonization and the foundation of cities. The importance of these has not always been understood correctly.[59] "Foundation" was often no more than a legal and financial transaction: the city, for a price, got the right to call itself after some member of the royal family, to revise its constitution along Greek lines, and to govern itself by its own representatives, elected according to the revised system. It thus got rid of the royal civil governor and his staff—no small saving, both in money and in face, even though the royal military commander, treasury officials, and the like remained.[60] Also, the opportunity to revise the constitution was an opportunity to change the franchise and so diminish the civil rights of the opposition. Since factional quarrels were endemic in hellenistic cities, this opportunity was not overlooked. Kings who needed money were therefore able to persuade many cities to accept such "foundation." Antiochus Epiphanes founded half a dozen cities in Palestine and Trans-Jordan alone, most of them self-governing before his foundation.[61] His efforts were not always taken kindly. In 2 Macc. 4:7–5:26 and 1 Macc. 1:11–64 we have accounts (from the opposition!) of the events which attended his foundation of Antioch-in-Judea (formerly Jerusalem).[62]

On the other hand, foundation might mean the creation of an entirely new city on a site formerly empty or occupied only by a village. The great examples of this were Alexandria and Antioch. It seems that no Palestinian city of the first importance was founded in this way

on the passage). The other places are small Jewish settlements known from Josephus or later sources and most of them are located in Galilee or northern Trans-Jordan (where Jewish settlements would probably not have survived the anti-Maccabean reaction; see 1 Maccabees 5). Behind Greek colonization was the poverty and overpopulation of Greece. The Persians had no such motivation.

59. Contrast Tcherikover, *Hellenistic Civilization*, 90–116. with Jones, *Cities*, 227–95; see also A. Jones, "The Urbanization of Palestine," *JRS* 21 (1931); 78ff.; Schlatter, *Geschichte*, 12ff.; and A. Alt, "Galiläische Probleme," *PJB* 33–36 (1937–40): 6.78ff.

60. Jones, *Cities*, 250–52.

61. Ibid., 251–52, credits him with five or six Antiochs (Gerasa, Gadara, Hippos, Ptolemais [?], and Jerusalem) and three Seleucias (Abila, Gadara [*sic*], and Seleucia in the Gaulan). This last may or may not be identical with Seleucia by Lake Huleh (Tcherikover, *Hellenistic Civilization*, 101) and Antioch near Huleh (Alt, "Probleme," 2.78). Gerasa, Gadara, Hippos, and Ptolemais, at least, were probably self-governing cities before his foundation.

62. Cf. E. Bickerman, *Der Gott der Makkabäer* (Berlin, 1937), chap. 3, with Tcherikover, *Hellenistic Civilization*, 188–89; Jones, *Cities*, 252; Abel, *Histoire* 1:122–23; etc.

before the Herodian period,[63] but a number of minor places[64]—and, in
Trans-Jordan, some considerable cities, notably Dium, Pella, and Gerasa[65]—may have been. Also, Gaza and Samaria were destroyed by the
forces of Alexander or his successors and rebuilt, so as to be practically
new foundations.[66]

Between these extremes, many procedures were possible. In general,
however, a city might hope to get, by "foundation," not only a Greek
(usually dynastic) name, a constitution of Greek form providing for
government by elected representatives, and autonomy in domestic,
civil affairs, but also help with municipal building (especially fortifi-
cation) and perhaps a grant of territory around the city.[67] However,
many cities without either Greek or dynastic names seemed to have
enjoyed these privileges (Ascalon, Joppa, etc.). In particular, almost all
of them seem to have had considerable territories under their authority
and therefore subject to the influence of their citizens. Moreover, when
records become sufficient to make a check possible, we find similar
privileges extended even to villages, which often were fortified, held
public lands from which they received income, had important buildings
(baths, markets, etc.), and had a good deal to say as to the administration of their own affairs—their inscriptions refer not only to the
royal officer in charge but also to a series of municipal magistrates and
occasionally to a local council or assembly.[68] We find such fortified

63. That Scythopolis was not entirely a new creation (in spite of its alternative
name, Trikomia) is argued by the survival of the name Beth Shan (S. Klein, *Sepher
Hayeshub* [Jerusalem, 1939], *s.v.*). Cf. Jones, *Cities*, 233. A. Rowe, *The Topography and
History of Beth Shan* (Philadelphia, 1930), 44, knows nothing of any interruption of
settlement. Strato's Tower was probably a Sidonian settlement, Tcherikover, *Hellenistic Civilization*, 93.

64. Seleucia by Huleh, Tcherikover, *Hellenistic Civilization*, 101. Philoteria, ibid.,
102; Abel, *Histoire* 1:57; cf. Alt, "Probleme," 3.86. Atabyrion, Alt, "Probleme,"
6.81; W. Oehler, "Die Ortschaften und Grenzen Galiläas nach Josephus," *ZDPV* 28
(1905): 6–7. Arethusa, Tcherikover, *Hellenistic Civilization*, 95; Jones, *Cities*, 259 n.42;
Schlatter, *Geschichte*, 13. Anthedon, Tcherikover, *Hellenistic Civilization*, 95; cf. Jones,
Cities 447 n.16.

65. Tcherikover, *Hellenistic Civilization*, 109; Jones, *Cities*, 239; Abel, *Histoire* 1:57;
C. Kraeling, ed., *Gerasa* (New Haven, 1938), 30–31.

66. Tcherikover, *Hellenistic Civilization*, 95–96, 103–4, 105; Abel, *Histoire* 1:54;
Jones, *Cities*, 238; but contrast Arrian *Anabasis* II.27, end.

67. Tcherikover, *Hellenistic Civilization*, 107–10; Jones, *Cities*, 242, 252; Abel,
Histoire 1:122–23.

68. G. Harper, *Village Administration in the Roman Province of Syria* (Princeton, 1928),
20ff., esp. 46–57. Jones, *Cities*, 285–86, tries to explain the councilmen as honorific;
D. Sourdel, *Les cultes du Hauran* (Paris, 1952), 11 n.1, has followed Harper; so too, M.
Rostovtzeff, "La Syrie Romaine," *Revue Historique* 175 (1935): 11–12.

villages already in the first century A.D.,[69] and from the earlier period we find a string of Greek place names for places which can never have been more than villages, but which evidently had Greek settlers and therefore may have had Greek cultural forms.[70] This suggests that the difference between "cities" and towns cannot have been sharp, and the same conclusion is suggested by Josephus's carelessness in describing places now as cities and again as villages,[71] and by the fact that rabbinic Hebrew never developed or adopted a special word for "city" in the Greek sense, but used 'ir for cities, towns, and villages alike.[72]

Thus the cities founded by the hellenistic dynasts formed no distinct class by themselves—nothing like the later Roman colonies—but were only one aspect of a policy intended to provide for the Greek followers of the kings and to establish centers of loyal population throughout the land. That there was no intention of limiting such centers to the cities is proved by the settlement of old soldiers through the countryside as small landholders—*cleruchs*—in rural colonies. The Ptolemies used this method widely in Egypt and (probably) in Palestine. We know of one such colony in Trans-Jordan, at Birta; Rostovtzeff has inferred another, somewhere near Gaza, and he remarks that Ptolemy III Euergetes threatened to turn the city land of Jerusalem into small holdings and send cleruchs to occupy it.[73]

Therefore the contrast commonly drawn between the Greek cities and the Semitic countryside has been exaggerated. The countryside was permeated by Greek elements and influences. They came to it not only through military operations and military and municipal settlements but also through economic and administrative channels. Both administrative and economic interests were represented for example, by Zeno, an agent of Apollonius, the finance minister of Ptolemy II. In 259–258 B.C.

69. L. Haefeli, *Samaria und Peräa bei Flavius Josephus* (Freiburg im Breisgau, 1913), 98–99 on Josephus *War* IV.420ff.

70. Homonoia on the Sea of Galilee (the name can hardly be post-Maccabean), Oehler, "Ortschaften," 11; Pella in Judea (E. Nestle's conjecture, "Judea bei Josephus," *ZDPV* 34 [1911]: 75, is unconvincing; a Macedonian settlement is more likely than such a scribal error); Berenike in Gaulan and Berenike in the coastal plain, Alt, "Probleme," 4.80 n.1; Pegai and Patras, Schlatter, *Geschichte*, 13; Arsinoe, V. A. Tcherikover, "Palestine under the Ptolemies," *Mizraim* 4–5 (1937): 43.

71. E.g., Gabara; see Thackeray's ed., vol. 1, index, s.v.

72. Cf. *Ta'anit* 21a (a small 'ir is one which can put five hundred men in the field) with *'Erubin* 60a (the minimum required for an 'ir is three dwellings).

73. Rostovtzeff, *Social and Economic History*, 348 (the inference is based on *Pap. Cairo, Zen.* 59006, which Edgar refers to a settlement near Gaza; cf. Tcherikover, "Palestine," 37). See further *Social and Economic History*, 346–51, 496–502.

Zeno visited Gaza, Marisa, Jamnia, Strato's Tower, Jerusalem, Jericho, Birta, Abila, several towns in the Hauran, Kadesh, Beth Anath,[74] and Ptolemais. Further, his correspondence shows him in touch with Ascalon, Joppa, Pegai, Tyre, Sidon, Berytos, Tripolis, Adora, and Philadelphia.[75] In many of these places he had agents. In so far as these represented the government (and not the private interest of Apollonius and Zeno) they were probably members of the special staff of the royal department of finance, and so apart from the regular administration, which was itself threefold: the country seems to have been divided into a number of major districts, each of which had a civil administrator and his subordinates, a military commander in charge of the troops quartered there, and a revenue officer in charge of the tax collectors.[76] (This last branch of the government was by no means the least. The activities of tax collectors sometimes amounted to small military campaigns: Josephus gives us a picture of one setting out with two thousand troops and beginning his operations by the capture of Ascalon.)[77] Besides these three main branches, there were (1) special officers of the king or of his great ministers—as remarked above, Zeno belonged to this class; (2) a judiciary system of some sort;[78] (3) officials of special royal institutions, for example, the royal bank; (4) the secret service, using a body of informers to whose efficiency Tarn attributes Eccles. 10:20, "Even in your thought (?) do not curse the King, . . . for a bird of the air will carry your voice"; (5) officials of the local administrative units (cities, temples, etc.) who were either appointed or confirmed by the royal government. Thus in Jerusalem, just before the outbreak of the Maccabean revolt, the government's chief officers were a civil administrator (Philip, the Phrygian), a military commander (Apollonius) with twenty-two thousand men, a chief tax collector (this same Apollonius), a

---

74. On Beth Anath see S. Klein, "Notes on the History of Large Estates in Palestine I–II," in *BIES Reader B*, ed. E. Stern (in Hebrew; Jerusalem, 1965), 139ff., who (for dubious reasons) would locate it in Trans-Jordan on the Syrian border.

75. See the study of his correspondence by Tcherikover ("Palestine"); also Abel, *Histoire* 1:67ff.; and J. Herz, "Grossgrundbesitz in Palästina im Zeitalter Jesu," *PJB* 24 (1928): 107.

76. The question is complicated. Cf. Abel, *Histoire* 1:60ff.; Tcherikover, "Palestine," 36ff.; and Jones, *Cities*, 248–49, 274. Jones thinks this essential structure lasted through Seleucid and Maccabean times and was taken over by Herod. Rostovtzeff, *Social and Economic History*, 348ff., comes, with reservations, to the same conclusion.

77. Josephus *Ant.* XII.180ff. The story must have been at least an exaggeration of recognized methods.

78. The relation of royal to local law remains one of the most obscure and important problems of this history.

special royal commissioner to oversee the religious reformation, and the High Priest (Menelaus) who was a royal appointee.[79] In Jamnia (?) in 259 B.C. we find a special royal representative, two officers of the garrison, the chief paymaster, a judge, and a clerk.[80] The papyrus which gives us the information for Jamnia is not a complete roster of the officials of the town but merely a business document which happens to mention a few of them.

Zeno's letters testify not only to this omnipresent administrative system but to business and banking connections equally extensive. Wherever he went, he acted as a purchasing agent. He also kept an eye on the interests of Egyptian Greeks who had loaned money to Palestinian villagers. All this business, of course, was conducted in Greek, and Bickerman has admirably summed up the gist of the linguistic evidence in his statement that "even in the villages there must have been persons able to draft a contract in Greek, or to write a request in the style required for a Greek petition."[81]

Many of the villages must have been located in estates owned by the king or by great courtiers and managed, therefore, by their enterprising Greek appointees. Such estates had been given already by the Persian kings to persons they wished to favor, among them Greeks.[82] In Zeno's day we know of an estate owned by Apollonius at Beth Anath in Galilee.[83] Evidence for many other such estates, from the Maccabean and later periods, has been collected by Herz, *Grossgrundbesitz*.[84] Estate management was made a science in the hellenistic period; consequently these large holdings and the larger royal domains, which were also managed by the latest methods, served as centers for the dissemination of the Greek language, Greek technical advances, and the Greek businessman's attitude.[85]

In all this we have discussed only the direct ways by which Greek influence came to Palestine. But in the Persian period, especially, the indirect influence of Greek culture—that exercised through neigh-

---

79. 2 Macc. 5:21—6:1; cf. 1 Macc. 1:29.

80. *Pap. Cairo, Zen.* 59006.

81. Bickerman, "Foundations," 93–94.

82. Rostovtzeff, *Social and Economic History*, 1339 n.8; Bengtson, *Geschichte*, 156.

83. Rostovtzeff, *Social and Economic History*, 1403 n.149.

84. Herz, "Grossgrundbesitz," esp. 99ff., 109ff. See also Alt, "Probleme," 3.80ff. Alt's attempt to prove, from these estates, the prior existence of royal domain land (p. 88) is contradicted by his own statements in "Probleme," 5.70, and refuted by Rostovtzeff, *Social and Economic History*, 1403 n.149.

85. Rostovtzeff, *Social and Economic History*, 351ff.; G. Bertram, "Der Hellenismus in der Urheimat des Evangeliums," *ARW* 32 (1935): 270–71.

boring peoples—must have been even greater than that exercised directly by Greeks. To the north of Palestine, Tyre and Sidon had been profoundly penetrated by Greek influence long before the fifth century (when, for instance, they began to buy even their copies of Egyptian sarcophagi from Greek factories).[86] Prior to Alexander's conquest they seem to have controlled the coastal plain of Palestine and to have established trading colonies in the cities of the central mountains.[87] There was a Tyrian colony in Jerusalem in the days of Nehemiah (13:16). In Marisa there was a colony of Sidonians, of which the preserved remains date from the third to second centuries B.C. and are full of imitations of Greek material.[88] The Samaritans of Shechem are represented by Josephus as calling themselves Sidonians—especially when they asked permission to dedicate the temple on Mt. Gerizim to Zeus Hellenios.[89] Whatever truth there is in the story,[90] it testifies to a tradition of Sidonian influence on the city. Coins minted in Phoenicia—especially in Tyre—and in the Palestinian coastal cities are frequent in Palestinian and Transjordanian sites from the end of the fifth century on.[91] Tyrian coins are prominent in the recent finds from fourth-century Samaria, and they were the customary currency both in Palestine and in Trans-Jordan throughout the Ptolemaic period (300–200 B.C.).[92] From a yet later period, a hoard of them has been found at Qumran. For Palestinian Judaism the general rabbinic rule reads: "The money mentioned by the Law [in specifying penalties, etc.] is always Tyrian money. What is Tyrian money? It is Jerusalem money."[93]

To the south of Palestine the Greek influence was even stronger in

86. F. Cumont, *Recherches sur le symbolisme funéraire des Romains* (Paris, 1942), 389. On the importance of the Phoenicians in hellenizing Palestine see Stern, "Eretz-Israel," 121.

87. Alt, "Probleme," 2.73ff. By the late fifth or early fourth century a Phoenician trader was established in Elath, J. Naveh, "The Scripts of Two Ostraca from Elath," *BASOR* 183 (1966): 27ff.

88. Goodenough, *Symbols* 1:65ff., 3:7–16.

89. Josephus *Ant.* XII.257–64; cf. 2 Macc. 6:2 (Zeus Xenios).

90. Alt, "Probleme," 4.83, and Abel, *Histoire* 1:56, supposed a Sidonian colony existed at Shechem. Contrast E. Bickerman, "Un document relatif à la persécution d'Antiochus IV Epiphane," *RHR* 115 (1937): 188ff.; idem, "Foundations," 87.

91. Sellers, *Beth Zur*, 69ff.; Reisner, *Samaria* 1:252–53; Rostovtzeff, *Social and Economic History*, 1324 n.16. A. Kindler, "The Mint of Tyre" (in Hebrew), in *E. L. Sukenik Memorial Volume*, ed. N. Avigad et al. (Jerusalem, 1967), 318ff., declares that Tyre was the major supplier of coins to Palestine through more than four hundred years.

92. Cross, "Discovery," 116–17; A. Kirkbride, "Currencies in Transjordan," *PEQ* 71 (1939): 153.

93. *t. Ketubot* 13 (12), end (ed. Zukermandel, 275).

Egypt than it was in Phoenicia to the north. The Phoenicians, it is true, were supported by the Greeks in their revolts against Persia in 385–381 and 351–350.[94] But Egypt, as we saw above, already relied on large-scale Greek assistance in its struggle against the Assyrians in the seventh century B.C. By the beginning of the sixth century the Greeks there reportedly numbered in the thousands. Driven out by the Persians, they came back again and again to support the revolts of the fifth century. When those revolts succeeded they came in even greater numbers and were the strength of the Egyptian armies which beat off the repeated Persian attacks throughout the fourth century. In 343, when Artaxerxes III finally conquered the country, the Egyptians opposing him had twenty thousand Greeks in their service, there were Greek garrisons in "all the cities" of the Delta, and Pelusium, the key fortress on the east mouth of the Nile, seems to have been predominantly Greek.[95]

To the north and to the south, then, Palestine was bordered by countries where the Greeks were numerous and Greek influence important. Even to the east, the Arabs had felt the effects of Greek influence in statuary as early as the fifth century and by the third century were minting coins after Greek models.[96] Each of these countries exercised its influence on Palestine, but, as far as the Palestinian Jews were concerned, the most influential foreign group were presumably the Jews of the diaspora, which had already begun in northern Syria in the eighth century, in Egypt at the latest in the seventh.[97] During the fourth and third centuries, especially, vast numbers of Jews were carried abroad by repeated deportations (we hear of five),[98] constant enslavement (not only in military campaigns; slaves were one of the country's main exports throughout the Ptolemaic period and the trade had already been considerable in Persian times),[99] military conscription (which they

---

94. Tarn, "Persia," 20ff.; P. Dikaios, *A Guide to the Cyprus Museum* (Nicosia, 1953), 40; Galling, "Denkmäler," 65ff.

95. Diodorus XVI.47.6, 49.1, XLIX.7; Hall, "Egypt," 153.

96. W. Phillips, *Qataban and Sheba* (New York, 1955), 277; G. Hill, *A Catalogue of the Greek Coins of Arabia* (London, 1922), 45, 47.

97. Drioton and Vandier, *L'Egypte*, 677.

98. By Artaxerxes III to the Caspian and Babylonia, Schürer, *Geschichte* 3:7. By Alexander to Alexandria, Josephus *C. Ap.* II.42. By Ptolemy Lagos to Cyrenaica, ibid., II.44 (defended by J. Juster, *Les Juifs dans l'Empire Romain* 2:226 n.2). By Ptolemy Lagos to Egypt, Josephus *Ant.* XII.7; cf. Deut. 28:68. By Seleucus Nicator to Antioch, Abel, *Histoire* 1:42; cf. Josephus *Ant.* XII.119. Passages predicting a new dispersion may or may not be prophecies *ex eventu*, e.g., *Testament of Issachar* 6.2.

99. Neh. 5:1–13; Joel 4:6ff.; Josephus *Ant.* XII.24–33 (from *Aristeas* 12–27), 144. Herz, "Grossgrundbesitz," 108; Tcherikover, *Hellenistic Civilization*, 68; Rostovtzeff, *Social and Economic History*, 341ff., 1262; Juster, *Juifs* 2:17–18 and nn.; E. Urbach,

often welcomed),[100] and more or less voluntary emigration (Palestine was a country oppressed by constant movements of armies and naturally poor).[101] The Jews thus carried abroad soon adopted the language and ways of thought of their Greek neighbors. Their continued loyalty to Jerusalem linked that city by the closest ties of financial interest, as well as kinship, to the great centers of Greek influence, especially Alexandria, Antioch, and the Aegean.

Gifts from the diaspora to Jerusalem began with the return of the exiles in the late sixth century, if not before.[102] Some time after the canonization of the Law came the payment of regular taxes prescribed by its interpreters. By the first century this tribute was customarily sent every year from every province of the Roman Republic and from Mesopotamia.[103] With these gifts came tens of thousands of pilgrims whose expenditures in Jerusalem were a substantial part of the city's income.[104] Tacitus[105] thought the importance of the Jewish state was due to these contributions from abroad, and Josephus[106] attributed to the Emperor Titus the opinion that the right to collect them was the greatest of the many great privileges the Romans had given the Jews. Only this external support can account for the recurrent recovery of the city after its recurrent lootings. Can one suppose that so important a source of income as the diaspora did not make its intellectual and religious influence felt?[107]

"Halakot Regarding Slavery as a Source for the Social History of the Second Temple and the Talmudic Period" (in Hebrew), *Zion* 25 (1961): 141ff. On the date of Joel, J. Myers, "Some Considerations Bearing on the Date of Joel," *ZAW* 74 (1962): 177ff., makes a good case for the late sixth century, and collects much material on Greek contacts with Palestine then and before; W. Rudolph, "Wann wirkte Joel?" in *Das ferne und nahe Wort,* ed. F. Maas (Berlin, 1967), 193ff., pleads for 590, but with too many false arguments.

100. Evidence collected by Juster, *Juifs* 2:265–68 and nn.; add Josephus *Ant.* XII.119 (intended to suggest service under Seleucus Nicator). Many references from papyri in Launey, *Recherches,* 541–56. That even Maccabean Jews desired such service is shown by the wishful thinking in 1 Macc. 10:36–37.

101. 2 Kings 25:26 and parallels; Josephus *Ant.* XII.9, XII.119; idem *C. Ap.* I. 194. Not all the Greco-Roman disapora came direct from Palestine, *Ant.* XII.147ff.

102. Ezra 1:4–11; 2:68–69; etc.; Jer. 41:4ff.

103. Cicero *Pro Flacc.* 28.67; Philo *De Spec. Leg.* I. 76–77; Josephus *Ant.* XVIII.313; J. Jeremias, *Jerusalem in the Time of Jesus* (Philadelphia and London, 1967), 1:73ff.; Juster, *Juifs* 1:377ff.

104. Jeremias, *Jerusalem* 1:73ff., 96; 2.A.50ff.

105. Tacitus *Historiarum* V.5.

106. Josephus *War* VI.335.

107. G. Kittel, *Die Probleme des palästinischen Spätjudentums und das Urchristentum* (Stuttgart, 1926), 74ff.

When all these factors are considered—repeated military conquest, constant military occupation, Greek settlement both in cities and in the countryside, economic and administrative penetration which reached every village, systematic exploitation of the countryside through landed estates, Palestinians' dealings with Phoenicians and Egyptians, and Jewish ties with Jews of the diaspora—when all these factors are considered it is clear that the cultural history of Palestine from the beginning of the Persian period is one of constant subjection to Greek influence, and that already in the Ptolemaic period every sector of the country must have been shaped by that influence more or less. "More or less" implies differences of degree which were undoubtedly important, but they were only differences of degree. As the evidence has shown, some of the most important elements of Greek culture had everywhere come to be taken for granted: typically Greek artifacts and techniques were everywhere in use; the country had a monetary economy, foreign trade was a major concern, the frame of thought had ceased to be the land of Palestine and become the civilized world, and Greek had become—as it was throughout that world—the normal language of business and politics.

Yet in spite of all this it would be a serious error to ascribe merely to imitation of Greek ways the great cultural change which took place, throughout the Near East, between the sixth and second centuries B.C. To understand this change we must realize that the world of the Greeks and Persians, Jews and Philistines, was a world of invaders. The invasions had taken place chiefly in the period 1250–950 B.C. Before that time, there had existed, throughout some two thousand years, a more ancient world, that of the Babylonians and Egyptians, the Semitic-speaking empires of the great river valleys, essentially concerned to maintain systems of irrigation, conservative as to the law of real property, and stabilized by the landed endowments and hereditary personnel of the immense temples. This more ancient world had been weakened and transformed, but not wholly destroyed, by the invasions. In Mesopotamia, especially, it retained the strength for a final effort to restore the old order. This effort continued to the sixth century, and Nebuchadnezzar was its last great figure. Within fifty years after his destruction of Jerusalem (587) the Neo-Babylonian Empire was itself destroyed by the Persians (539).

It was the Persian, not the Greek, conquest which marked the beginning of a new era in the Near East. Admittedly, Cyrus made no drastic changes. In religious affairs he came as a restorer of the old order; his conquest of Babylon was welcomed by the priesthood of the great temple of Marduk.[108] In political matters he permitted much local independence.[109] Political reorganization came only with Darius, and the power of the Babylonian priesthood was not broken until the reign of Xerxes (486–465).[110] Even after Darius and Xerxes the Persians left local institutions generally undisturbed and governed largely through local officials who were not Persians.[111] And even to decorate their own palaces they employed artists from their subject peoples who most often repeated and refined the clichés of ancient near eastern tradition.[112] Nevertheless, the mere fact of their conquest resulted in differences from the old order which were of epoch-making importance.

In the first place, the new empire they created was of vastly greater extent than any previous one. The biggest of the previous ones—those of Egypt and Assyria—had been river valley empires, which pushed beyond their valleys to conquer neighboring territories, but remained practically and psychologically centered in their valleys with their central river transport and irrigation systems. With the Persian conquest these valleys became merely parts of a much greater empire, stretching from the Danube across Thrace, Anatolia, Armenia, Media, eastern Persia, and Afghanistan, to the upper Indus. The lifelines of this new empire were overland trade and military routes, and its psychological as well as its geographical center was not in the river valleys but in the uplands along the Zagros. Its population was far more numerous and more various than that of any previous empire, and the ruling people, instead of being the largest body of people in their own territories, were a military minority spread thin over the multitude of their diverse subjects.

In the second place, from the Persian conquest on, for the next thousand years, the great powers of the Near East were Indo-Europeans (Persians, Greeks, Parthians, and Romans) whose languages never re-

---

108. *ANET* 315b–16b; Ghirshman, *Iran*, 132–33; see my "II Isaiah and the Persians," *JAOS* 83 (1963): 415ff.

109. Probably exaggerated by G. Holscher, *Palästina in der persischen und hellenistischen Zeit* (Berlin, 1903), 1–4; cf. Ghirshman, *Iran*, 142ff.

110. J. Duchesne-Guillemin, *Zoroastre* (Paris, 1948), 128–29.

111. G. Driver, *Aramaic Documents of the Fifth Century* B.C. (Oxford, 1954), 15ff.

112. Ghirshman, *Iran*, figs. 60, 63, 64; pls. 15(d), 17(a), 18. But elements of Greek style were also introduced; see H. Frankfort "Achaemenian Sculpture," *AJA* 50 (1946): 6ff.; and G. Richter, "Greeks in Persia," ibid., 15ff. Persian readiness to appropriate alien cultural elements is remarked by Herodotus I.135.

placed completely the Semitic tongues of masses of their subjects.[113] This difference of language exacerbated natural conflicts of interest. The resultant tension between the rulers and the Semitic-speaking population was henceforth (until some time after the Arab conquest in the seventh century A.D.) characteristic of this area and was one of the major factors which shaped its history.

Moreover, the new rulers did not establish their seats of government usually—or, at least, exclusively—in the river valleys where had formerly been the chief centers of population. Even the Ptolemies called the city from which they ruled "Alexandria *by* (not *in*)[114] Egypt" and their interest (as opposed to their interests) was often in the Aegean area. The new locations and concerns of the governing groups contributed further to the differences between them and the native populations. In these differences the priesthoods of the great temples located in the former centers of population found themselves on the side of the natives. Their endowments were usually maintained and sometimes extended, but they had become groups alien to the ruling class.[115]

Thus the political and institutional foundations of the old order were undermined by the Persian conquest. Similarly the development of trade fostered by the Persian Empire—by road building, establishment of a gold currency of universal circulation, and so on[116]—diminished the relative importance of the agricultural interests in the state, impoverished many small farmers, produced a landless proletariat in the cities it financed, and resulted in a uniform pattern of social and religious adjustments. Although this process had already begun in the Assyrian empire, it was much accelerated by the enormous extension of unified political control and the consequent facilitation of travel under the Persians. That Greeks played a large part in the development of trade and that the universal circulation of Greek silver matched and supplemented that of Persian gold[117] is true, but the social and religious

113. Jones, *Cities*, 230, and Tcherikover, *Hellenistic Civilization*, 34–35, argue that the survival of Aramaic place names proves the persistence of Semitic-speaking populations. If so, then in Gaza, Acre, Sidon, and Tyre, Greek never became the exclusive language; cf. E. Bevan, *The House of Seleucus* (London, 1902), 1:225ff.

114. Rostovtzeff, *Social and Economic History*, 415.

115. A. Nock, *Conversion* (London, 1933), 37; J. Bidez, "Les écoles chaldéennes sous Alexandre," *AIPHOS* 3 (1953): 41ff.

116. Ghirshman, *Iran*, 185ff.; Schlumberger, *Argent*, 13ff.

117. Schlumberger, *Argent*, 17–18.

changes resulted from the trade, not from the Greeks' part in it, let alone from their personal influence as Greeks.

Thus the forces which produced the changes called "hellenization" were not universally nor even primarily Greek. As for the forces which conditioned the change, they were often not only independent of Greek influence but resistant to it—so, for instance, the institutional inertia of the Near East[118] and the self-perpetuating pattern of peasant life. Even when a change can be attributed to Greek influence—as, for instance, the spread of silver coinage along the Phoenician and Palestinian coasts[119]—it remains a question whether the cultural element diffused by the Greeks was of Greek origin (coinage, for example, seems to have been originally Lydian).[120] And it was not only the Greeks who appropriated and disseminated elements of neighboring cultures. We have seen that Greek influence came to Palestine largely through the Phoenicians; Palestine, in its turn, must have been a center from which Greek influence spread through Arabia. At the same time, within the Greek tradition some important developments which mark the change from the classical to hellenistic culture were due to oriental influence (for instance, the rise of the cults of Adonis, Isis, and Sarapis). As the people of the Near East changed both by adoption of Greek ways and by resistance to them, so the Greeks changed both by adoption of oriental ways, and by careful efforts to preserve classical usages which, when classical, had been spontaneous.

Thus "hellenization" in the Near East and Greece[121] cannot be described simply as the adoption of Greek ways by the peoples of the Near East and of oriental ways by the Greeks, though both these processes were parts of it. Instead, we have a vast tissue of change, in which innumerable strands of independent, but parallel, development are interwoven with a woof of influence and reaction to produce a single, new culture, the hellenistic, which is no less different from

118. Shown, for instance, by the history of boundaries, Alt, "Probleme," 2; idem, "Judas Gaue unter Josia," *PJB* 21 (1925): 100ff.; etc.

119. Schlumberger, *Argent,* 22.

120. P. Ure, *The Origin of Tyranny* (Cambridge, 1922), 127ff. Further Greek borrowings: Olmstead, *Persian Empire,* 208ff.; S. Mazzarino, *Fra oriente e occidente* (Florence, 1947), chap. 1.

121. The question of hellenization as a whole, involving the West also, is a larger problem, with which this study is not concerned. Cf. the Greek provincialism of R. Laquer, *Hellenismus* (Giessen,1925), and the following list of differences between "classical" and "hellenistic."

classical Greek culture than from the cultures of the more ancient Near East. To mention only the most important differences from classical Greek culture: (1) In the classical world the principal form of land tenure was the relatively small holding of the ordinary citizen; in the hellenistic world it was the large estate of the king, the temple, or the great official. (2) In the classical world the chief political form was the city-state of small extent and homogeneous population, with some form of conciliar government; in the hellenistic world—though the appearance of legal autonomy was often preserved, and the fact occasionally survived—the chief political form was the absolute monarchy ruling various peoples and a vast territory. (3) In the classical world the structure of society was regulated chiefly by local custom and tradition; in the hellenistic world a much larger part than before was played by explicit, written laws.[122] (4) In the classical world the cult of the gods of the city was the center of both petition and patriotism; in the hellenistic world patriotism found expression in the cult of the divine ruler, while petitions were more often directed to deities whose political affiliations, if any, were of minor importance. (5) In the classical world, because the economic and political units were so small, private individuals were of relatively great importance; this both encouraged their concern for the state and made their activities matters of public concern; consequently the artistic and philosophical life of the period was closely connected with politics and politics was a major concern of the average man. In the hellenistic world, because the units were so big, private persons were generally of no importance; accordingly they neglected the state and the state them; therefore the artistic and philosophic life of this period was generally nonpolitical (except when inspired by patronage or the hope of patronage) and the average man was less interested in politics, more in his private affairs. (6) In the classical world the civil administration and the army were both run largely by amateurs (citizens ordinarily employed in private occupations) and professionals were rarely used except as subordinates; therefore the internal histories of the states were full of struggles between political factions. In the hellenistic world both the administration and the army were staffed almost entirely by professionals and the internal history was therefore one of bureaucratic intrigues and palace revolutions. (7) In the humanities, arts, and sciences, too, the hellenistic world

122. Rostovtzeff, *Social and Economic History*, 1101.

was distinguished by the growth of professionalism and the consequences of the professional approach.[123] These consequences were:
collection of previous knowledge, systematization and consequent discoveries (mostly minor), reduction of the system to a handbook and a
set of rules, consequent decline of originality and standardization of
product.

In all the above points except number 3 (the importance of written
law) the hellenistic world resembled Persia or Egypt rather than classical Greece. This resemblance is not accidental, nor was hellenistic
culture an imitation of the classical, which failed, in these points, to
achieve its goal. The hellenistic rulers had no intention of imitating the
political forms of the classical city-states.[124] The religious changes,
which took place also in Greece, were due to deliberate adoption. The
growth of professionalism was already begun in the classical world, but
was there felt to be incompatible with the ideal of the gentleman and
was attacked accordingly.[125] It is true that hellenistic culture comes to
include among its *new* elements the recognition of bodies of "classics"
and the deliberate imitation of "classical" models: the canonization of
the plays of the Greek tragedians, the chapters of the Book of the
Dead,[126] and the books of the Old Testament,[127] the imitation of
Homer by Apollonius Rhodius, of Ramesside documents by the Ben-
tresh stele, and of Judges by the author of 1 Maccabees, are cases in
point. But the culture as a whole was not, and was not intended to be,
an imitation of the classical. It was a new way of life, with its own
structural unity.[128] We can trace the social and cultural changes which
were to produce this way of life, we can see them at work before the
new culture emerges as a totality, and therefore we can speak of the
process of hellenization as at work even in the Persian period, or even in
classical Greece.

An important element in hellenistic culture was the tension already
remarked between the primarily Semitic-speaking masses of the population (many of whom, as we have seen, must have understood some

123. Ibid., 1134–1301.
124. Antiochus Epiphanes' playing at democracy was only an apparent exception
to this rule. See Bevan, *House of Seleucus* 2:148–61.
125. E. Gardiner, *Athletics of the Ancient World* (Oxford, 1930), 71, 102ff.; Plato's
attacks on professional teachers of philosophy.
126. J. Breasted, *Development of Religion and Thought in Ancient Egypt* (New York,
1912), 293–94.
127. E. Bickerman, "La chaine de la tradition pharisienne," *RB* 59 (1952): 46–47.
128. W. Ferguson, "The Leading Ideas of the New Period," *CAH* 7:1–2.

Greek) and the primarily Greek-speaking upper class (most of whose members could probably understand a little Semitic).[129] But this was not the only tension in the society. Another existed between the city dwellers and the village dwellers, and yet another between those who lived in Greek fashion and those concerned to preserve native ways. We have seen that not all the primarily Greek-speaking were city dwellers. No doubt many of the primarily Semitic-speaking lived in cities, and many of them liked Greek ways and were determined to follow them, just as some Greeks went native.[130] So the common equations: Greek-speaking = city-dwelling = grecizing, and Semitic-speaking = village-dwelling = anti-Greek, are true only as loose generalizations. Semitic languages continued to be used in and by some of the cities where Greek customs were most generally adopted: Sidon, until 150 B.C., issued coins bearing only Semitic inscriptions; its coinage was bilingual until A.D. 75; Tyre's coinage remained bilingual until the city was made a Roman colony, A.D. 198;[131] numerous Phoenician inscriptions from these cities date from the last three centuries B.C.[132] On the other hand, some of the most violent anti-Greek propaganda was written in or translated into Greek, not only by Jews (the Books of the Maccabees, the Sibylline Oracles),[133] but also by pagans (the Potter's Oracle, which happily prophesies the ruin of Alexandria).[134]

Thus the cultural tensions within the society—to say nothing of the political—were complex and are misrepresented when simplified to a single conflict. But such oversimplification errs more seriously when it represents the whole society as the result of a conflict between "Greek" and "oriental" cultures,[135] and neglects the existence of hellenistic culture as a thing in itself, different from either of its sources. The resultant confusion can be illustrated by a passage from Rostovtzeff—the more striking because it occurs in the works of so great a scholar. In discussing the policy of Antiochus Epiphanes which occasioned the

129. Meleager of Gadara greets the visitors to his grave in two Semitic dialects, as well as Greek, *Palatine Anthology* VII.419.

130. Nock, *Conversion*, 34.

131. G. Hill, *A Catalogue of the Greek Coins of Phoenicia* (London, 1910), 156, 174, 168.

132. Z. Harris, *A Grammar of the Phoenician Language* (New Haven, 1936), 157ff.

133. Schürer, *Geschichte* 3:545ff.

134. U. Wilcken, "Zur Aegyptischen Prophetie," *Hermes* 40 (1905): 556ff.

135. So Rostovtzeff, equating "hellenistic" with "Greek," *Social and Economic History*, 1053, 1057-73, 1098-1107, etc., though he recognizes the danger of this equation, 1063ff., 1069, 1071ff., etc.; cf. Abel, *Histoire* 1:276.

Maccabean revolt, he writes: "The existence of Greco-Semites, either hellenized Semites or orientalized Greeks, was a fact, and Epiphanes endeavored to make use of it . . . to transform his realm . . . into a network of cities with Greek organization and a Greek mentality." The religious aspect of this program was the introduction of the cult of Zeus Olympios, "a counterpart of the Ptolemaic Sarapis . . . bearing a Greek name . . . worshipped in semi-oriental temples. . . . represented in a semi-oriental dress and with semi-oriental attributes . . . as much the Pansemitic Baalshamin as the Greek Zeus, the symbol as it were of the growing Syrian solar henotheism."[136] This is an amazing series of statements: Epiphanes hoped, by using "hellenized" and "orientalized" subjects, to product a "*Greek*" mentality, therefore he introduced a "semi-oriental" religion: This confusion underlies Rostovtzeff's further statements that the breakup of the Seleucid Empire was due to rural reaction against hellenism, yet "the new rulers [who replaced the Seleucids] were certainly not hostile to Greek civilization as such. Most of them belonged to the hellenized upper class of the native population . . . therefore . . . the states they set up were of the hellenistic pattern."[137] We shall do better to recognize "hellenistic" as a cultural classification distinct both from "Greek" and from "oriental," and to see the civil conflicts of the Seleucid and Ptolemaic empires as conflicts between various groups of a single cultural continuum: the hellenistic.

---

136. Rostovtzeff, *Social and Economic History*, 703ff.
137. Ibid., 848; cf. 705. These generalizations are applied specifically to Judea, 852–53.

Arnaldo Momigliano

6

The Hellenistic
Discovery of Judaism   (1975)

The Greeks enjoyed an "ethnographical" literature as far back as the time of Herodotus, in the sixth century B.C. In the Hellenistic world created by Alexander, however, Greeks and orientals lived side by side, and both parties faced the problem of presenting the oriental cultures in terms appropriate to the dominant Hellenistic culture. One of the more interesting aspects of this issue is the question of how Jews and Judaism were perceived by the Greeks.

Arnaldo Momigliano discusses this "discovery of Judaism" by the Greek-speaking world. His survey of the relationship between Greeks and Jews prior to the Maccabean revolt highlights the problematic aspects of literary and cultural contact between the two communities. The author sensitively probes the self-imposed limitations which severely curbed any true or deep knowledge of Jews and Judaism on the part of intellectuals in the Hellenistic world. The consequently limited and generally one-sided communication between the two groups played a considerable role in the frustration (and ultimate rejection) which many Jews faced in their encounter with an increasingly Hellenized environment. Momigliano's perceptions provide yet another window on the period we are considering.

1

THE GREEKS were perhaps the first to study the peculiarities of foreigners. They began by collecting information as traders or colonists but by the end of the sixth century B.C. they were already writing books on ethnography and geography to satisfy their taste for enquiry—for *his-*

toria, as they called it. As Herodotus shows, their enquiries extended to territories no Greek had ever visited (4.25). On the other hand, we have noticed that the Greeks were much less curious than we would expect them to be about certain countries within their reach and indeed well inside their sphere of economic and cultural influence. Their interest in Celtic lands and civilization became apparent only in the fourth century B.C., though they had founded the important colony of Marseilles as early as the end of the seventh century. Even more paradoxically, that distinguished son of Marseilles, Pytheas, who discovered the north of Europe, seems never to have traveled inside France. The historians Ephorus and Timaeus, who in the fourth and third centuries B.C. were the first to collect extensive information about Gaul and Spain, do not seem ever to have visited these countries.

Ancient travelers did not find it easy to go into the interior of countries. We must consequently not expect Greek callers at Palestinian ports to go up to Jerusalem for the pleasure of observing Jewish festivals. But trade relations between Greeks of some sort and Palestinians started in the Mycenean period; Greek mercenaries represented another point of contact.

It is probable that David employed Cretan mercenaries (2 Sam. 20:23; 1 Kings 1:38); they presumably spoke Greek. About 840 Joash was put on the throne either by Carian or by Cretan mercenaries, according to which interpretation one prefers of 2 Kings 11:4. Greek ships with Greek traders certainly reappeared along the coasts of Palestine in the ninth and eighth centuries B.C. At Samaria Greek pottery antedates the destruction of the city by Sargon II in 722. At Tell Sukas between Tripolis and Laodikeia (Latakia), the Danish excavator P. J. Riis found a Greek settlement with a temple which seems to have been built in the seventh century and rebuilt about 570 B.C. The Greeks remained at Tell Sukas at least until 500 B.C. to trade with Palestinians of any religious and national variety. There were Greek mercenaries in the Egyptian army of Necho son of Psammetichus who killed Josiah— allegedly at Megiddo—in 608 B.C. There were thirty thousand Greeks, according to Herodotus, in the army of Necho's grandson Apries who tried to relieve Babylonian pressure on Palestine in 588 (Jer. 37:5) and probably precipitated the final onslaught of Nebuchadnezzar on Jerusalem in 586 B.C. It has even been suggested that a king of Judah had Greek mercenaries. The excavations of J. Naveh at Mesad Hashavyahu, not far from Yavneh in central Judea, yielded a great deal of Greek pottery from the last decades of the seventh century. The place looks like a fortress and may have been occupied by Greek mercenaries rather than by Greek traders. When Jeremiah fled to Egypt he went to Tahpanhes (43:7; 44:1) which was known to the Greek world under the name of Daphne and was probably already garrisoned by Greek mercenaries, as it certainly was a little later under King Amasis (570–526). It is tempting to imagine Jeremiah being received by Greek soldiers on Egyptian soil.

Contacts survived the exile. Finds of Greek pottery at Bet-Zur on the road from Jerusalem to Hebron are signs of brisk trade in the first part of the fifth century. Attic sherds of En-gedi belong mainly to the late fifth and early fourth centuries. We know from the orator Isaeus that an Athenian mercenary had accumulated a fortune of two talents at Akko about 370 B.C. (4.7). The earliest coins of Judea imitate Greek coins in the interest of trade with the Greeks. We do not know what authority was responsible for them. Money of Yavan—of Greece—it will be remembered, is mentioned in one of the papyri, dated 402 B.C., of the Jewish colony of Elephantine in Egypt (*Brooklyn Pap.* 12).

The Jews had other opportunities for contacting Greeks in Mesopotamia as well as in Egypt. It is symbolic that a Babylonian text records a payment of oil to Jehoiakin, the son of the king of Judah, and to seven Greek carpenters who worked for the Babylonian court (*ANET*, 2d ed., p. 308). In Egypt native and Persian kings attracted not only Greek and Carian but also Jewish mercenaries. The origins of the military colony of Elephantine are unknown, but the author of the letter which goes under the name of Aristeas must have found somewhere the piece of information that Jewish soldiers helped Psammetichus in his campaign against the king of the Ethiopians (13). The Psammetichus in question is Psammetichus II who had the support of Greeks, Carians, and perhaps Phoenicians in his expedition of 589 against Nubia. The graffiti left by these soldiers at Abu Simbel in Lower Nubia are famous. If the information of Aristeas is correct, Jewish and Greek soldiers must have rubbed shoulders in the same campaign. The absence of Hebrew graffiti at Abu Simbel is perhaps not sufficient to throw doubt upon Aristeas. A recent papyrological discovery shows that in the fourth century B.C. a story like the judgment of Solomon was known in Greece (*Pap.Oxy.* 2944), but there is no sign that it came from the Bible.

Such being the direct evidence for contacts between Greeks and Jews before the time of Alexander, we ask the obvious question: what did Greeks and Jews make of these various opportunities for meeting and knowing each other? As for the Greeks, the answer is simple. They did not register the existence of the Jews. The little nation which was later to present the most radical challenge to the wisdom of the Greeks is mentioned nowhere in the extant pre-Hellenistic texts. The absence of references to Jews in Greek literature disturbed Hellenized Jews, as we can read in the Letter of Aristeas (31; 312). Flavius Josephus made a diligent search for references to Jews in Greek literature when he compiled his *Contra Apionem*; and no doubt he had many predecessors in this hunt. The results were negligible. The most ancient author Josephus could find was the poet Choerilus, a contemporary of Herodotus. Choerilus mentioned Solymian mountains inhabited by warriors speaking the Phoenician language. Unfortunately, the tonsure Choerilus attributed to these people was explicitly forbidden to the Jews by Mosaic Law (Lev.19:27), which was clearly in operation at the time of Jeremiah (Jer. 9:26). It is practically certain that Choerilus had in mind the eastern Ethiopians, and that he combined several passages from Homer (*Odys.* 5.283) and from Herodotus (7.79; 7.89 and possibly 3.8) to form his fanciful picture. Nor does Herodotus necessarily refer to the Jews when he mentions Syrians and Phoenicians of Palestine, who acknowledge that they learned circumcision from the Egyptians (2:104).

Modern scholars who have tried to imitate Josephus in his search for references to Jews in pre-Alexandrian Greek literature have had no better luck. A fragment of the poet Alcaeus (50 Diehl = 27 Lobel and Page) has been taken to imply that his brother Antimenides fought against a gigantic Jew during one of the two sieges of Jerusalem by Nebuchadnezzar. But S. Luria—who proposed, or rather re-proposed this conjecture (*Acta Antiqua* 8 [1960]: 265–66)—had to postulate that Alcaeus called Jerusalem Hierosylyma, not Hierosolyma, and his only evidence for this was an etymological joke with antisemitic undertones quoted by Josephus (*C. Ap.* I.311), according to which the word Hierosolyma came from *hierosylos*, "temple robber." No doubt Antimenides fought in Palestine for the Babylonians, but his brother Alcaeus was not interested in specifying against whom he fought. Another text with allusions to Jewish ethical norms attributed to Phocylides was recognized long ago to be a Jewish forgery of the Hellenistic age. Franz Dornseiff, a German scholar who proved his courage and independence in difficult times, tried hard to persuade us that it was in fact authentic Greek poetry of the sixth century B.C. He also tried to show that a long description of the Jews attributed by Photius to Hecataeus of Miletus was really composed by this late sixth-century writer, and not (as is generally admitted) by the younger Hecataeus of Abdera who lived after Alexander. In both cases Dornseiff failed to convince. These texts attributed to Phocylides and to Hecataeus of Miletus are at least two centuries later—with the difference that "Phocylides" covers a forgery, whereas "Hecataeus of Miletus" is a wrong attribution, little more than a slip of the pen. Nothing so far has disproved the contention that the classical Greeks did not even know the name of the Jews.

In short, as far as we know, the Greeks lived happily in their classical age without recognizing the existence of the Jews. As for the Jews of the biblical period, they of course knew of Yavan, which designated all the Greeks rather than specifically the Ionians. Where Yavan is more precisely defined, as in the genealogy of Noah, Yavan is father of Elisah, Tarsis, Kittim, and Dodanim; that is, probably, of Alashiya and Kition in Cyprus, of Rhodes and of Tarsus—rather than Tartessus. There is no indication that Athens, Sparta, Thebes, or even Miletus and Ephesus were consciously connected with the name Yavan. This table of the Nations in Genesis 10 can hardly be more ancient than the seventh century B.C. Not much later Ezekiel or one of his disciples included Yavan in the lamentation for Tyre (27:13–19). Here Yavan is one of the merchants who trade with Tyre, and slaves are among the merchandise. Ezekiel's motif of the Greeks as merchants is taken up by Joel who accuses Tyre and Sidon and "all the coasts of Palestine"—that is the Philistines—of trading with Yavan and of selling them "the children of Judah and the children of Jerusalem" (3:6). It is a well-known problem whether Joel—or at least this section of Joel—belongs to the postexilic period. Yavan is mentioned in the last chapter of Isaiah, 66:19, among the peoples to whom God will reveal his glory. This is probably a late sixth-century text. Finally, Yavan appears in the Messianic promise of Zech. 9:13: "I have raised up thy sons of Zion, against thy sons of Greece." But this text clearly belongs to the period after Alexander, though I would not commit myself to a Maccabean date. The few biblical texts with the mention of Yavan which can be dated with probability before 336 B.C. know the Greeks only as traders—or more generically as one of the nations of the world. The Greeks are known, but they appear rather remote and insignificant. In the pre-Hellenistic sections of the Bible there is no notion that can be ascribed to Greek influence: indeed there is no certain Greek word. The first certain Greek words in the Bible are in the Book of Daniel (3:5), which in its present form belongs to the third and second centuries B.C. It is further-more probable that in Kohelet (Ecclesiastes) the Persian word *pardes*

(2:5) is used in a meaning, orchard, given to it by the Greeks under the form παράδεισος. But Kohelet, too, is probably Hellenistic.

The picture does not really change if we turn from the Bible to those seals and bronzes from the Persian period with which the Archaeological Museums of Jerusalem have made us familiar. There we meet Athena, Heracles, satyrs, and other Greek deities. We do not know who were the owners, nor what the objects meant to the owners. Those of us who display Buddha in the drawing-room are not necessarily Buddhists. There is indeed no indication that any Jew ever worshiped a Greek god before Alexander. This is interesting, because we know that even in the postexilic period a considerable proportion of the Jews was for all practical purposes polytheistic. Pure monotheism was by then securely established in the Second Temple of Jerusalem, but remained shaky elsewhere. During and after the exile Ezekiel (33:23), the Third Isaiah (57:1–10; 65:11–12), and the Second Zechariah (10:2; 13:2) denounced the worship of idols, the slaying of children, and the practice of ritual prostitution. In the Babylonian Murashu documents of the fifth century B.C. unmistakably Jewish names alternate in the same family with Babylonian theophoric names. The colonists of Elephantine in Egypt combined observance of the Passover and perhaps of the Sabbath with a devotion to Eshembethel and Anathbethel which my late colleague and friend Umberto Cassuto was unable to explain away. Greek gods are conspicuous by their absence in these documents of the declining Jewish polytheism of the fifth century B.C.

One document still defies interpreters. I allude of course to the mysterious figure on a coin now in the British Museum. The coin belongs to the Persian period, bears the inscription "Judea" (YHD), and shows a figure on a winged throne or on a chariot: this figure apparently confronts a Dionysiac mask (B. Kanael, *BA* 26 [1963]: 40 and fig. 2). This is something unique; and it is not surprising that somebody should have thought of the mystical chariot of Ezekiel. I am sure that everyone in this room satisfies the Rabbinic condition for discussing the chariot of Ezekiel (*ma'ase merkava*)—namely to be wise and able to deduce knowledge through wisdom of his own—but I do not propose to indulge in this subject. All the other Judean coins of the Persian period have non-Jewish symbols; there is no particular reason to believe that this coin bears a Jewish symbol. As I have already said, we do not know under what authority the coins were issued.

Before Alexander the Jews knew a little more about the Greeks than the Greeks knew about the Jews. After all, the Greeks traded in

Palestine, but apparently no Jew traded in Greece. This difference did not amount to any assimilation of Greek culture among the Jews. Yet the developments which took place in Judea in the fifth and fourth centuries B.C. offer many points of comparison with contemporary Greek developments. Both Greeks and Jews were living on the borders of the Persian Empire. Nehemiah's work can best be understood if compared with Greek events. In political terms Nehemiah was a tyrant imposed by the Persians just as much as Histieus and others had been imposed as tyrants over Greek cities by the Persian government. Nehemiah rebuilt Jerusalem, as Themistocles had to rebuild Athens. His remission of debts had obvious analogies in Greek practice of the sixth and fifth centuries. Nehemiah's law against mixed marriages was paralleled in Athens by Pericles' legislation against foreign wives. Even Ezra's and Nehemiah's autobiographies were new in Judea, as Ion of Chios's memoirs were new in Greece—practically at the same time. E. Bickerman once compared the work of the Chronicler with that of Herodotus. It was perhaps a wrong comparison. The technique by which in the fourth century B.C. the Chronicler rewrote and modernized the Books of Kings reminds us of the technique by which in the late fourth century Ephorus and Theopompus rewrote and modernized Herodotus and Thucydides. Other parallels can be adduced and have been adduced. The table of the Nations in Genesis 10 reminds us of the map of Anaximander; the Book of Job, probably an exilic work, has often been compared with Aeschylus's *Prometheus*.

One can speculate why, with so much in common, Greeks and Jews do not seem to have spoken to each other. One explanation is only too obvious. They had no language in common. The Greeks were monolingual; the Jews were bilingual, but their second language, Aramaic, gave them access to Persians and Babylonians, even to Egyptians, rather than to Greeks. Yet language difficulties have never been insurmountable barriers. Perhaps we have to reckon with an element of chance. Herodotus did not happen to visit Jerusalem. A page of Herodotus would have been sufficient to put a battalion of biblical scholars out of action. Ultimately, however, we must perhaps admit deeper obstacles. Under the guidance of Nehemiah and his successors the Jews were intent on isolating themselves from the surrounding nations. They trusted in God and his Law. For the same purpose, the Greeks trusted their own intelligence and initiative, were unceremoniously aggressive, and contributed everywhere to disturbing the peace of the Persian Empire on which the reconstruction of Judaism depended. One hundred and twenty years after Nehemiah and Pericles Greeks and Jews found themselves under the control of Alexander the Great—a Greek-speaking Macedonian who considered himself the heir of the Persian kings.

2

We have no idea of how the Jews reacted to the news that Persepolis was burning. Alexander never went to Jerusalem. But Jewish legends which found their way into the Alexander romance fondly narrated the encounter between the High Priest and the new King of Kings. Jewish legend also suggested that Alexander proclaimed the unity of God from the tower of this new city, Alexandria (Ps.-Callisth. II.28, p. 84 Müller). In Christian writers there is a story, probably of Jewish origin, that Alexander brought the bones of the prophet Jeremiah into Alexandria to keep snakes and crocodiles out of it (*Suda,* s.v. ᾽Αργόλαι). These legends prove at least that in Palestine the transition from Persian to Macedonian rule had been smooth. The memory of Alexander remained one of those pieces of folklore the Jews could share with their neighbors.

Alexander had certainly done one thing for the Jews which proved to be irreversible. He put the majority of them into a Greek-speaking, instead of an Aramaic-speaking, world. After his death Palestine was a bone of contention for more than twenty years. One of the rivals for the succession, Ptolemy, occupied Jerusalem in 320—perhaps by taking advantage of the Sabbath (Josephus *Ant.* XII.5 and *C. Ap.* I.205; Appian *Syr.* 50). From 301 to 198 the Ptolemies ruled Palestine. Greco-Macedonian governors, soldiers and traders came to live in Palestine by right of conquest. Philosophers and historians looked into Jerusalem, and, on the whole, they were pleased. Judaism became suddenly known—and respectable.

The conquerors of the Persian Empire found it advisable to get to know and, if possible, to win over the natives. Not everywhere had the previous rulers been popular. The Egyptians had a most successful record of rebellions against the Persians; the Babylonians had repeatedly revolted. Even in Palestine, where the Persians had been good rulers, there had been troubles, if our confused evidence is to be trusted at all (*C. Ap.* I.194; Syncellus I.486A). The Greco-Macedonians tried to present themselves as more sympathetic masters than their predecessors. They were helped by trends of thought which had developed in Greece in the fourth century. Here the interrelation between ideology and action is particularly complex. Platonic and Pythagorean philosophy had prepared the Greeks to understand and appreciate rigorously hierarchic, indeed hieratic communities. The philosopher-king was not far removed from the priest-king. Platonists were aware of Zoroaster. The historian Theopompus wrote on him. Alexander's teacher Aristotle did not share this liking for priests, but his scientific curiosity which was truly universal extended to the wisdom of the East. We shall meet several Aristotelians in our path.

Thus the new interest and sympathy were not specifically directed towards the Jews. But the other barbarians—Egyptians, Persians, Babylonians, and even Indians—had been known to the Greeks for centuries. There was much previous information available, now to be reassessed and brought up to date. The Jews were the newcomers. Everything had still to be learnt about them. It is perhaps not by chance that the first Greek book to speak extensively about the Jews was written by an adviser of Ptolemy I in the years in which he was campaigning for the conquest of Palestine. Hecateus of Abdera included a section on the Jews in a book about Egypt which he wrote in Egypt before 300 b.c., probably about 315 b.c. Hecateus idealized the Egyptians and especially their priestly class. He spoke about the Jews in an Egyptian context, though the fragment preserved by Diodorus and quoted by Photius does not allow us to see the exact place of the Jewish excursus in the plan of his book. According to Hecateus, the Jews were among the people—including the illustrious Danaus and Cadmus— who had been expelled by the Egyptians during a pestilence. Moses, a man distinguished by wisdom and courage, had guided the emigration, founded Jerusalem, built the Temple, divided the people into twelve tribes, established the priesthood, and altogether enacted praiseworthy laws. He had ensured a large population by making the land inalienable and by prohibiting the exposure of children, a practice common among the Greeks. He had prescribed an education of almost Spartan rigor; the comparison with Sparta is obvious, but only implicit. If the type of life Moses had introduced was slightly unsocial and hostile to strangers, this was understandable after the painful experience of leaving Egypt. Hecateus ended his excursus by noticing, in conformity with a well-known pattern of Greek ethnography, that the Jews had modified their customs under the influence of Persian and Macedonian rule. Hecateus did not know of the patriarchs and apparently had never heard of Hebrew kings. One of the intriguing features of his account is that he seems to have heard or read at least one quotation in Greek from the Pentateuch. He says that at the end of the Laws of Moses one finds the following words: "Moses, having heard the words of God, transmitted them to the Jews." This seems to be an echo of Deut. 29:1. A pre-Septuagint translation of some sections of the Torah is not altogether incredible and is, in any case, given as a fact by Aristobulus, an Alexandrian Jew writing in Greek during the second century B.C. (Eusebius *Praep. Ev.* 13.12.1).

More or less in the same years about 300 B.C. the greatest pupil of Aristole, Theophrastus, became interested in Jewish customs within the context of his comparative researches on Piety. Jacob Bernays was the first to notice, in 1866, that a fragment of Theophrastus's book *On Piety* concerning the Jews was quoted by Porphyry in his treatise *On Abstinence* (2.26). Theophrastus spoke of the Jews as philosophers who had by now discarded human sacrifice and performed their holocausts while fasting and talking incessantly about God. Besides, the Jews inspected the stars by night, turned their eyes towards them, and invoked them in their prayers.

The notion that the Jews were philosophers recurs in a book about India by Megasthenes who was an ambassador to that country on behalf of Seleucus I in about 292 and who reported what he had seen. His idea that the Jews were to the Syrians what the Brahmans were to the Indians gained favor (*F. Gr. H.* 715 F.3 Jacoby). Clearchus of Soli, another pupil of Aristotle, who must have read his Megasthenes, went a step further and suggested that the Jews were in fact the descendants of the philosophers of India, whom he called *Kalanoi*. The *Kalanoi* in their turn were descended from the Persian *magi* (fr. 5–13 Wehrli). Oriental wisdom was thus unified in a genealogical tree in which the Jews were the descendants of the Persian wise men. Clearchus wrote a dialogue on sleep, in which he introduced his master Aristotle as the main speaker. Aristotle was made to report what was obviously an imaginary conversation with a Jewish sage whom he supposedly met somewhere in Asia Minor. The Jew had left Judea, where the capital has a name difficult to pronouce (they call it Ierusalem) and had come down to the sea. He had visited many nations and was a Greek not only in language, but in soul. Having talked to so many sages, he was able to instruct Aristotle. What his wisdom was about we are not told directly; but Hans Lewy (*HTR* 31 [1938]: 205–36) argued plausibly that it was about experiments in induced lethargy (as after all the title of Clearchus's dialogue about sleep suggests). Such experiments had a bearing on the problem of the nature of the human soul. We now know a little more about Clearchus of Soli, thanks to an unusual inscription which was recently published and admirably illustrated by Louis Robert. In the French excavations at Ai Khanoum in Afghanistan an inscription was found with a series of sentences of Delphic wisdom. An introductory epigram states that Clearchus copied them exactly in Delphi and brought them to this remote place of Bactriana. There seems to be little doubt that Robert is right in identifying this Clearchus with the pupil of Aristotle (*CRAIBL* [1968]: 416–57). This means that he traveled widely and explored the East in which he was interested.

The picture is consistent. In the first thirty or forty years after the destruction of the Persian Empire, Greek philosophers and historians discovered the Jews. They depicted them—both in fact and in fiction— as priestly sages of the type the East was expected to produce. The writers were important and responsible persons. They certainly meant to impress the Greek readers with the wisdom of the Jews. They probably expected to have Jewish readers too. We have no way of measuring the immediate impact of this writing on Jewish readers because we have no document we can safely date about 300 B.C. But if it is true that Kohelet, Ecclesiastes, wrote in the early third century B.C., one must acknowledge that at least one of the Jewish sages was not prepared to play the part the Greeks had assigned to him. Whatever may be said about Ecclesiastes—and many things have been said about him—he decried traditional wisdom. He was certainly a God-fearing man but the God of his fathers was above him, not with him—exactly the opposite position to that of Spinoza. He saw little sense in life. He had nothing of the self-assurance the Greeks liked to attribute to wise Jewish men. At the other end of the social scale Moschos, the son of Moschion, the Jewish slave, has now emerged from a most improbable place—from the temple of Amphiaraus in Boeotia. Anxious about his prospects of liberation, the slave Moschos went for a night of incuba-tion to the temple and had a dream in which the divine pair Amphiaraus and Hygieia ordered him to write down what he had seen and to set it up in stone by the altar. This inscription must be roughly contemporary with Kohelet—that is, not later than 250 B.C. "The first Greek Jew," as David Lewis called him (*JSS* 2 [1957]: 264–66), shows himself as a frightened little being who had been sold into slavery in a remote land. He had not forgotten that he was a Jew, but had recognized the power of the gods of his masters and had acted in accordance with their orders. He was not ready for the role of the philosopher-priest either.

3

Behind Kohelet and Moschos the world had moved fast, and what was already at the start a semi-utopian picture by Greek philosophers soon became absurd.

More and more Greeks and Macedonians moved into Palestine, either on royal initiative or by choice: they encouraged the Hellenization of the natives. Greek cities developed, especially along the Mediterranean coast and near the Sea of Tiberias. Some of the cities—such as Acco, Dor, Jaffa, Ascalon, Gaza, Pella, Philadelphia, Scythopolis, Samaria— were ancient towns which changed style and occasionally names: Phila- delphia is the new name for Rabbat-Ammon; Scythopolis for Bet-Shean. The Greek cities were fortresses, markets, and intellectual centers. Saul Weinberg's exploration at Tel Anafa in Upper Galilee is now beginning to give us an idea of a small Hellenistic center of the second century B.C. in its intercourse with Phoenician towns and with the Greek world of the eastern Mediterranean. Menippus, the Greek counterpart of Kohe- let, came from Gadara in Transjordan; he was Hellenized rather than Greek. The same applies to his later fellow-citizens Meleager, the subtle writer of eipgrams, and Philodemus the Epicurean. Meleager was very conscious of his Semitic origins. From his imaginary tomb he greeted the passer-by trilingually: "If you are a Syrian, Salam; if you are a Phoenician, Naidios [the word is certainly corrupt]; if you are a Greek, Chaire; and say the same yourself" (*Anth. Gr.* 7.419). One of Meleager's rivals in love was a Jew, and Meleager commented with resignation: "Love burns hot even on cold Sabbaths" (5.160). This is the idyllic part of a transformation which had far harsher sides. As the events of the second century were to show, Jews and Gentiles could be beastly to each other on Palestinian soil.

In the third century B.C., Judea proper was a small part of Palestine: it was almost identifiable with the territory of the city of Jerusalem, and as such it was still envisaged by Polybius in the middle of the second century B.C. (16, fr.39). Samaria and Galilee were outside it. The Samari- tans—or at least those of them who were not entirely Hellenized—had built up a religious center of their own on Mount Gerizim in circum- stances which contradictory legends have rendered unrecognizable. A council of laymen and priests under the presidency of the High Priest had a large measure of autonomy in its government of Jerusalem, but the presence of Ptolemaic garrisons in the country must be assumed. The Zenon Papyri have shown how in about 259 B.C. the agents of the finance minister Apollonius operated in the interests of their master: one of his estates was at Bet Anat in Galilee (*CPJ* I:1–5). From the same papyri we learn that the Ptolemies had picked up the well-known Sheikh of Transjordan, Tobiah, to command the military settlers in his territory. Tobiah was a Jew by religion but had his own temple on his own land—and nobody seems to have questioned his orthodoxy. One of his ancestors was Tobiah "the Ammonite slave" who gave trouble to Nehemiah (Neh. 2:10; 13:4). One of his sons, Joseph, became the chief tax-collector for Judea about 230 B.C. (Josephus *Ant.* XII.160ff.). The High Priest and his council had to reckon with the Tobiads. They were not in a position to remind them that "an Ammonite and a Moabite shall not enter the congregation of the Lord" (Deut. 23:4)—if it is true that the Tobiads were Ammonites. The slave trade was as rampant as ever, and Ptolemy Philadelphus had to intervene to prohibit attempts at enslaving the free people of Palestine (*SB* 8008).

The pressures of the new society were equally manifest in the emigration of Jews from Judea. Here again compulsion and free choice combined. Egypt was a traditional and obvious place for needy Jews to go. The basic figures we have for this emigration—one hundred thousand prisoners of war brought from Palestine into Egypt by Ptolemy I (*Aristeas* 12–14) and one million Jews in Egypt at the time of Philo (*In Flaccum* 43)—are almost certainly both false. Jews went into Egypt to exercise the old professions at which they were good—they were soldiers, tillers, shepherds. The transition from soldier to peasant and vice versa was normal. The strongly centralized administration gave Jews opportunities to enter the king's service as policemen and tax-collectors; foreigners were preferred in such posts. Papyri are less informative about economic life in Alexandria. We know therefore less about Jews as artisans, traders, and bankers in the city; but they existed. The Third Book of Maccabees (3:10) has a reference to Greeks who were business partners of Jews in Alexandria about the end of the third century. Egypt was probably the point of departure for further emigration to Cyrene, to Greece, and to Italy. There were Jewish communities of some size in Sicyon, Sparta, Delos, Cos, and Rhodes in the second part of the second century B.C. In 139 B.C. Jews were thrown out of Rome for obnoxious religious propaganda (Valerius Maximus 1.3.3). The creation of a vast diaspora favored the priestly class in Jerusalem, as it increased the number of those who paid tribute to the Temple. Pilgrimages to Jerusalem became a much more solemn and expensive occasion. But the description of these pilgrimages in Philo (*De Spec. Leg.* 1.69), in the Acts of the Apostles (2:5–11) and in Josephus clearly reflects the later conditions of the *pax romana*, and the commercialization of religious devotion by Herodes.

The figure of 2,700,000 pilgrims per year, which is given by Josephus (*War* VI.9.3), is another of those impossible data with which the historian of antiquity has to learn to live. Even on a far smaller scale the pilgrimages to Jerusalem of the third century B.C. must have represented important events. They provided a meeting point for people who were increasingly diversified in language, manners, status, and even political allegiance. The Babylonian Jews were loyal to the Seleucids; eight thousand of them fought off an attack of marauding Galatians, according to the Second Book of Maccabees (8:20). Louis Finkelstein has shown to my satisfaction—but not, I must admit, to everybody's satisfaction—that the Midrash of the Passover Haggadah reflects these conflicts of political allegiance. Legends about the Babylonian and Persian period were revived—or perhaps invented for the first time—to encourage faithfulness to the Mosaic Law in the new conditions. The first part of the Book of Daniel (approximately chaps. 1–6) and the Books of Esther and Judith are more likely to belong to the third than to the second century B.C. They combine edification with entertainment. They show concern for the preservation of the Law, but no pressing anxiety. There is not in them that somber atmosphere of a mortal struggle which we find in the second part of Daniel.

The fact that the Mediterranean diaspora had rapidly become Greek posed a problem about the knowledge of the Torah. In Palestine and Babylonia Hebrew had remained a literary language. Oral translation of the Bible into Aramaic was sufficient to keep the ignorant informed. In Egypt knowledge of Hebrew became exceptional, while there were all the attractions of Greek literature. The Torah had to be made accessible in Greek both for religious service and for private reading. That meant a written translation. From the Torah the translation was later extended to the rest of the Bible. The process may have taken two centuries. The Book of Esther was probably translated only in 78/77 B.C.

The translation must also have helped proselytism, which acquired quite different dimensions as soon as the Jews began to speak Greek. I do not know of any Hellenistic evidence to show that a Gentile became a Jew or a sympathizer because he had read the Bible. But Philo says that many Gentiles—that is, I presume, sympathizers—took part in the annual festival on the island of Pharos to celebrate the translation of the LXX (*Vita Mosis* 2.41). The sacred books had become accessible to those who were interested in Judaism. There is, however, no sign that the Gentiles at large ever became acquainted with the Bible: it was bad Greek. No Hellenistic poet or philosopher quoted it, although modern scholars have sometimes deluded themselves on this subject. The first certain quotation of the Bible in a Greek philosopher is to be found in the treatise *On the Sublime* attributed to Longinus which is usually dated in the first century A.D. (9.8). Behind it there is probably the teaching of the rhetorician Caecilius of Calacte, who was a Jew. It is the parochial character of the LXX—its obvious derivation from the methods of oral translation in the Synagogue—which makes it improbable that it should have been translated by command of Ptolemy II. I never disagree lightly with Elias Bickerman who has defended this tradition, already current in the second century B.C.—only one century after the alleged event. Bickerman argued that in antiquity big enterprises of translation were due to public, not private, initiative. But he could quote only the case of the thirty books on agriculture by the Carthaginian Mago which were translated into Latin by order of the Roman Senate (Pliny, *N. H.*18.22). The Romans had a different attitude to translations from that of the Greeks. In the third century B.C. Livius Andronicus was brought to Rome to be a semi-official translator of Greek poetry into Latin. In the absence of anything comparable among the Greeks, I hesitate to attribute to royal initiative a translation so clearly born within the precincts of the synagogue. The LXX remained an exclusive Jewish possession until the Christians took it over. We do not even know whether it was deposited in that great Ptolemaic foundation, the library of Alexandria.

The consequence must now be faced. About 300 B.C. Greek intellectuals presented the Jews to the Greek world as philosophers, legislators, and wise men. A few decades later, the alleged philosophers and legislators made public in Greek their own philosophy and legislation. The gentile world remained indifferent. Other Semites, the Phoenician Zeno of Citium and Chrysippus of Soli, came to Athens and easily established themselves as masters of wisdom in the very center of intellectual life in Greece, because they accepted polytheism and made the traditional language of Greek philosophy their own. The contrast was glaring. The failure of the LXX to arouse the interest of the pagan intelligentsia of the third century B.C. was the end of the myth of the Jewish philosopher.

Let us consider more closely what was implied in the Greek refusal to look at the Bible. It meant that the Greeks expected the Jews not to translate their holy books, but to produce an account of themselves according to the current methods and categories of ethnography. This was an old practice in the Greek world. In the fifth century B.C. Xanthus of Lydia had written in Greek a book on Lydian history and customs which was probably inspired by Herodotus. In the third century books of this kind were multiplying. The Egyptian Manetho, the Babylonian Berossus, and the Roman Fabius Pictor wrote the histories of their respective countries in a suitable version for the benefit of the Greeks. It was easy for the Jews to comply with this custom because Hecateus of Abdera had produced a little model of what was expected of them. Thus, in a sense, the Jews were asked to perpetuate their own myth in the terms in which the Greeks had invented it. Some Jews obliged. We know that a Demetrius (whom Flavius Josephus foolishly calls Demetrius of Phalerum) composed a biblical history, including the chronological enquiries which were fashionable. This must have happened in the late third century. Not much later a man who was probably a Samaritan composed another history of biblical times. But the most famous of such treatises about the Jews were written in the middle of the second century. Eupolemus, who was Judas Maccabeus's envoy to Rome in 161 B.C., composed a work in which one could read an exchange of letters between the twelve-year-old Solomon and his client kings Vaphres of Egypt and Suron of Tyre (Eusebius *Praep. Ev.* 9.31–4). Another historian, the very mysterious Malchus or Cleodemus, whose Jewish origin is only probable, presented the sons of Abraham as companions of Hercules who married the daughter of one of them (Josephus *Ant.* I.240). Aristobulus of Paneas allegorized Hebrew tradition in a dialogue in which Ptolemy VI (181–145 B.C.) asked questions about the Bible. This approach made it inherently possible for the Jews to claim to have been the teachers of the Greeks owing to their own greater antiquity. About 200 B.C. the biographer Hermippus accepted without difficulty the nation that Pythagoras had been a pupil of Jews and Thracians. The Jews were also entitled to seek respectable genealogical connections with the Greeks. Somebody—either Jew or Greek—invented a common descent of Jews and Spartans from Abraham. It is apparent from the Second Book of Maccabees that at least some Jewish circles admitted the claim—which had many parallels in the Hellenistic world. It was also established that the Jews had been friends of the inhabitants of Pergamum in the time of Abraham (*Ant.* XIV.255). Indeed, Abraham, more cosmopolitan and less legalistic than Moses, became the favorite hero of such concoctions.

All this was not only demoralizing. It was positively dangerous because it involved the Jews in a game in which they were bound to be discredited. The game, as I have indicated, was played in an atmosphere of mounting tensions. In Palestine the Jews had to face the intruding Greeks. In Egypt they were the intruders. In the third century B.C. they were still cooperating with the Greeks in Egypt, but they were becoming unpopular with the natives. Two theories about the Jews circulated under the name of Manetho. One identified them with the invading Hyksos, the other with lepers. It is a famous question whether the well-deserving historian Manetho was responsible for either of these theories. The Jews defended themselves by quoting Hecateus of Abdera. Here again it is a famous question whether what Flavius Josephus and Eusebius quote under the name of Hecateus is authentic. Hans Lewy is another scholar with whom one can disagree only at one's peril, and Hans Lewy maintained in an admirable paper that at least what Josephus quotes is authentic Hecateus. I am, however, inclined to believe that the authentic Hecateus could not have stated, as Josephus makes him state, that Alexander gave the Samaritan territory free of tax to the Jews. Whether authentic or not, this material from Manetho and Hecateus was used for mean purposes of reciprocal abuse. Forgeries of Greek poetry completed this work.

The worst was still to come. In the second century the religious and social conflicts became far more acute. When Palestine was turned into Syrian territory in 198, it was soon involved in the process of decomposition of the Hellenistic system under Roman pressure. In Egypt the Jews had to take sides in the hostilities between the various factions which competed for whatever power was left under the virtual protectorate of Rome. Accusations of ritual murder and of anti-Greek oaths were levelled against the Jews. Somebody insinuated that the Jews worshipped a donkey's head in their Temple. The story goes back to Mnaseas, a writer of the second half of the second century B.C. (*C. Ap.* 2.112). It became widely known through the book written against the Jews by Apollonius Molon, one of Cicero's teachers.

It is not my purpose to follow up in detail the story of the literary abuse which accompanied and followed the Maccabean rebellion and the much less glorious establishment of the Hasmonean dynasty. I shall, however, discuss the tradition about the Maccabees in my next lecture. What is clear is that with the elimination of the only authentic document—the Bible—from the picture, the discussion was bound to degenerate. The philosophers were not allowed to produce their philosophy. The *Ersatz* they were asked to give, and gave, was of low quality.

While peace still lasted, but with some expectation of trouble to come, Simon ben Jesus ben Eleazar ben Sira, as he was apparently called, wrote his meditations—the *Ecclesiasticus*. They must belong to the period 190–170 B.C. Ben Sira had wandered abroad (51.13), and his ideal scribe was a man who had traveled "through the lands of the peoples" and had tested "good and evil among men" (39.4). I do not see any clear trace that Ben Sira had read Greek books, and I do not believe that he needed the *Iliad* to learn that men "sprout and fade like leaves of a tree" (14.18). But he had certainly seen something of the Greek civilization, with its philosophic schools, theatres, and gymnasia. He foresaw a war and prayed for the victory of his people. He also saw social antagonisms growing in Palestine and advised charity and justice. But he had really no message, either for victory or for reform. His book, steeped as it was in the Proverbs and in the Psalms, quietly reaffirmed Jewish traditional faith against the temptations of Hellenism: "Fear God with all your heart and reverence his priests" (7.29). Ben Sira praised the fathers of old and described the High Priest Simon son of Jochanan in his majestic appearance when he went up to the altar (50.11). He concluded (if this is the correct reading) "May my soul delight in my Yeshibah" (51.29).

As a personal evaluation of a hundred years of Jewish-Greek contacts this was a remarkable statement. It was a return to the Bible by a scribe who had seen the consequences of Hellenization. By writing in Hebrew and preserving their spiritual independence, men like Kohelet and Ben Sira saved the Jews from the intellectual sterility which characterized Egyptian and Babylonian life under the Hellenistic kings. The Romans, too, avoided total absorption in Hellenistic modes of thought, but after all they were politically independent and soon became more powerful than any Hellenistic kingdom. The Jews remained alive by sheer obstinacy of faith. There is, however, another side of the story—and this will be our end for today. The Hebrew text of Ben Sira, which accompanied the sectarians of Qumran and the defenders of Masada, was lost in the early Middle Ages and was only partially recovered in the Cairo *Geniza* at the end of the last century. The book by the man who had repudiated Greek wisdom lived on through the centuries in the Greek version made by his grandson—an émigré to Egypt in 132 B.C.

7

The Influence of Hellenistic Civilization in Palestine down to the Maccabean Period (1980)

In his massive and controversial work *Judaism and Hellenism* (1970), Martin Hengel marshaled evidence in support of the claim that the tumultuous events of the second century in Judea must be understood against the background of a formative Hellenistic influence on Judaism during the preceding centuries. The argument ultimately addresses the causes of the Maccabean revolt. Was it Jewish opposition to the forcible and unprovoked imposition of repressive anti-Jewish regulations? Could it have been, instead, the response to an extreme movement of Hellenization within the Jewish community which was eventually supported by the Seleucid house? In treating this issue, Hengel assembled and analyzed all available evidence concerning the relationship between Judaism and Hellenism down to the outbreak of the Maccabean uprising.

The following chapter (from a later study by him) provides an accurate and terse summary of the positions advanced in *Judaism and Hellenism*. Hengel surveys the various types of evidence we have been considering for the fourth and third centuries in order to assess the degree to which Judaism had been Hellenized. Deeply influenced by Bickerman's views on the nature of Jewish religion and society, Hengel's essay forms a fitting epilogue to this anthology.

IT WAS IN PALESTINE that the Jews made the acquaintance of the Macedonians and Greeks in the time after Alexander's expedition. Not only did they discover them as a cultural force; they were also confronted with their absolute military and political superiority. Even more markedly than under Persian rule the Jews now became the passive object of history and were the helpless victims of the changing configurations of power in Syria and Palestine during the struggle of the Diadochoi. The fact that they are either not mentioned at all in the Greek sources of the time, or only appear on the periphery (Agatharcides and Hecateus of Abdera), only shows their political impotence. The renewal of prophetic prediction in the early "apocalyptic" of the anonymous author Deutero-Zechariah[1] or the Isaiah apocalypse shows that under the impact of the cruelty of war and the arrogance of the new rulers, God's intervention to save his people was a matter of intense expectation. Now the Greeks could take the place of the traditional opponents, the Assyrians and the Babylonians, as the eschatological enemies of the people of God.[2] That means that the first stage was not cultural encounter but polemical confrontation, which is continued in the image of the cruel and godless "fourth kingdom" of later apocalyptic. The emigration of Jews to Egypt under the rule of Ptolemy I Soter, reported by Pseudo-Hecateus, will—as Pseudo-Aristeas suggests—have largely been the result of external compulsion. By contrast, the writings of the Chronicler show that what made an impression was above all the military power of the Macedonians and the fortresses built by the Ptolemies, along with their agriculture based on large estates;[3] at the same time, the greater harshness of the foreign rule led to a picture of the past painted in ideal colors, with a heightened contrast between good and evil.

Whereas the destruction of Samaria and the foundation of a Macedonian military colony considerably reduced the political and economic supremacy of their northern fellow-countrymen akin in descent and religion, the specifically Jewish region of the old Persian subsatrapy of Yehud suffered no ill consequences from the foundation of Greco-Macedonian military colonies on the coastal plain and in Transjordania.[4] The great trade routes bypassed Jerusalem, and the zeal with which the

1. Cf. H. Gese, "Anfang und Ende der Apokalyptik dargestellt am Sacharjabuch," *ZThK* 70 (1973): 20–49, esp. 41ff.

2. Zech. 9:13; Dan. 7:7ff.; 8:5ff.; Ethiopian Enoch 90.1ff.; cf. also the allegory of the shepherds in Zech.11:4ff.

3. 2 Chron. 26:9–15.

4. A. Alt, *Kleine Schriften* 2:396ff.

Phoenician coastal cities adopted Greek language and Greek ways of life—at least outwardly—need not necessarily have been imitated immediately in the hill-country of Judea. However, once political conditions had been stabilized at the beginning of the third century B.C., a turning point will have come. The new ruler Ptolemy I Soter was concerned to further military and economic development in the newly won bulwark formed by Palestine, a policy in which he was followed by his no less brilliant son Ptolemy II Philadelphus; in the wake of this, Palestinian Judaism, which was conservative simply by virtue of its geographical setting, could no longer escape the spirit of the new age. The small area of the Jewish territory around Jerusalem and the relative poverty of the population compared with the rich Phoenician and Palestinian coastal cities should not blind us to the fact that there was a vigorous intellectual life in the various Jewish wisdom schools in the country, stimulated not least by the growing Jewish Diaspora in Egypt, Babylonia, and Syria. Since, as we saw, the Jews adopted the Greek language and a Greek way of life relatively quickly in Egypt, because they came as military settlers, merchants, craftsmen, peasants, or slaves, this influence will in turn have had an effect on the home country through those who returned.[5] The fragments of the Jewish literature of the fourth and third centuries as they have come down to us in the late works of the Old Testament canon and in the apocrypha, show a great variety of content and literary forms; nor was this literature all religious in character: some of it took the form of secular belles lettres.[6] Even though we must be very careful about arguing for "Hellenistic influence" in this early period, here at least we come up against an intellectual climate that was prepared to be stimulated and influenced in a number of ways; in particular some tendencies in the development of Jewish wisdom and also in apocalyptic made them particularly open to such an encounter with Greek ideas.[7] In the papyrus documents connected with the journey to Palestine made by Zeno as agent of Apol-

5. M. Hengel, *Judaism and Hellenism* (Philadelphia, 1974; London, 1970), 1:37–38, 248; M. Smith, *Palestinian Parties and Politics That Shaped the Old Testament* (New York, 1971), 71.

6. M. Smith, in *Fischer Weltgeschichte 5 (Griechen und Perser*, ed. H. Bengtson [Frankfurt am Main, 1965]), 364ff.; idem, *Palestinian Parties*, 158ff.; he wants to ascribe this literature to "pious members of the assimilationist party" (p. 159); Hengel, *Judaism and Hellenism* 1:113ff.

7. Hengel, *Judaism and Hellenism* 1:107ff., 247ff.

lonius the finance minister in 259 B.C., we find a great many contacts between Greek officers, officials, merchants, and adventurers, and the local Semitic inhabitants, including Jews. The Ptolemaic administration sought to administer its colony just as strictly and exploit it with just as much thoroughness as the Egyptian mother country itself. Greek agents and "excisemen" visited every last village for this purpose. The numerous garrisons and military colonies which had to protect the frontier province against the Seleucids in the north and the Arabic tribes in the East, and against inner unrests, were ethnically mixed and furthered the process of economic and cultural integration. Jerusalem, too, seems to have had a permanent garrison with which the Jewish population had to live. In addition there were regular contacts with the numerous armies which crossed Palestine and, say in winter, were billeted among the local population in the villages. It was probably contacts of this kind which made young Jews, too, want to be mercenaries so that they could enjoy the same privileges as the foreign soldiers. Between the death of Alexander the Great and the Roman conquest by Pompey (323–63 B.C.), Morton Smith counts "at least 200 campaigns fought in or across Palestine."[8] One difference from Egypt, where the native aristocracy no longer had a role, was that the Ptolemaic officials and military forces were prepared to work in close collaboration with the local upper classes in the province and to allow them to have a share in its produce.[9] Thus we find a mixed Macedonian-Jewish military colony in Ammanitis in Transjordania commanded not by a Greek but by the Jewish magnate Tobias, whose family controlled the area even in Persian times and whose predecessors had once caused Nehemiah very great difficulties.[10] According to Josephus he was the brother-in-law of the high priest. Zeno paid a visit to his citadel in Ammanitis with great success, and he later appears in correspondence with Apollonius and the king in Alexandria, treating them almost as his equals. He sends the king rare animals for his zoo, and provides Apollonius with young slaves. In this correspondence he also proves himself to be a very liberal Jew. Of course he has a Greek secretary. As commander of a Ptolemaic unit

8. Smith, *Palestinian Parties*, 63ff. (quotation is from p. 64 and see pp. 111–112 above); Hengel, *Judaism and Hellenism* 1:14–15.

9. M. Rostovtzeff, *Social and Economic History of the Hellenistic World* (Oxford, 1941), 213ff.; V. Tcherikover, *Hellenistic Civilization and the Jews* (Philadelphia, 1959), 64ff., 132ff.

10. Tcherikover and Fuks, *CPJ* 1:115ff., nos. 1–5; B. Mazar, "The Tobiads," *IEJ* 7 (1957): 137–45, 229–38; Smith, *Palestinian Parties*, 92, 132–33, 258 n.38.

with Macedonian subordinates he himself must have also been capable of both speaking and writing Greek.[11]

According to the Tobiad romance in Josephus, his son Joseph became a figure of great political and economic significance in Jerusalem—presumably under Ptolemy III Euergetes. Not only did he become *prostatēs*, representative of the Jewish *ethnos* to the Ptolemaic kingdom, but he also succeeded in securing for himself supervision of tax collection throughout the whole province of "Syria and Phoenicia," as he had particularly good connections with the royal house. He forcibly overcame individual Hellenistic cities which sought to resist the new tax authority. He maintained a permanent agent in Alexandria who administered his gigantic fortunes and kept relations happy by sending "gifts" to the court and royal officials. We may take it for granted that this Joseph was thoroughly Hellenized and also brought up his sons in Greek ways. That is the only explanation for his rapid rise. His youngest son, Hyrcanus, later became supreme commander of the family possessions in the Ammanitis including the Ptolemaic military settlement, where he "levied tribute from the barbarians" (*kākei dietriben phorologōn tous barbarous*); in other words, he subjected the Nabataean and Arabian tribes there. His brothers continued to have great political influence in Jerusalem.[12] Their descendants became the protagonists of the radical Hellenistic reform which followed the accession of Antiochus IV Epiphanes in 175 B.C.[13] Through the Tobiad family in particular, remote and retrograde Jerusalem was introduced to a new, luxurious life style which was certainly in conflict with the strict principles of ancient Israelite tradition and which Koheleth describes tersely and aptly: "Feasts are held at will, and wine gladdens life, and money answers everything."[14]

The gradual invasion of Hellenistic civilization is also clear from the appearance of Greek names. In Phoenician territory we find numerous Greek names and Greco-Semitic double names as early as the third century. We find a vivid mixture of Phoenician, Idumean, Jewish, and Greek names in the Phoenician colony of Marisa, founded in the middle of the third century. It was the chief center in Idumea, only about

11. V. Tcherikover, "Palestine under the Ptolemies," *Mizraim* 4/5 (1937): 37, 49–50; Hengel, *Judaism and Hellenism* 1:59–60, 267ff.

12. Josephus *Ant.* XII.160ff. Quotation from XII.222.

13. Josephus *War* I.31ff.; *Ant.* XII.239–40; the sons of Tobias support the radical Menelaus. Cf. Schürer, Vermes, and Millar, *History* 1:149–50, n. 30.

14. Koh, 10:19; cf. Hengel, *Judaism and Hellenism* 1:47ff.

twenty-five miles southwest of Jerusalem and in a cultural milieu which had already been fully Hellenized.[15] There was also presumably a Sidonian colony of the same kind, in Samaritan Shechem (Sikima). Individual fragments of inscriptions of Greek names have also been found there.[16] Goodenough's verdict on the tombs of Marisa may also be applied to Shechem, and indeed to large areas of Palestine at the beginning of the second century: "It seems reasonable to suppose that we have here a picture of the sort of syncretizing Hellenization against which, as it affected Jews, the Maccabees revolted. Had syncretism gone on in this way among the Jews, Judaism would probably be now as little known as the other religions of the ancient Levant."[17]

We find Greek names even among "conservative" Jews in Palestine: the fathers of the delegates sent to Sparta or Rome by the Maccabeans Jonathan and Simon, Numenius, son of Antiochus, Antipater, son of Jason, and Alexander, son of Dorotheos, will all have been born at the end of the third century, B.C.[18] The second son of the high priest Simon the Just appears under the name Jason. He displaced his conservative brother Onias III and in 175 became the real power behind the Hellenistic reform, which sought to transform Jerusalem into a Greek *polis*. With royal consent, and to the general approval of the aristocracy of Jerusalem, he established a gymnasium alongside the Temple and had the sons of the high-born educated there as ephebes.[19] However, after a few years he had to give way to the even more radical brothers, Menelaus, Lysimachus, and Simon, from the priestly family of Bilga, who were closely associated with the Tobiads. After an unsuccessful attempt at rebellion, Jason fled via Petra and Egypt to his supposed relatives in Sparta.[20] According to rabbinic accounts, because of this the priestly order of Bilga was later excluded from service at sacrifices "for all time," allegedly because the daughter of a priest, Miriam, had married a Greek officer and had desecrated the altar in the Temple.

15. J. P. Peters and H. Thiersch, *Painted Tombs in the Necropolis of Marissa* (London, 1905); F.-M. Abel, "Tombeaux récemment découverts à Marisa," *RB* 34 (1925): 267–75; Hengel, *Judaism and Hellenism* 1:62ff.

16. G. E. Wright, *Shechem* (London and New York, 1964), 183; Hengel, *Judaism and Hellenism* 1:62–63.

17. E. R. Goodenough, *Jewish Symbols in the Greco-Roman Period* (New York, 1953), 1:74.

18. 1 Macc. 12:16; 14:22, 24; 15:15; cf. Josephus *Ant.* XIII.169; XIV.146. On this and what follows see Hengel, *Judaism and Hellenism* 1:64–65.

19. 2 Macc. 4:7ff.; 1 Macc. 1:11ff.; cf. Hengel, *Judaism and Hellenism* 1:73ff., 277ff.

20. 2 Macc. 3:4; 4:23ff., 29, 39ff.; and Hengel, *Judaism and Hellenism* 1:279ff.

Evidently at the time of the reform the members of this order had been unconditionally in favor of assimilation. In his enumeration of the priestly orders, Eleazar Kalir stills calls them "the Greek order." There are a few other indications of Jewish mixed marriages in early Hellenistic Palestine.[21] There was even free love. Meleager of Gadara in Transjordania complains in an epigram that his beloved Dema is warming herself with a Jewish lover on the cold sabbath.[22] The otherwise unknown Antigonus of Socoh, who according to Pirqe Aboth 1.3 received the Law from Simon the Just and rejected the expectation of reward as slavish, was probably also a contemporary of Jason and Menelaus. At a later date he was made the spiritual father of the Sadducees. The only two officers of the Maccabean cavalry from Transjordania, presumably from the cleruchy of Tobias and Hyrcanus, to be mentioned by name are called Dositheos and Sosipatros.[23] John, from the priestly family of Haqqoṣ, who negotiated with Antiochus III about 200 b.c., called his son Eupolemus. Under Judas Maccabeus he became leader of the first embassy in Rome and composed what was presumably a historical work about the Jewish kings in Greek.[24] Under the Hasmoneans this predilection for Greek names and Greek culture continued in the upper class, despite all the resistance from the circles faithful to the Torah. It is striking that we find foreign names equally among the advocates of the Hellenistic reform and their Maccabean opponents. A large number of the seventy-two elders of the Letter of Aristeas, who come to Alexandria to translate the Torah, have Greek names like Theodosius, Theodotus, Theophilus, Dositheus, and Jason. The author of the letter evidently took this for granted.[25]

Even more important than the Greek names of individual translators is the fact that the author also takes it for granted that the seventy-two Jewish scholars from Palestine "not only had a thorough knowledge of Jewish literature but also had a thorough knowledge of Greek."[26] That means that at about the middle of the second century b.c. the author thought it quite possible that educated Palestinian Jews could have a perfect knowledge of Greek. As early as the first half of the third

---

21. *T. Sukka* 4.28 (line 200): *j. Sukka* 55d, 40ff.; *b. Sukka* 56b. For mixed marriages see Smith, *Palestinian Parties*, 84ff., 154, 174, 195, though of course he exaggerates.

22. *Greek Anthology* 5, 160; cf. 172–73.

23. 2 Macc. 12:19, 24, 35; see Hengel, *Judaism and Hellenism* 1:276.

24. 2 Macc. 4:11; cf. 1 Macc. 8:17; see p. 158, n. 44 below.

25. Ps. Aristeas 47–50.

26. 121: *alla kai tēs tōn hellēnikōn ephrontisan ou parergōs kataskeuēs.*

century B.C., Clearchus of Soloi presupposes that Jews from Jerusalem had a Greek education.[27] Furthermore, one of the foundations of the political success of the various Jewish delegations, first in Antioch and then in Sparta and Rome, was that their members could speak and write perfect Greek.[28]

The same is true of communications with Diaspora Judaism in Egypt, Asia Minor, and the Aegean, where the knowledge of Aramaic had quickly been lost. If the Temple in Jerusalem wanted to maintain and develop its significance as the religious center of Judaism in the Hellenistic world, it had to keep in touch with the communities there. The pilgrims who came to the feasts in Jerusalem from the West brought their Greek mother tongue to Jerusalem.[29] The various documents in Greek from the second century B.C. in Josephus and in Maccabees indicate an experienced Greek chancery in the Temple. The Hasmoneans later attempted quite deliberately to strengthen the religious and political influence of the Jerusalem sanctuary on the Diaspora, and to this end even encouraged the dissemination of nationalistic Jewish literature in the Greek-speaking Diaspora and probably also its translation into Greek. Herod gladly continued this policy, and even more markedly than the Hasmoneans made himself the political advocate and protector of Diaspora Judaism. Under him Jerusalem became even more of a Greek-speaking city—at least as far as the upper classes were concerned.[30]

We find the first slight traces of the influence of Greek in Koheleth, in Ben Sira, and with the musical instruments in the Book of Daniel. They are then extraordinarily numerous in later Jewish rabbinic literature.[31] Literary Hebrew and Aramaic as we find them, say, in the writings of the Qumran library, give the impression of being almost artificially pure in comparison with the spoken idioms of later Talmudic literature. This suggests that foreign words had found their way into the vernacular substantially earlier, a fact which is now also confirmed by the Aramaic copper scroll of Qumran.[32]

27. Josephus C. Ap. I. 176–81.

28. 2 Macc. 4:5–6; 14:4ff.; 1 Macc. 8; 12:1ff.; 14:16ff.; etc.

29. A good example of this from Roman times is the Theodotus inscription CIJ II.333 no. 1404, cf. Sevenster, Do You Know Greek? 131ff.; Hengel, ZThK 72 (1975): 184–85; cf. 156ff. on the significance of Greek in Jerusalem in the New Testament period.

30. Cf. 2 Macc. 2:15; cf. also the colophon to the Greek Book of Esther, and E. Bickerman, "The Colophon of the Greek Book of Esther," JBL 63 (1944): 339–62.

31. Daniel 3:5, 7, 10, 15; Hengel, Judaism and Hellenism 1:60.

32. Hengel, Judaism and Hellenism 2:44 n. 24.

The establishment of a gymnasium with ephebes in Jerusalem in 175 B.C. would have been unthinkable had not the knowledge of Greek and in some respects of Greek literature not already been widespread among the Jerusalem aristocracy at this time. This also presupposes the existence of a Greek elementary school—presumably on a private basis—in the Jewish capital.[33]

A further indication of the penetration of Greek thought into Jerusalem is the claim that the Jews were related to the Spartans through Abraham, which presumably arose as early as the third century B.C. among circles which were well-disposed toward the Greeks. The starting point is the letter from the Spartan king Areus to the high priest Onias II. As King Areus I was killed at Corinth in 265 B.C., in the Chremonidean war, and the initiative in questions of affinity is hardly likely to have come from the Spartans, this letter may be a forgery. The Phoenicians similarly appealed to their affinity with the Greeks through Cadmus; according to Hecateus the ancestors of the Greeks once emigrated from Egypt with the Daneans under the leadership of Cadmus at the time when Moses set out for Palestine. According to the Jewish historian Cleodemus Malchus, Heracles married a granddaughter of Abraham in Libya. In Asia Minor the Pergamenes called attention to the former friendship of their ancestors with Abraham. Whereas the Romans claimed that they were descended from fugitives from Troy, various cities in southwestern Asia Minor claimed to be Lacedemonian colonies. A letter from the people of Tyre to Delphi, preserved on an inscription, calls the Delphians "kindred."[34] According to E. Bickerman, this sort of thing was regarded as an "entrance ticket into European culture,"[35] i.e., into the community of Hellenes. Constructions of this kind in the third century thus served as an ideological preparation for the transformation of Jerusalem into a Greek *polis* after 175 B.C. It is striking that even Jonathan the Maccabee referred to this Jewish Hellenistic legend in his attempt to strike up a political alliance with the Spartans, which certainly went against his hatred of the Greeks and

---

33. Ibid. 1:74ff.

34. 1 Macc. 12:6–23 (10:21); 2 Macc. 5:9; Josephus *Ant.* XII.226–27; XII.167; earlier literature in R. Marcus, *Josephus*, Loeb Classical Library (1961), 7:769; Hengel, *Judaism and Hellenism* 1:72–73; B. Cardauns, "Juden und Spartaner," *Hermes* 95 (1967): 317–24; S. Schüller, "Some Problems connected with the Supposed Common Ancestry of Jews and Spartans . . . ," *JSS* 1 (1956): 257–68; Schürer, Vermes, and Millar, *History* 1:184–85 n. 33. Smith, *Palestinian Parties*, 177–78, transfers the first contacts as far back as the Persian period.

35. *PW* XIV.1, 786, alluding to a saying by Heinrich Heine.

the national self-consciousness of his Hasidic compatriots. It is evident here that the Hasmoneans did not really slow down the "process of Hellenization" in Palestinian Judaism, but in fact continued it as soon as they themselves came to power.[36] The assertion of an affinity between the Jews and the Spartans may of course also be connected with the conservative attitude of both peoples towards their law given on the one hand by Moses and on the other by Lycurgus, along with their xenophobia and their pride in their military past.

Higher, literary Greek education also gradually began to find a footing in Palestine. Thus for example in Gaza and Sidon we find two extensive verse inscriptions in impeccable form from the period round about 200 B.C. The one from Gaza is the epitaph of two Ptolemaic officers and members of their family;[37] the one from Sidon is in honor of the suffete Diotimus for his victory in the panhellenic Nemean chariot race in Argos. The poem lays special emphasis on the mythological affinity between Argives, Thebans, and Phoenicians.[38] A graffito from one of the tombs of Marisa contains a skillful erotic poem in the genre of the Locrian hymn.[39] The fortress of Gadara in Transjordania was a special seedbed of Greek culture. Strabo, who in fact confuses Gadara with Gazara (Gezer), which had become Jewish in the Maccabean period,[40] mentions four famous writers who come from this city, remote from all other centers of ancient culture: "Philodemus the Epicurean, Meleager, Menippus the satirist, and Theodorus the Rhetorician from our days."[41] Menippus was presumably born towards the end of the fourth century and is said to have been sold as a slave to Sinope, in Pontus in Asia Minor. We might conclude from this that he was descended, not from new Greek settlers, but from Syrians, were not the theme of slaves and celebrated literary figures quite so widespread. This

36. Cf. also the tomb in Modein, 1 Macc. 13:25ff.; Josephus Ant. XIII.210ff.; C. Watzinger, Denkmäler Palästinas (Leipzig, 1935), 2:22–23, and Jason's tomb, L. Y. Rahmani et al., Atiqot 4 (1964).

37. P. Roussel, "Epitaphe de Gaza commémorant deux officiers de la garnison ptolémaïque," Aegyptus 13 (1933):145–51; W. Peek, Griechische Grabgedichte (Darmstadt, 1960), 112 n.162. Presumably an epidemic caused a number of deaths in the family. Cf. Hengel, Judaism and Hellenism 2:20 n.79.

38. E. Bickerman, "Sur une inscription grecque de Sidon," Mélanges R. Dussaud (Paris, 1939), 1:91–99; Hengel, Judaism and Hellenism 1:71–72.

39. W. Cronert, "Das Lied von Marisa," RheinMus 64 (1909): 433–34, Hengel, Judaism and Hellenism 2:56 n.192.

40. Schürer, Vermes, and Millar, History 1:191; cf. also the curse inscription, CIJ 1184.

41. XVI.2, 29 (759).

would in that case be an example of the degree to which even then Semites could become assimilated to Greek culture. Later he became a citizen of Thebes. According to Diogenes Laertius, who calls him a "Phoenician," he became the pupil of the Cynic Metrocles. He is the creator of the polemic philosophical genre of the satire. The new stylistic form combining prose and poetry which he introduced evidently has Semitic roots. A later Syrian, Lucian of Samosata, then completely transformed the Greek satire, with reference to Menippus. Meleager, the creator of the Greek Anthology, was born in the middle of the second century and educated in Tyre, where the "Phoenician school," which was significant for Greek lyric poetry, developed under Antipater of Sidon (about 170–100 B.C.). Meleager himself called his native city "Assyrian Attica," and a later epitaph gives it the honorific title *chrēstomousia*.

In the second century B.C., significant philosophers like the Stoic Boethus of Sidon and the Epicurean Zeno of Sidon taught in Phoenician cities. Meleager and the younger Philodemus were both marked by Epicurean *joie de vivre*. Ashkelon, too, became an intellectual center alongside Gadara in the second century B.C. and produced a series of significant philosophers and writers.[42] Of course the intellectual development of Hellenistic Palestine suffered a severe blow as a result of Jewish-Hasmonean and Arabic-Iturean expansion. Almost all the Palestinian poets and philosophers emigrated to the West, especially to Italy. The papyrus library of Herculaneum, some of which survives, goes back to the Epicurean Philodemus of Gadara. How far the lively intellectual milieu of the Phoenician cities, as of individual Greek settlements, like Gadara, extended its influence into the Jewish world must remain an open question. However, events during the Hellenistic reform show that the Hellenists in Jerusalem thought it particularly important to have good contacts with the Phoenician cities, as centers of Hellenistic civilization. Because of that, the citizens of the newly founded *polis* of Antiocheia in Jerusalem participated in the quinquennial festivals in Tyre which had been founded by Alexander, under the aegis of the high priest Jason. However, at that time they did not dare give directly to the Tyrian god Heracles Melkart the three hundred drachmae which the high priest had provided for a sacrifice, so the money was used to equip ships.[43] Even the pro-Maccabean Jewish

---

42. Hengel, *Judaism and Hellenism* 1:83–88.
43. 2 Macc. 4:18ff.; cf. 4:32, 39.

Palestinian "historian" Eupolemus still tells proudly how Solomon had once sent king Syron of Tyre a golden pillar which Syron had erected in "the temple of Zeus," that is, of the Phoenician Baal Shamem; this report is also confirmed by Tyrian historians.[44] Thus for example the Phoenician "historians" Laitos and Menander reported that Solomon had married the daughter of the Phoenician king when king Menelaus of Sparta visited Tyre after the capture of Troy.[45] Such elaborations of their own national history made it possible for Phoenicians and Jews on the one hand to stress their connection with superior Greek culture while at the same time pointing to the greater antiquity of their own tradition, which made them teachers of the Greeks. On a similar level is the assertion of Meleager of Gadara that Homer had been a Syrian, "since in accordance with the customs of his homeland he never has the Achaeans eating fish, although the Hellespont is full of them."[46] The Hellenistic-type designation of Jerusalem as Hierosolyma, which appears for the first time in Hecateus and in the Zeno papyri, but only late on in the Septuagint and in Hellenized authors,[47] may well be more than a fortuitous piece of nomenclature; it may be a deliberate Greek interpretation made by earlier Jewish Hellenistic circles which is connected with Homeric tradition. The first part of the word, *hiero-*, showed the holy city, like Hiera- or Hieropolis in Phrygia or like the Syrian Hierapolis-Bambyce or the various *Hierai-kōmai* in Asia Minor, to be a temple city. This corresponds with the report of Polybius quoted

44. Eusebius *Praep. Ev.* IX. 34, 16=Jacoby, F. Gr. Hist. 723 F 2; Hengel, *Judaism and Hellenism* 1:94; cf. Dio in Josephus *C. Ap.* I.112–13; Menander, *C. Ap.* I. 118; Theophilus, Eusebius *Praep. Ev.* IX.34.19 = Jacoby F. *Gr. H.* 733. The theme already occurs in Herod. II.44.1. See M. Hadas, *Hellenistic Culture*, 95–96, who sees in this reference a sign of a "considerable latitudinarism, or perhaps a tendency towards syncretism."

45. Clement of Alexandria, *Stromata*, I.114.2, and Tatian, *ad Graecos* 37 = Jacoby, F. *Gr. H.* 784 F1a and b.

46. Athenagoras IV.157b; cf. Hadas, *Hellenistic Culture*, 83.

47. PCZ 59004 = CPJ no. 2a/col. I, 3: PCZ 59005 = CPJ no. 2b; Hecateus of Abdera according to Diodore 40 fr. 3.3 = Jacoby, F. *Gr. H.* 264 F 5.3. Of course we do not know for certain whether Photius, who has preserved this fragment for us, or Diodore later "Graecized" the names. Ps. Hecateus (second century B.C.) also knows the Greek form of the name, see Josephus *C. Ap.* I.197. On the other hand, Clearchus of Soli (first half of the third century B.C.) still has *Hierousalēmē, C. Ap.* I.179. This is probably a "Graecism" from the Latin translator (*hierosolyma*). The Greek name was taken over by all the later non-Jewish writers from the third century B.C. on (Berossus, Ps. [?] Manetho, Agatharchides of Cnidus). See J. Jeremias, *ZNW* 65 (1974): 273ff., and Reinach, *Textes*, index *s.v.* "Jerusalem," 370. In the LXX the new form appears in the later writings: 1–4 Maccabees; 1 Esdras; Tobias.

by Josephus (*Ant.* XII.136): "The Jews who live around the sanctuary (*hieron*) called Hierosolyma . . ." On the other hand, the second half of the word, -solyma, connects the inhabitants with the "famed people of the Solymians" (*Solymoisi . . . kydalimiosi*), already mentioned by Homer in *Iliad* VI.184, a people who, according to Eratosthenes (Pliny *N.H.* V.127) no longer existed. As Homer, *Odys.* V. 283, also speaks of "mountains of Solymi" in the vicinity of Ethiopia, in his account of the antiquity of the Jewish people in *Contra Apionem*, Josephus can describe its inhabitants, who according to a poem of Choïrilos of Samos were part or Xerxes's army, as Jews (*C. Ap.* I.173–74); Pseudo-Manetho also calls the later inhabitants of Hierosolyma *Solymitai* (*C. Ap.* I.248, cf. 241). The fourth Sibylline oracle (115, 126) and Philostratus in his *Vita Apollonii* (6, 29) also similarly call Jerusalem simply Solyma; Tacitus (*Histories*, 5, 2, 3) finally gives the ancient reader an illuminating explanation for this: "Others (*alii*) attribute a glorious origin (*clara . . . initia*) to the Jews. The Solymians, a race celebrated in the poems of Homer, called the capital which they founded Hierosolyma, taking up their own name." The *alii* is presumably a reference to Hellenistic Jews. The Greek interpretation of the holy city along these lines was surely meant to heighten its significance in Greek eyes. Thus the alteration of the name follows the same line as the alleged affinity to the Spartans.

Alexander Polyhistor has preserved for us fragments of a Jewish-Samaritan historical work which praises similar tendencies and which was presumably written in Palestine after the conquest by the Seleucids, but before the outbreak of the Maccabean revolt. According to this, Enoch, whom the Greeks call Atlas, received the secrets of astrology from the angels and handed them down to posterity. Abraham, "who surpassed all men in nobility and wisdom," then brought them at God's command to the West and first taught the Phoenicians, and later the Egyptian priests in Heliopolis. This is a deliberate reversal of the biblical pattern of Abraham's journeying. As later, in the Sibylline writings, the pagan gods are devalued in a euhemeristic way and made to serve the greater glory of the Jews through the theme of the "first inventor" (*prōtos heuretēs*). The Samaritan origin of the history emerges from the stress on the "city sanctuary of Hargarizim," as the place where Abraham "received gifts" from the priest-king Melchizedek.[48]

---

48. Eusebius *Praep. Ev.* IX.17 and 18.2 = Jacoby, *F. Gr. H.* 724; cf. Hengel, *Judaism and Hellenism* 1:88–89; A.-M. Denis, *Introduction aux pseudépigraphes grecs d'Ancien Testament* (Leiden, 1970), 261.

The spirit of the new age and indeed the direct influence of Greek thought can even be found in some parts of Hebrew wisdom literature. This is true above all of the book Koheleth, which is puzzling in so many ways, and in which earlier scholars traced the influence of Greek philosophy. The work was probably written in the third century, in Jerusalem, under the Ptolemies; to some degree it has an aura of the early Hellenistic enlightenment.[49] This is already evident from certain linguistic affinities. Thus terms for destiny which Koheleth is fond of using, like *miqreh*, death, and *ḥeleq*, man's due portion, recall Greek *moira* and *tychē*. The often recurring "under the sun" was regarded as another Grecism. It was supposed that a Greek equivalent of the decisive term *hebel*, nothingness, was *typhos*; *'āśāh ṭôb* represented the Greek *eu prattein* or *eu drān*, while *ṭôb 'ašer yapeh* was thought to be the well known *kalos kāgathos* or *to kalon philon*.[50] There are also Greek parallels to the stress on time as a term for destiny. Other features are the impersonal conception of God, restraint towards prayer and worship, the complete absence of Jewish history with the exception of the disputed mention of Solomon at the beginning, the omission of the tradition about the Law, and above all the almost fatalistic notion that man is the victim of his fate and that the only thing for him to do is to enjoy his portion as long as he may. In particular, this invitation to *carpe diem* and the conception that after death "the breath of man ascends on high" has a wealth of Greek parallels.[51] A comparison with the Greek gnomic tradition shows that Koheleth must have been acquainted with it. The question remains open whether he knew it from oral tradition or in a literary form. Presumably both were available. Parallels can be produced from Greek poetry and popular philosophy for almost every verse.[52] It should, however, be stressed that Koheleth combined these new stimuli coming from outside with traditional Jewish, Eastern wisdom teaching, with which he is engaged in a critical discussion, to produce a coherent work with a character all of its own and a considerable degree of artistic skill. Presumably his provocative work, which

---

49. Hengel, *Judaism and Hellenism* 1:115–30; R. Braun, *Kohelet und die frühhellenistische Popularphilosophie* (Berlin, 1973), passim; Smith, *Palestinian Parties*, 159ff. "Though there is no reason to suppose that he knew Epicurus's work, the similarities of temper and attitude are unmistakable" (p. 160). Cf. also E. Bickerman, *Four Strange Books of the Bible* (New York, 1984), 139–67.

50. Braun, *Kohelet*, 44ff.

51. Hengel, *Judaism and Hellenism*, 1:123ff.

52. See the surveys in Braun, *Kohelet*, 146ff., 158ff.

above all broke with the old pattern of a just connection between act and consequence brought about by God, and thus raised doubts as to God's righteousness and goodness, was later revised and toned down by another hand.[53]

Another wisdom teacher is Ben Sira, who presumably lived a generation or two later than Koheleth, whose work he knew and used. In contrast to Koheleth, he does not hide behind a mysterious nom de plume, and is the first writer in Hebrew literature to give his own name. This too is a sign of a new age.[54] Awareness of the nature of intellectual originality now also found its way into Palestinian Judaism. Furthermore, the author openly presents himself as a "wise man" and a "scribe" who invites the young into his "school" and —in contrast to the earlier wisdom of a Job or a Koheleth—deliberately takes his place in the tradition of the salvation history of Israel. Perhaps he was one of the "temple scribes" mentioned in the decree of Antiochus III. Sometimes he speaks with the claim of prophetic authority and includes the interpretation of the prophetic writings in his task as a scribe.[55] More than that, however, for him the Torah given by God on Sinai is central; he boldly identifies it with preexistent wisdom which God poured out on all creation.

At God's bidding, this primal and universal wisdom found its dwelling place on Mount Zion in Jerusalem: here the mediating form of wisdom, which by virtue of its universality could be compared with the Platonic world-soul and the Stoic Logos, is exclusively connected with Israel, God's chosen people, and his sanctuary. In the hymn to wisdom in chapter 24, the centerpiece of his work, Ben Sira follows Prov. 8:22ff. by taking over aretalogical forms known to us from the Egyptian Isis aretalogies and which were perhaps used in Palestine in honor of Phoenician-Canaanite Astarte.[56] Here we have a characteristic which distinguishes him markedly from Koheleth. However, he uses new "Hellenistic" forms and material just as much as Koheleth, not to criticize the traditional religious heritage of Israel but to defend it in the contemporary intellectual struggle. Thus he attacks the wicked

---

53. K. Galling, *Der Prediger,* HAT 1, 18, 2d ed. (Tübingen, 1969), 75ff.: "The corrections made by QR[2] contradict the scope of the sentence in question" (p. 76).

54. Sir. 50:27, see Hengel, *Judaism and Hellenism* 1:79.

55. Sir. 24:30–31; 33:16a, 25ff.; 38:34—39:8 (numeration following V. Hamp); Hengel, *Judaism and Hellenism* 1:134ff.

56. 1:1–20; 24:1–34; cf. Hengel, *Judaism and Hellenism* 1:157ff.; J. Marböck, *Weisheit* (Bonn, 1971).

men and apostates, i.e., the Hellenists among the Jewish aristocracy, who want to forsake the Law;[57] those who deny free will, who make God himself responsible for their failure, and above all those who doubt the justice of God's recompense. He defends the purposefulness of the world and God's providence and justice with Stoic arguments; that is, he tries to develop something like a theodicy in terms of popular philosophy. Like Chrysippus, he argues that the evil in the world is there for the just punishment of sinners.[58] Ben Sira can describe the relationship of God to the world in almost pantheistic-sounding formulas: "and the sum of our words is: 'He is the all.'"[59] While on the one hand he takes up themes from the social preaching of the prophets, by attacking the exploitation of the poor by the rich landowners,[60] on the other hand he can value riches, is familiar with the etiquette of Greek meals, defends consultations with doctors, and praises the reputation and the political significance of the wise man who travels to foreign lands on behalf of the great.[61] Like Koheleth, he also knows Greek gnomic literature,[62] but does not glorify the wisdom and the heroes of alien peoples; his praise is reserved for the Torah and the great men of God from the sacred history which reaches from Adam and Enoch to his contemporary, the high priest Simon the Just,[63] whose sons he warns about division:[64] round about 180 B.C., when he was finishing his book, the Hellenistic reform was already casting a shadow forward. The eschatological prayer, with its petition for liberation from the gentile yoke, clearly shows that he was very critical of alien Seleucid rule. However, with the caution of a wise man, he knows how to disguise his criticism, and this prayer, too, is set in the framework of an almost universalist philosophical concept of God. It begins with the petition, "Have mercy upon us, O Lord, the God of all . . ." and ends, "and all who are on the

57. 41:8–9; 10:6–25; 16:4; Hengel, *Judaism and Hellenism* 1:150ff.

58. 39:24–34; Hengel, *Judaism and Hellenism* 1:141ff.; cf. Marböck, *Weisheit*, 134ff.; R. Pautrel, "Ben Sira et le stoïcisme," *RSR* 51 (1963): 535–49; J. L. Crenshaw, "The Problem of Theodicy in Sirach . . . ," *JBL* 94 (1975): 47–64.

59. 43:27, cf. Marböck, *Weisheit*, 150 n. 13; 170 n. 46.

60. 34 (G31): 24–27; 13:2–5; 4:1ff., 8ff.; 21:5; Hengel, *Judaism and Hellenism* 1:136–37; Tcherikover, *Hellenistic Civilization*, 144ff.

61. 10:27; 13:24; 25:3; etc.; 31:12ff.; 32:3ff.; 34:9ff.; 38:1, 12 (but cf. 2 Chron. 16:12, which is a little earlier) see Marböck, *Weisheit*, 160ff.

62. Middendorp, *Die Stellung Jesu ben Siras zwischen Judentum und Hellenismus* (Leiden, 1973), 7–34, gives a large number of parallels.

63. 44:1—50:24; T. Maertens, *L'Éloge des Pères (Ecclésiastique XLIV–L)* (Bruges, 1956): E. Bickerman, "La chaîne de la tradition pharisienne," *RB* 59 (1952): 44ff.; Hengel, *Judaism and Hellenism* 1:136.

64. Sir. 50:23–24.

earth will know that thou art the Lord, the God of the ages."[65] There has been much discussion as to whether Ben Sira was pro-Hellenist or anti-Hellenist, but this is to pose a false alternative.[66] It must be viewed in the light of the divided historical situation in Judea in the pre-Maccabean period. Furthermore, a distinction needs to be made between a Hellenistic-type form and the basically xenophobic tendency.[67] Ben Sira was a religious conservative, a Jewish *sōper* (scribe), faithful to the Torah and thinking in nationalistic terms, who believed that he had an obligation to ancestral tradition but was nevertheless more influenced than he was aware by the spirit of his time, i.e., the thought-world of Hellenism. However, in addition there can be no doubt that he was consciously an opponent of the Hellenistic reformers in the city and that if he was still alive to experience events after 175 B.C. he would have been on the side of the Maccabees and certainly not on that of Jason, Menelaus, Alcimus, or the Tobiads. In him we find that spirit which we later meet again among the early Sadducees, who were also conservative, nationalistic Jews, put up bitter resistance against the Romans and Herod's seizure of power, and yet did not despise Hellenistic civilization and its resources, supporting the transformation of Judea into a "Hellenistic" monarchy which was brought about by the Hasmoneans.

To conclude, it is also important to consider the opposition movement of the Hasidim[68] which began to organize itself shortly before, or at the beginning of, the Hellenistic reform. The influence of the new age can be seen even in those who rejected the spirit of Hellenism with particular vehemence; indeed, it can be seen here above all. That is true of the free form of organization which they adopted, that of the religious association, which was later adopted by the *yaḥad (koinon)* of the Qumran Essenes and the *ḥᵃbūrōt* of the Pharisees:[69] we must understand it as the sign of a new religious individualism which rested on the

65. Sir. 36:1–22.

66. Most recently, Middendorp, *Stellung*, has tried to describe Ben Sira as an out-and-out "Hellenist." But even he has to concede that Ben Sira stands on the side of the high priest Simon and is an opponent of the Tobiads, 167ff. Marböck, *Weisheit*, 168ff., is more restrained in his judgment. See my review of Middendorp's book in *JSJ* 5 (1974): 83–87.

67. See Smith, *Palestinian Parties*, 79ff., and his warning against false alternatives.

68. 1 Macc. 2:42; 7:13; and 2 Macc. 14:6; cf. Hengel, *Judaism and Hellenism* 1:175ff.; Schürer, Vermes, and Millar, *History* 1:157.

69. Hengel, *Judaism and Hellenism* 1:244ff.; W. Tyloch, "Les Thiases et la Communauté de Qumran," in *Fourth World Congress of Jewish Studies, Papers* 1 (Jerusalem, 1967), 225–28.

free decision—the "conversion"—of the individual. Other signs of the spirit of a new age are many of their religious views, which have been recorded above all in the apocalyptic literature, produced from their circles. The Essenes, of course, vigorously rejected gentile, Hellenistic civilization. However, they in particular show signs of varied influence from this alien spirit of the age and therefore their teaching was especially suitable for a philosophical and apologetic interpretatio graeca.[70] It would be wrong to see the ḥasidim, molded by apocalyptic thought, as being in conscious opposition to Jewish wisdom or to the Temple cult.[71] In reality the division of the people ran through the priests and Levites as well as through the scribes. A new phenomenon in ḥasidic apocalyptic was the claim it raised to special revelations of divine wisdom. Here the concept of the secret took on central theological significance.[72] A "higher wisdom" appeared alongside the wisdom handed down by tradition, which was received through a special revelation, through dreams and visions, through journeys to heaven and hell, through the appearances of angels, and through inspiration. Here we find the same forms of revelation as in the Hellenistic world; to some degree the same "religious koinē" is spoken.[73] The heyday of Jewish apocalyptic, from the second century B.C., which then quickly spilled over to the Diaspora in the form of the Sibylline oracles, runs parallel to the renewal of a "religion of revelation" in the Hellenistic world. Of course it began there rather later, and reached its climax only from the second century A.D. onward, in the time of the Empire. A further essential point was the emergence of the individual's hope of overcoming death, along with the conception of the judgment of the dead. The development of a future hope beyond death then in turn exercised an essential influence on burial customs and the form of tombs, which underwent a particularly intensive development in the late Hellenistic and Roman period. In Palestine this expectation assumed the typically Jewish form of the physical resurrection from the

70. Hengel, "Qumran und der Hellenismus," in Qumrân. Sa piété, sa théologie et son milieu, ed. M. Delcor (Paris and Louvain, 1978), 333–72.

71. Thus rather one-sidedly in the otherwise valuable book by O. Plöger, Theokratie und Eschatologie, WMANT 2 (Neukirchen, 1959). This is already clear from the significance of the Temple in the Book of Daniel and the fight of Ḥasidim, Essenes, and Pharisees for the purity of the Temple and its worship.

72. Thus above all the Persian loanword raz Dan. 2:18–19, 27–30, 47, and the Qumran writings and Ethiopian Enoch 16.3; 38.3; 103.2, 104.12. Cf. Hengel, Judaism and Hellenism 1:202–3.

73. Hengel, Judaism and Hellenism 1:209–18.

dead; alongside it, certainly under the Greek influence, there developed the idea of the immortality of the soul, which was influential above all in the Diaspora. However, both were variable and could be combined. The development of a hope beyond death is closely connected with the question of theodicy, which was raised especially as a result of persecution. In Greece the hope of immortality, the expectation of a judgment of the dead, and the conception of places of reward and punishment for the dead were very much older. We must not rule out influence from here on early Jewish apocalyptic. This is especially true of the idea of astral "immortality" and future hope for the wise teachers, which we find as early as the end of the book of Daniel.[74] Lastly, mention should also be made of the concept of the unity of world history, which is closely bound up with the idea of world kingdoms; this developed in the controversy with the Hellenistic monarchies. The imminent kingdom of God will soon make an end to the overwhelming arrogance of the world empire. The imagery of the four metals of successively inferior quality as symbols for the world kingdoms in Nebuchadnezzar's dream recalls the four metals in Hesiod's picture of the ages of the world, which had a decisive influence on ancient historical thinking.[75] The notion of universal mission to be found, with its eschatological proviso, in Greek-speaking primitive Christianity, and the thinking of Paul in particular, both of which represent something completely new in the history of religion, are a last consequence of the universalist, Hellenistic, apocalyptic conception of the one *oikoumenē*, the unity of the inhabited, civilized world. On the other hand, Jewish and Iranian apocalyptic in turn influenced ancient poetry. The best example of this is Virgil's Fourth Eclogue.[76]

Thus the adoption of Hellenistic civilization, its language, its literature and its thought, by ancient Judaism and the conflict which resulted is a complex development involving a great deal of tension. The development in Palestine differed only partially from that in the Dia-

74. Dan. 12:2–3; Ethiopian Enoch 104.2. T. F. Glasson, *Greek Influence in Jewish Eschatology* (London, 1961); Hengel, *Judaism and Hellenism* 1:196–202; G. W. E. Nickelsburg, *Resurrection, Immortality and Eternal Life in Intertestamental Judaism* (Harvard diss., 1972); G. Stemberger, *Der Leib der Auferstehung*, Analecta Biblica 56 (Rome, 1972); E. M. Meyers, *Jewish Ossuaries, Reburial and Birth*, Biblica et Orientalia 24 (Rome, 1971).

75. Hengel, *Judaism and Hellenism* 1:181ff.; B. Gatz, *Weltzeitalter, goldene Zeit und sinnverwandte Vorstellungen*, Spudasmata 16 (Hildesheim, 1967).

76. H. C. Gottoff, "On the Fourth Eclogue of Vergil," *Philologus* 111 (1967): 66–79; Gatz, *Weltzeitalter*, 87ff.

spora; it affected almost all strata and groups of the population and involved both the political and economic and the intellectual and religious spheres. The reactions of individual classes and groups was also very different. The aristocracy proved to be most open to the new life-style and the education that went with it; this upper class was also particularly threatened with assimilation. However, the opposition too, the Hasidic apocalypticists or the Jewish Hellenistic apologists, all of whom wanted to preserve the ancestral heritage intact, did not escape the influence of the thought of the new age in this political and intellectual struggle. Precisely by accepting new ideas and working intensively with them, ancient Judaism acquired the inner strength to pull itself out of the morass of alien and seductive civilization and even in a different garb and in connection with new forms of thought and expression to preserve the traditional religious heritage and to remain true to its divine task in history. Thus by and large we may term Judaism of the Hellenistic Roman period, both in the home country and the Diaspora, "Hellenistic Judaism."[77]

77. Hengel, *Judaism and Hellenism* 1:104ff., 311ff.; Smith, *Palestinian Parties*, 81: "We shall do better to recognize 'Hellenistic' as a cultural classification distinct both from 'Greek,' and from 'oriental,' and see the civil conflicts of the Seleucid and Ptolemaic empires as conflicts between various groups of a single cultural continuum—the Hellenistic."

Conclusion

In the introduction we characterized the fourth and third centuries B.C.E. as a "dark age" in the history of Judaism. In this anthology we have sought to cast some light on various aspects of the age. New perceptions have been catalyzed often by new physical evidence, chiefly archeological and epigraphic, but also sometimes by new conceptions and ways of perceiving the previously known odds and ends of information. These new perceptions, partly because of the glimpses they have granted us, make us still more sensible of the obscurity of the period. The literary evidence from this period is slight and highly restricted in its nature. There is little by way of systematic knowledge of the nature of Jewish society in Palestine during these centuries; we enjoy no true sense of the range of religious and intellectual expression which may have flourished at that time.

In the modern historiography of Judaism, as we have noted, the third and fourth centuries have not received the attention warranted by their significance. Only in the last generation has there been some redress of this imbalance, and much still remains to be done. The problematic nature of the evidence has brought to light varied and deeply divergent interpretations of the history of Judaism at that time. Indeed, it is the basic recognition of the "darkness" of the period that lends so great an interest and excitement to the articles presented above. The varied remains from the Zenon archive, the Wadi Daliyeh cache, and the Qumran scrolls have illuminated the fourth and third centuries in a considerable and not altogether expected fashion.

The chapters by Cross and Tcherikover deepen our appreciation of the complex relations between the inhabitants of Judea (Judeans, Judahites) and the non-Judeans in this period. The local aristocracies which dominated the three chief Israelite areas (Samaria, Judea, and Ammon) were related by marital connections, family interrelations, and common political and economic interests. At the same time, the local aristocracies of Samaria and Ammon were consciously independent of, and often opposed to, Jerusalemite society.

In these studies, too, the issue of the many temples of the God of Israel arises—God was worshiped not only in Jerusalem. Centuries after the reforms of Josiah (621 B.C.E.) that had finally consolidated the cult in Jerusalem, a series of Temples to the God of Israel sprang up. The Samaritan Temple at Gerizim was one; the Temple built by the exiled Onias IV at Leontopolis (Egypt) in the early second century B.C.E. is another. A number of authors speak of a third Temple at Araq el-Emir in Transjordan, built by the Jewish Tobiad dynasty of Ammon, though recent discoveries have cast doubt on this identification.[1] Rather later, Josephus talks of a Jewish sanctuary in Antioch as having characteristics of a Temple; an inscription discovered at Sardis (Asia Minor) is another indication of the conduct of the sacrificial cult of God outside Jerusalem.

At a quite different level of discussion, Stone's reading of the Enoch material raises fresh questions regarding the nature of intellectual speculation during these centuries and the nature of the intellectual culture. These insights bear on certain aspects of the intellectual world of Judea in this period that are not witnessed by the biblical documents. Not only were there new religious concepts, but also more general "scientific" concerns, often using Mesopotamian conceptual structures and terminology.

These discoveries are doubly important: they not only enrich our understanding of the period, but also serve a a renewed warning not to try to place unwarranted limits on the religious and intellectual creativity of Jewish society in Palestine. This needs be stressed in light of persistent attempts to "map" the development of Judaism during these dark centuries in terms of theological streams or traditions. Some scholars extrapolate these forward from the period of the Restoration and the days of Ezra and Nehemiah. One variation on this theme is

1. In favor of the identification of a temple structure at the site, on the basis of preliminary excavation reports, see M. Hengel, *Judaism and Helenism*, trans. J. Bowden (London: SCM Press, 1973; Philadelphia: Fortress Press, 1974), 273–74, and E. F. Campbell, "Jewish Shrines of the Hellenistic and Persian Periods," *Symposia: Celebrating the 75th Anniversary of the American Schools of Oriental Research [1900–1975]*, ed. F. M. Cross (Cambridge, Mass., 1979), 159–67. Strong doubts are raised by E. Will, however, in *The Excavation at Araq el-Emir*, ed. N. L. Lapp, Annual of the American Schools of Oriental Research 47 (1983), 1:150–51.

Wellhausen's classic presentation of Judaism in this period as the growth of the ascendancy of "the Law" and "legalism."A more subtle attempt in this direction is that by Paul D. Hanson, who tries to isolate a prophetic party and a hierocratic one, and traces the history of this period in terms of the conflict between them.[2] At the other extreme, Otto Plöger and Martin Hengel, in different ways, use the streams they discern in the conflict over Hellenism in the early second century to characterize Judaism in the third century.[3] In general, such characterizations have been far more indicative of the theological agenda of their proponents! The discoveries of the last half-century should put us on guard against theories based on the "natural" development of Jewish religion or society. Every new piece of evidence provides witness for increased diversity and diminished predictability.

The structure and scope of this anthology should not be misapprehended as a narrowing vision of the fundamental diversity and creativity of Judaism during this period. By focusing on the phenomenon of Hellenism in the final chapters, we make no presumption that this is the sole, or even the most important, religious and intellectual development during the fourth and third centuries in Palestine. We present it as a crucial question which has been the subject of keen debate during the last two decades, and concerning which we have a relative plenitude of sources.

In another anthology we could deal with other equally important issues. Perhaps the most glaring omission is a treatment of the influence of Iranian religion and culture on a region that was part of the Persian empire for centuries. This is a much-debated subject, and its absence from this collection reflects primarily the fact that little innovation has been made on the traditional views as far as they relate to the situation in the fourth and third centuries. Much more could be said about the question of Iranian influence that many would claim is evident in Judaism in the Land of Israel in the second and first centuries B.C.E., particularly in the Dead Sea Scrolls. But that should be left for another book.

We might also concern ourselves with the question of the "pre-Qumran" documents among the Dead Sea Scrolls. By all views the Dead Sea Sect originated sometime in the second century. In recent years,

---

2. P. D. Hanson, *The Dawn of Apocalyptic: The Historical and Sociological Roots of Jewish Apocalyptic Eschatology* (Philadelphia: Fortress Press, 1975).

3. O. Plöger, *Theocracy and Eschatology,* trans. S. Rudman (Oxford: Basil Blackwell & Mott, 1968); Hengel, *Judaism and Hellenism.*

however, many documents from the Qumran library have been recognized to originate from an earlier period than the sect itself and, although they have some sectarian features, do not bear the distinctive mark of the Qumran sect. These pre-Qumranian documents also present types of Judaism and Jewish thought which fit none of the traditional pictures of Judaism in the fourth and third centuries. Such intriguing features include a deviant calendar, special sacrificial cult, and expectation of one Messiah from the tribe of Levi.

An obviously crucial matter excluded from the present anthology, but which might well form the basis of another collection, is Diaspora Judaism. The development of Judaism in Palestine in the fourth and third centuries must be complemented, in any full description, by portraits of the communities in Egypt, Asia Minor, Mesopotamia, and Persia, and their literature and culture. A number of works written in the Diaspora survive, including the Greek translation of the Pentateuch, the Chronography of Demetrius, and most probably certain other books, such as Tobit, Daniel (chaps. 1—6), and Esther. The direct historical sources are even thinner than those surviving for Palestine, but there exists enough evidence to raise many fascinating issues.

In spite of these exclusions, the present collection presents central aspects of Judaism of this age, highlighting a number of its new and unexpected features.

Bibliography
An Annotated Guide
to Further Reading

The following works of general reference are indispensable:

The Interpreter's Dictionary of the Bible. Nashville: Abingdon Press, 1962. 4 vols. and "Supplementary Volume" (1976).

The Oxford Classical Dictionary. 2d ed. Ed. by N. G. L. Hammond and H. H. Scullard. Oxford: Clarendon Press, 1970.

Introductions and Surveys

Bickerman, E. J. *From Ezra to the Last of the Maccabees.* New York: Schocken, 1962.

Bickerman's account—the first part of which opens the present anthology—is both concise and thought-provoking.

Davies, W. D., and L. Finkelstein, eds. *Cambridge History of Judaism: The Persian Period.* Cambridge: Cambridge Univ. Press, 1984.

This new "standard" history of the period is of uneven quality yet rich in references and bibliography.

Hayes, J. H., and J. M. Miller, eds. *Israelite and Judaean History,* 489–538 ("The Persian Period" by G. Widengren), 539–604 ("The Hellenistic and Maccabean Periods" by P. Schäfer). OTL. Philadelphia: Westminster Press. London: SCM Press, 1977.

The chapters by Widengren and Schäfer provide discussions of central problems with valuable guides to both primary and secondary sources.

Nickelsburg, G. W. E. *Jewish Literature between the Bible and the Mishnah.* Philadelphia: Fortress Press, 1981.

This introduction to postbiblical Jewish literature is both accessible and broad in scope.

Nickelsburg, G. W. E., and M. E. Stone, *Faith and Piety in Early Judaism.* Philadelphia: Fortress Press, 1983.

The authors highlight central features of the period of the Second Temple through an anthology of texts and documents in translation.

Schürer, E. *The History of the Jewish People in the Age of Jesus Christ (175 B.C.– A.D. 135).* 3 vols. Trans. and ed. by G. Vermes, F. Millar, et al. Edinburgh: T. & T. Clark, 1973–87.

Schürer's classic work, now revised and updated, treats both the religious life and the literature of the period.

Smith, Morton. *Palestinian Parties and Politics That Shaped the Old Testament.* New York: Columbia Univ. Press, 1971.

This highly original study of postexilic Judaism is no less important than it has proved controversial.

Stern, E. *Material Culture of the Land of the Bible in the Persian Period, 538– 332 B.C.* Jerusalem and London, 1982.

Stern surveys a wide range of archeological evidence with important cultural and social implications.

Stone, M. E. *Scriptures, Sects, and Visions.* Philadelphia: Fortress Press, 1980.

This concise "profile" of Judaism in the Second Temple Period challenges various aspects of the orthodox consensus.

————, ed. *Jewish Writings of the Second Temple Period.* Compendia Rerum Judaicarum ad Novum Testamentum II.2. Philadelphia: Fortress Press; Assen: van Gorcum, 1984.

The contributors to this volume provide in-depth surveys of a broad range of postbiblical Jewish literature.

Judeans and Samaritans

Coggins, R. J. *Samaritans and Jews.* London: Oxford Univ. Press, 1968.

Cross, F. M. "The Discovery of the Samaria Papyri." *BA* 26 (1963): 110–21.

Cross's initial survey of this important find, which he is publishing.

————. "A Reconstruction of the Judean Restoration." *JBL* 94 (1975): 4–18.

In this article Cross draws detailed conclusions from the Daliyeh papyri for the history of Judea and Samaria and brings them into relationship with some biblical data.

Dexinger, F. "Limits of Tolerance in Judaism: The Samaritan Example." In *Jewish and Christian Self-Definition,* ed. by E. P. Sanders, with A. I. Baumgarten and A. Mendelson, 2:88–112. Philadelphia: Fortress Press, 1981.

Dexinger deals with important aspects of the attitudes of Jews and Samaritans to one another.

Talmon, S. "Polemics and Apology in Biblical Historiography—2 Kings 17:24–41." In *The Creation of Sacred Literature,* ed. by R. E. Friedman, 57–68. Berkeley and Los Angeles: Univ. of California Press, 1981.

The story in 2 Kings 17 tells, purportedly, of the origins of the Samaritans. Talmon critically examines the chapter, and discusses the implication of this examination for the understanding of Samaritan origins.

Wright, G. E. "The Samaritans at Shechem." *HTR* 55(1962): 357–66.

The excavator of Shechem puts the implications of his discoveries into the context of the founding of the Samaritan sanctuary there and of Alexander's conquests of the land of Israel.

Apocalyptic

Collins, J. J. *The Apocalyptic Imagination: An Introduction to the Jewish Matrix of Christianity.* New York: Crossroad, 1984.

A general introduction to the Jewish apocalyptic literature in an up-to-date fashion.

Hanson, P. D. *The Dawn of Apocalyptic.* Philadelphia: Fortress Press, 1975.

An influential book that has attempted to trace the origins of apocalyptic eschatology in the experience of the exilic and postexilic period.

Hellholm, D. *Apocalypticism in the Mediterranean World and the Near East.* Tübingen: J. C. B. Mohr (Paul Siebeck), 1983.

A rich volume investigating apocalyptic literature from a variety of perspectives and cultures. Besides looking at Jewish and Christian sources, the volume examines Greek, Persian, and other ancient Mediterranean and Near Eastern literatures.

Koch, K. *The Rediscovery of Apocalyptic.* Naperville, 1972.

Koch in this book attempted to bring clarity into a much confused area of definition and characterization of such entities as "apocalypse," "apocalypticism," etc.

Momigliano, A. "The Origins of Universal History." In *The Poet and the Historian,* ed. by R. E. Friedman, 133–54. HSS 26. Chico, Calif.: Scholars Press, 1983.

A work setting out some of the developments in the history of ideas that enabled the apocalyptic view of history to emerge.

Russel, D. S. *Method and Message of Jewish Apocalyptic.* Philadelphia: Westminster Press; London: SPCK, 1964.

A standard introduction to the apocalypses giving a sound survey of their contents and character.

Stone, M. E. "Lists of Revealed Things in Apocalyptic Literature." In *Magnalia Dei,* ed. by F. M. Cross, W. Lemke, et al., 414–25. Garden City, N.Y.: Doubleday & Co., 1976.

This article attempts to penetrate certain aspects of the apocalypses, particularly their interest in "scientific" and speculative knowledge, previously little stressed.

The Tobiads

Goldstein, J. A. "The Tales of the Tobiads." In *Christianity, Judaism, and Other Greco-Roman Cults: Studies for Morton Smith,* ed. by J. Neusner, 3:85–123. SJLA 12. Leiden: E. J. Brill, 1975.

Goldstein offers a detailed analysis of the stories in Josephus's *Antiquities* concerning the Tobiad family.

Lapp, N. L., ed. *The Excavations at Araq el-Emir* I. Annual of the American Schools of Oriental Research 47, 1983.

The final report on the archeological excavations conducted at the site of the Tobiads' stronghold in Transjordan.

Mazar, B. "The Tobiads." *IEJ* 7 (1957): 137–45, 229–38.

Mazar examines the early history of the Tobiad family.

Tcherikover, V. A., and A. Fuks, eds. *CPJ* 1:115–30 ("Jews of Palestine in the Zenon Papyri"). Cambridge: Harvard Univ. Press, 1957–64.

The text and translation (with introduction and notes) of the papyri from the Zenon archive which shed light on third-century Palestine and the activities of Tobiah.

Hellenization

Auscher, D. "Les relations entre la Grèce et la Palestine avant la conquête d'Alexandre." *VT* 17 (1967): 8–30.

This article is the basic survey of Greek influences in Palestine prior to the onset of the Hellenistic period.

Bickerman, E. J. *The Jews in the Greek Age.* Cambridge: Harvard Univ. Press, 1988. A posthumously published collection of a great scholar's researches and reflections.

Collins, J. J. *Between Athens and Jerusalem.* New York: Crossroad, 1983.

Collins provides an authoritative introduction to the literature and culture of Hellenistic Judaism.

Goldstein, J. "Jewish Acceptance and Rejection of Hellenism." In *Jewish and Christian Self-Definition* (see above), 2:64–87, 318–26.

A stimulating reappraisal of Jewish attitudes toward Hellenistic practices and influence.

Hengel, M. *Jews, Greeks, and Barbarians.* Trans. by J. Bowden, Philadelphia: Fortress Press; London: SCM Press, 1980.

Hengel develops and summarizes his principal conclusions regarding the Hellenization of Judaism.

———. *Judaism and Hellenism.* Trans. by J. Bowden. Philadelphia: Fortress Press, 1974; London: SCM Press, 1970.

This volume is both a valuable work of reference and a daring statement of the interaction between Judaism and Hellenism in the pre-Maccabean period.

Millar, F. "The Background to the Maccabean Revolution: Reflections on Martin Hengel's *Judaism and Hellenism*." *JJS* 29 (1978): 1–21.

Millar presents some telling criticism of central aspects of Hengel's thesis.

Momigliano, A. *Alien Wisdom: The Limits of Hellenization*. Cambridge: Cambridge Univ. Press, 1975.

An important and elegant study of the contacts between classical cultures and their neighbors.

Stern, M. *Greek and Latin Authors on Jews and Judaism*. 3 vols. Jerusalem: Israel Academy, 1974–84.

The first volume of this superb collection contains the evidence (introduction, texts, and translation) concerning Greek attitudes toward Jews and Judaism in the early Hellenistic period.

Tcherikover, V. *Hellenistic Civilization and the Jews*. Philadelphia: Jewish Publication Society, 1959.

Tcherikover's book remains a classic investigation of the relations between Jews and Greeks in the Hellenistic period, both in Palestine and in the Diaspora.

Index of Chief Subjects